My Spirit Guide, Francine, says, "If you can think of the question, the answer is available." May this book be full of available answers for many of your most heartfelt questions.

How likely is **Armageddon**?
Where did **Atlantis** go and when will it return?
How do you know if you have the gift of **clairvoyance**?
Is there something more to **coincidence**?
Are past lives the answer to the strange phenomenon of **déjà vu**?
Does each of us have a **doppelgänger**?
Who really are **ghosts and ghouls**?
How does **numerology** affect you?
Have I experienced r**eincarnation**?
Is **sorcery** something we should fear?
How do I find my **Spirit Guide**?
Are there really such things as **zombies**?

An A–Z compendium of all things on the Other Side, this is the perfect resource for anyone in search of signs or understanding of the paranormal.

"Sylvia Browne is more than a psychic—she is a master at conveying the truth that exists in the fourth dimension."
—Caroline Myss, Ph.D., author of *Anatomy of the Spirit*

SYLVIA BROWNE

with
Lindsay Harrison

PHENOMENON

Everything You Need to Know About the Paranormal

NEW AMERICAN LIBRARY

New American Library
Published by New American Library, a division of
Penguin Group (USA) Inc., 375 Hudson Street,
New York, New York 10014, USA
Penguin Group (Canada), 90 Eglinton Avenue East, Suite 700, Toronto,
Ontario M4P 2Y3, Canada (a division of Pearson Penguin Canada Inc.)
Penguin Books Ltd., 80 Strand, London WC2R 0RL, England
Penguin Ireland, 25 St. Stephen's Green, Dublin 2,
Ireland (a division of Penguin Books Ltd.)
Penguin Group (Australia), 250 Camberwell Road, Camberwell, Victoria 3124,
Australia (a division of Pearson Australia Group Pty. Ltd.)
Penguin Books India Pvt. Ltd., 11 Community Centre, Panchsheel Park,
New Delhi - 110 017, India
Penguin Group (NZ), cnr Airborne and Rosedale Roads, Albany,
Auckland 1310, New Zealand (a division of Pearson New Zealand Ltd.)
Penguin Books (South Africa) (Pty.) Ltd., 24 Sturdee Avenue,
Rosebank, Johannesburg 2196, South Africa

Penguin Books Ltd., Registered Offices:
80 Strand, London WC2R 0RL, England

Published by New American Library, a division of Penguin Group (USA) Inc.
Previously published in a Dutton edition.

First New American Library Printing, October 2006
10 9 8 7 6 5 4 3 2 1

 REGISTERED TRADEMARK—MARCA REGISTRADA

New American Library Trade Paperback ISBN: 0-451-21949-X

Library of Congress cataloging-in-publication data for the hardcover edition
of this title is available upon request.

Set in Fairfield Light
Designed by Helene Berinsky

Printed in the United States of America

FROM SYLVIA:

For Angelia,
whose research made all the difference
and whose love I cherish with all my heart.

FROM LINDSAY:

For Eugenie,
and the Angels she and Teddy will send next
to take care of George, Willie and me.

CONTENTS

B

C

D

Contents

I

J

K

L

M

N

O

P

W

X

Y

Z

INTRODUCTION TO *PHENOMENON*

This book is devoted to both defining and describing, with examples, many words that are commonly used in the world of the paranormal. Happily, some of these words have become part of the mainstream vocabulary. But I know you're still having experiences that confuse you, or frighten you, or that you simply don't understand. You're not eager to confide in anyone about these experiences, because you're sure they'll think you're crazy; but you'd feel so much better knowing there really is an explanation for what happened, that there are even words for these things and that there are other perfectly sane people they've happened to.

Fifty years ago, when I started doing readings and making public appearances as a psychic, the world wasn't sure whether to bless me or burn me. As time has gone on, more and more people are figuring out that so-called "psychic phenomena" aren't so unnatural or uncommon after all; that the worlds of the paranormal and spirituality are handmaidens to each other; and that both can actually deepen and enhance a whole spectrum of even the most devout religious beliefs. There's no devil's work involved in studying new ways to affirm our sacred, eternal connection to God, which is the real bottom line to my life's passion. In fact, the devil, if there were such a thing, would be furious.

Through my eyes, the paranormal world isn't all that mysterious, and it's certainly not scary. Come to think of it, there's only one story in this entire book in which you'll find me downright terrified. Other than that, this paranormal world in which I spend a great deal of my time is fascinating, informative, thrilling and God-centered at every turn. It's those adjectives that I would love to inspire in you, as well as have you make friends with the words and explanations you'll find between these covers. I would love to remove the mystery, lift the veil and shine a light on those monsters in your room you've spent your life being afraid of, to show you that it's just a harmless pile of clothes on a chair.

You'll find words in this book you might not be expecting. There are other words you might be expecting that you won't find here. The master list that Lindsay; our editor, Brian Tart; and I started with has been revised a hundred times, with the yardstick probably getting a little blurry in the process. I can promise you that I've either researched or had personal experience with every word, that I have strong and potentially controversial opinions on every word (there's a surprise) and that no opinion goes unexpressed (another surprise). For better or worse, the ship has sailed on my ability to appear wishy-washy about much of anything.

I genuinely hope this book won't just sit on a shelf in your home but that it will actually become your companion, something you'll reach for to find comfort, to satisfy a passing curiosity, just for fun or, most of all, to reavow your soul's certainty that there's Something and Someone magnificent beyond you, whom you're a part of and who's as much a part of you as your soul itself.

My Spirit Guide Francine says, "If you can think of the question, the answer is available." May this book be full of available answers for many of your most heartfelt questions, now and always.

Affirmations

Affirmations are declarations of our worthiest goals and our sacred responsibilities to ourselves as treasured children of God. Repeating those declarations often enough that our subconscious minds accept them as fact and guide our behavior accordingly is what makes affirmations a powerful spiritual tool that anyone can use. Through affirmations we can declare ourselves healthier, stronger, more positive, more successful, kinder, more patient, more confident, more courageous, more responsible, more spiritually attuned—whatever will help us love ourselves more. If prayers are acknowledgments of reverence to that God "out there" who's with each of us at every eternal moment, affirmations are those same acknowledgments to that God "in here," in the very genetic makeup of our souls.

Religion and literature have provided us with many beautiful affirmations, and I've included several of my own that appear at the end of this entry. By all means find, learn and use every affirmation that resonates in your soul. But affirmations you create yourself, spoken out loud or silently from the depth of your heart, will be just as effective as the most eloquent affirmations ever written.

If you're not sure you believe affirmations will really work, just think about the "negative affirmations" you've accepted as truth in your life. "You're useless/stupid/pathetic/an idiot." "You'll never amount to anything." "You can't do anything right." "You'd never make it without me." "You're fat/ugly/too short/too tall/too skinny." "You're such a loser." Sadly, you've probably heard some variation on at least one of those over and over and over again from a supposed loved one in your life. And even more sadly, you've learned to believe them. Why? Because you've heard them so often, right? Well, you can learn to believe their exact opposites if you hear them every bit as often, and that is where affirmations come in. Your first affirmations can be a counterattack to anything and everything negative about your self-image, no matter where it comes from.

And I do mean *no matter where it comes from*. Putting yourself down, even jokingly, or allowing anyone around you to insult you, through words or behavior, doesn't just cause erosive psychic damage; it's also a form of sacrilege when you think about it. Who does anyone think they are, after all, to be anything less than respectful to one of God's children?

For every insult anyone aims at you, or ever has aimed at you, by their words or by their actions, make it a habit to neutralize it with an affirmation, over and over again, until you believe your affirmation more surely than you could ever believe anything negative about yourself. Try replacing insults and negativity with affirmations for three short months, and I promise you will be amazed at the changes you'll see in yourself.

Once you've used affirmations to enhance your self-confidence and self-respect, and learned that affirmations really do work, you can start using them toward achieving your highest, worthiest aspirations. Of course, you can try it the other way around if you want—you can start with affirmations about that spouse or family or career or lifestyle you've always wanted. And if your goal is simply securing those things, it will probably work.

If your goal is actually *keeping* them, though, and finding the fulfillment in them that's exactly what's making you yearn for them in the first place, the answers lie in *you*, and in the certainty of your God-given worthiness that daily affirmations will help to create and help you never to forget.

To give you an idea of how limitless and personalized affirmations can be as you gather and compose your own, here are a few that I've used myself over the years. Please feel free to adopt any of them that resound in your soul.

* "Today, through every hour, I will picture myself being carried inside a perfect white bubble of God's pure loving light. And as a defense against my enemies, I will surround them with that same bubble of God's light, so that He may disarm and dissolve the negativity and darkness that I no longer tolerate or engage in."

* "Today I ask every cell in my body to respond and react as they did at the age I felt my healthiest, most energetic best. I will negate all illness, knowing that my mind is stronger than my body and my spirit mind can transcend them both and create miracles, with God's blessing."

* "I will move closer today to becoming the person I wish to be. By making a list of all the undesirable things that I've allowed to become my habits and my self-imposed obstacles, I will find the clear vision to affirm and celebrate all the wonderful things that I am and build on those toward spiritual perfection."

* "On this day I declare with the almighty strength of God's power that I deserve abundance and the financial means to be comfortable, and that I will joyfully use that abundance as a celebration of the law of karma—the more of it I share with the truly needy and deserving, the more of it will come back to me, multiplied by His grace and thanks."

* "I will listen closely today to my body. I will not negate any pain or illness that needs expert medical attention. But any chronic

or minor pain or illness I will condense into a ball of fire, release it from my body, secure it in a safe of thick lead and blow it up into a harmless impotent vapor."

* "I am from God. I am part of God, and God is part of me. Therefore I cannot be diminished. I am strong, I am loved and I am loving, because I am living this and every day in accordance with God's great plan."

* "As I face my grief today, I will not bury it, but instead I will consent to it. And by consenting to it, I ask God to help me draw strength from His divine plan and guidance and surround me with His Angels, knowing the truth that I will see and share eternity with my loved ones again in the perfect joy of the Other Side."

* "I will love myself completely today, regarding myself with pride and honor. Because my soul and my spirit come from God, I cherish myself too much to let anyone abuse or defame me in any way."

I've turned the use of affirmations into a ritual that I have found to be incredibly powerful and healing. This keeps me centered in an often maddening world, and I believe it provides protection, calm, reassurance and, most important, love. I hope you will join me in this ritual. It will help you. For nine nights, at precisely 9:00, light a candle and repeat:

> "I am a blessed child of God. I am well. I am happy.
> Great abundance is on its way because, as God's child,
> I am empowered to create miracles."

Akashic Records

There seems to be general agreement among the majority of the world's faiths, cultures and philosophies that the Akashic Records exist. What's not quite as unanimously agreed upon is where they exist and how to describe exactly what they are.

The Hindus, whose religion is thought to date back as far as 4000 B.C., believe in a universal substance called "akasha," from which the natural elements of fire, water, air and earth were created. Eternally imprinted on that substance is every thought, word and action in the history of the universe, collectively called the Akashic Records.

The brilliant prophet and clairvoyant Edgar Cayce wasn't as specific about the existence of an "akasha" substance. But he certainly believed in the existence of the Akashic Records, which he perceived to be the collective memories and histories of every thought, sound, physical and emotional vibration, major event and incidental moment in eternity, an atmospheric presence that affects us all and we all affect with every breath we take. In his "Reading 294-19 Report File," Cayce detailed one of his visits to the Akashic Records:

"I see myself as a tiny dot out of my physical body, which lies inert before me. I find myself oppressed by darkness and there is a feeling of terrific loneliness. Suddenly, I am conscious of a white beam of light. As this tiny dot, I move upward following the light, knowing that I must follow it or be lost. . . . I become conscious of sounds, at first indistinct rumblings, then music, laughter, and singing of birds. There is more and more light, the colors become very beautiful, and there is the sound of wonderful music. . . . Quite suddenly I come upon a hall of records. . . . I am conscious of seeing an old man who hands me a large book, a record of the individual for whom I seek information."

Carl Jung, the noted psychologist, preferred to describe the Akashic Records as a powerful, tangible force of nature throughout the universe that he called the Collective Unconscious, kind of an eternal and infinite embodiment of the principle that for every action there's an equal and opposite reaction.

My definition of the Akashic Records is consistent with those philosophies. The Akashic Records are the entire sacrosanct body of God's knowledge, laws and memories. They're absolutely imprinted on the ether of every planet, solar system and galaxy God created. But they also very literally exist in written form, perfectly printed in the universal language of Aramaic, in a magnificent building on the Other Side called the Hall of Records.

We have the honor of perpetual access to the Akashic Records when we're at Home on the Other Side. Our spirits, safely housed in our subconscious minds, have perpetual access to them as well during our fleeting incarnations here on earth. During sleep, hypnosis, meditation or physiological unconsciousness, when our noisy, chaotic, conscious minds are temporarily out of the way, our spirits know exactly where the Akashic Records are and how to get there. We turn to them more often than we consciously realize for answers, for clarity, for comfort and for the nourishment only God can provide.

Please don't let me create the mistaken impression that among the impossibly vast aisles of the Hall of Records, taking up an incomprehensible amount of space on shelves more endless than we can imagine, there are actual volumes entitled "Akashic Records." Instead, let the correct impression wash over you that as you stand inside this very real, unimaginably infinite structure and try to take in scrolls upon scrolls upon scrolls, volumes upon volumes upon volumes, lined on shelves upon shelves upon shelves far beyond what the eyes can begin to see, you're gazing at a fraction of the entirety of the Akashic Records. They have no beginning. They have no end. They are being added to with every passing moment of every life, every new thought, every spirit entering a fetus, every spirit returning Home. The Hall of

Records contains the Akashic Records, but it can also be said that every fluid word contained within the infinite Hall of Records *is* the Akashic Records, and that they've been added to considerably since you began reading this paragraph.

I was doing a hypnosis session many years ago with a client I'll call Susan, letting her spirit mind take her wherever it wanted. The more she talked, the more aware I was that her spirit was on a journey far, far away from the room we were sitting in. It's hard to describe how and why this particular session was so intense for me, but I remember an odd sense that something significant was happening when I finally asked, "Where are you, Susan?"

She began to describe a vast domed building, with aisle after aisle after aisle as far as the eye could see, containing an infinite number of shelves that held an even more infinite number of scrolls. As her description became more detailed, I recognized it as a place I'd traveled to myself—she was walking through the Hall of Records on the Other Side.

And to my shock, for the first and only time during a hypnosis session, I realized that I was with her, in those stunning, endless aisles full of charts and literature and maps and art and wisdom and thoughts that make up the body of God's Akashic Records.

I started to say something but immediately stopped myself, not wanting to lead her. It turned out I didn't need to say a word. She said it instead: "You're here with me."

She walked us through that amazing place beneath that magnificent dome until suddenly I noticed a beautiful dark-haired woman in blue gossamer in the distance, several aisles away, approaching us. I knew it was Susan's Spirit Guide, and I knew her name was Rachel. Still I kept my mouth shut. Again Susan spoke up. "Someone's with us."

I was straining to keep the excitement out of my voice at such immediate, undeniable validation that our spirits really were on this trip together. I simply, quietly asked her who it was. She answered, "It's a woman. She has dark hair. I don't know why, but I think she's my Spirit Guide."

At that instant Rachel saw us and called out, "Susan . . . !" I bit my tongue, determined not to make a sound and keep letting Susan, not me, stay in the lead. Sure enough, Susan breathlessly said, "Did you hear that?"

I asked what she'd heard.

She replied, "She said my name."

It was a heart-stopping moment. Almost as heart-stopping as the discovery we made when we played back the audiotape of that session. My voice clearly said, "Who's with us?" Susan's voice clearly said, "It's a woman. She has dark hair. I don't know why, but I think she's my Spirit Guide."

And then a third voice, clear as a bell on the tape, said, "Susan . . . !"

Her Spirit Guide, Rachel, as audible in my office through the tiny speaker of my mundane tape recorder as she'd been standing among the glorious sanctity of the Akashic Records beneath that white marble dome of the Hall of Records on the Other Side. Don't ever let anyone tell you the Akashic Records aren't real, that they're just a lovely bit of imagery or a philosophical metaphor. I've seen them. Whether you consciously remember or not, so have you, during astral trips here on earth and during your rich, full life at Home.

This is an eternal universe God has created for us, just as He Himself is eternal. There is no time in eternity, no past, present or future. There's nothing but now. So God's written body of knowledge includes everything that ever has been and everything that ever will be, in that most hallowed hall full of pages called the Akashic Records.

Alchemy

Alchemy is an ancient practice in which metallurgy, medicine, mysticism, chemistry and religion were blended together into an optimistic worldwide school of thought.

There were several goals involved in alchemy, but the most famous of them was the effort to transform base metals into gold or silver. As blatantly greedy as that motivation seems at first glance, alchemists' beliefs were consistent with the general belief systems of the ancient world. And among those beliefs was an inseparable bond between the physical and the spiritual/metaphysical. Trying to turn base metals into precious metals was symbolic of alchemists' simultaneous hope of bringing the universe closer to its highest potential, physically and spiritually. Gold was thought to be as close to perfection as an earthly substance could get, both beautiful and immune to corruption. So the alchemists' further hope was that if they could find the key to gold's durable longevity, maybe in the process they could also unearth the secret to curing diseases.

Essential to the process of changing base metals into precious metals was the elusive, mystical Philosopher's Stone. It actually wasn't a stone at all, but a "medicine," with a recipe so cryptic and filled with arcane symbolism that it's no wonder the Philosopher's Stone was so rare and the object of centuries of searching, speculating and fantasizing. Two of the ingredients, for example, were said to be "philosophical mercury" and "philosophical sulphur." How exactly to blend them is a whole series of mysteries in itself, but they're not properly combined until they've achieved perfect unity. Once the Philosopher's Stone was somehow achieved, its applications could be understood only "with the help of the Holy Ghost." The reward wasn't just creating gold out of lead, though. The Philosopher's Stone was also believed to be a source of great wisdom, power and healing, to have the ability to restore youth and to purify the body of potentially fatal germs and illnesses.

The Philosopher's Stone was the essence of the second genuine intention of ancient alchemy: to discover an elixir that would cure all diseases and indefinitely extend human life expectancy.

Last and certainly not least, it was the ultimate aspiration of alchemy to develop the ability to create human life.

The study and practice of alchemy and its variations managed to last for two thousand years before modern science, modern chemistry, modern medicine and modern metallurgy began unraveling the majority of the foundations on which alchemy was based.

It hasn't completely vanished from today's world, though—even now the concept of finding a way to purify the earth's resources and the human spirit at the same time, and to explore and validate through the sciences the connection between the soul and the Creator, is irresistible to some modern-day alchemists who quietly keep right on working—some with the most fraudulent intentions, but a handful still earnestly trying to keep an ancient discipline alive.

Altered State (of Consciousness)

This is a term that gained enormous popularity during the New Age era, which made it seem like something that's accessible only to a highly educated, highly experienced, very "in" handful of believers in trance, meditation or yoga.

Here's the truth: Altered states of consciousness happen to most of us one way or another on a regular basis.

An altered state of consciousness is simply a state in which the mind conceives, perceives and processes information in a different way than it normally does.

That includes trances, meditation, astral travel, hypnosis (regressive and otherwise), clairaudience, clairvoyance, clairsentience and most other forms of psychic and paranormal experiences.

It also includes dreams, daydreams, taking most recreational and prescription drugs and drinking enough alcohol that you feel its effects.

Now, obviously, those lists include voluntary altered states of consciousness we can control—essentially the items listed in that first paragraph—and those we can't control. And yes, you might look at items like drugs and alcohol and think you have control over those as well. After all, if you indulge at all, you choose what quantity over what length of time, right?

But what you don't control when your state of consciousness is altered by any foreign substance is the exact way and extent to which it will be altered on any given occasion. You know as well as I do that there are any number of variables involved in the effect your usual amount of alcohol or drugs has on you, and that even if you're mellow or hilarious eight times out of ten when you're high, you could turn angry, aggressive and obnoxious those other two times without having the slightest idea which way it might go before you choose to indulge. Let's face it—not having the slightest idea which way it might go is the antithesis of control.

And then there are the hallucinogens and club drugs—LSD, peyote, Ecstasy, crystal meth, an apparently resurging cocaine, GBX and other currently chic street pharmaceuticals, all of which are popular precisely for their reputation for being mind/consciousness altering. There again, while a temporary loss of control and break from reality might sound like a refreshing change of pace, not to mention a stress reliever to beat all others, the most conspicuous alteration you'll notice in your consciousness is that every one of your abilities to make choices, rational or just plain nuts, will go right out the window. Hallucinations might sound intriguing if you've never experienced them, but you'll have no control over how unforgettably horrifying those hallucinations might be. The rushes of Ecstasy or crystal meth or cocaine might sound, or even feel, like that first downhill plummet on a thrilling roller coaster, or they might just as easily make you so paranoid that you can no longer distinguish your friends from your enemies. GBX could possibly heighten a sexual experience, but more likely it will render you completely unconscious and subject you to the whim of whoever happens to be around at the moment. And in not one of those cases will the choice be yours, once you've stepped over those particular pharmaceutical lines. Will your mind conceive, perceive and process information in a different way than it normally does? Absolutely. Does that qualify drugs and other intoxicants as inducing an altered state of consciousness? Obviously. But with so many ways to arrive at altered states of consciousness available that don't rob us of our choices—and let's face it, choices equal freedom, which we can't forfeit at any cost—why on earth not opt for one of those that leave the control in our hands where it belongs?

Amulets

The word "amulet" can be traced back to a few Latin words and terms that translate to "means of defense." So appropriately, an amulet is a token of some kind worn in many cultures to ward off evil. Whether it's small bags of dust from tombs, pouches of tobacco, jewelry made of precious and semiprecious stones shaped like scarab beetles or rams or crescent moons, or crystals and bells sewn into the hems of garments, there's no limit to the forms amulets can take or the variety of faiths who wouldn't dream of leaving home without them.

An amulet serves a slightly different purpose from its cousin, a regularly worn token called a talisman, which is thought to bring good luck. Trying to trace the very beginning of belief in amulets is virtually impossible. But since they're depicted on walls of ancient Egyptian writings and were often buried with mummies, it's not a stretch to theorize that even the caveman might have carried a symbol of protection.

The Eye of Horus: an Egyptian amulet

I have to admit, it makes me smile when I travel, especially in Egypt, Greece and Turkey, and notice how sheepish people look when I ask them about the amulets they're wearing. They rush to tell me they don't really believe in them, they're not really superstitious, *but* . . . And to be fair, I'm not superstitious either, but I don't blame people for hedging their bets, and inevitably these same generous, sheepish people send me home with a fresh supply of amulets, not one of which I would ever part with.

With a couple of provisions, I actually think there can be some value in carrying or wearing amulets and other symbols. One of those provisions is moderation. I have a dear actress friend who was complaining one night at dinner that her neck was so stiff and aching she could barely move her head. I asked if it might have something to do with the twenty pounds or so of crystal necklaces she happened to be wearing.

"These?" she asked as if I were either crazy or stupid. "Don't you know how healing crystals are?"

I guess she didn't get the irony of that statement. She still insists on draping herself in healing crystal necklaces, her neck still hurts, and she's sure I don't know what I'm talking about when I try to explain to her that one crystal can be just as powerful as a hundred (and a lot less heavy).

Which leads to the other provision: Keep in mind that crystals, amulets and any other symbols you choose to carry or wear have no power at all of their own. They're exactly as blessed, protective, healing, energizing or calming as you believe them to be—no more, no less—because they can be wonderfully helpful, tangible reminders of priorities on which you want to focus your own God-given, God-centered energy. The one piece of jewelry I'm never without, for example, is my Celtic cross. You'll never see me without it, on TV, at lectures, traveling, anywhere. I don't wear it to please God so He'll give me more protection or better luck. I wear it because it's the symbol of Gnostic Christianity; I'm a Gnostic Christian, and as a Gnostic Christian I already have all the protection and all the luck I need. (At its most ridiculously oversimplified, Gnostic Christianity is the belief that we each have, not around us but *within* us, the divine spirit of our Creator. That divine spirit within us connects us all, and our most worthwhile spiritual journeys lead us not "outward" but "inward," where the answers lie.)

So when it comes to amulets, my position is, go right ahead and wear one if you want. Then, each and every time you so much as glance at it, let it cue you to surround yourself at that same moment with the sacred white light of the Holy Spirit. And what do you know, that amulet will end up having a dazzling ability to protect you after all.

Angels

One of the most common misconceptions about Angels is that if we and/or our loved ones live fine, pure, reverent lives here on earth, we can aspire to become Angels someday when we're on the Other Side again. While it's a lovely thought, it just happens to be impossible.

Please don't let that fact be discouraging, as if our worth in God's eyes is somehow diminished by our inability to ascend to membership in that divine, glorious legion of winged protectors. God doesn't place greater value on His Angels than He places on us. He cherishes us equally and unconditionally. We're not prevented from becoming Angels because He finds us unworthy. We're prevented by simple physiology: Angels and people are two different species.

The easiest way to remember the distinction between Angels and us is that Angels never incarnate as people. They never live a life on earth in a human body. They're able to take human form to accomplish brief missions here on earth, but you'll notice that in every one of the literally millions of stories of earthly Angel encounters, the person/Angel seems to appear out of nowhere and vanish again just as quickly. That's because Angels come and go for our benefit from their Home, which is exclusively on the Other Side.

Angels also never speak. Their communication is exclusively telepathic, although it's so powerful that humans often come away from contact with them convinced that words were actually spoken. It's not that they don't have voices. They certainly do, and the beauty of their voices is impossible to capture with any adjectives in our

Angels

vocabulary. But the voices of Angels are reserved for only one purpose: to celebrate the glory of God through soaring hymns of praise that resound throughout heaven and the universe and have, on at least one occasion, found their way to earth. (See "Hall of Voices.")

While some Angels are given proper names in the Bible and other religious works—Michael, Gabriel and Raphael, for example—the truth is, Angels are androgynous. There aren't male Angels and female Angels. Their bodies and facial features are identically exquisite. They transcend and encompass all races when it comes to coloring, and they vary their coloring appropriately for their brief visits here. But everyone who sees them, both on earth and at Home, notices that their skin seems almost to sparkle, as if the sun is perpetually glistening off of it. In fact, the source of this very special effect isn't external, but internal. Angels are quite literally illuminated from within by the loving, sacred, perfect light of their Creator, which is their essence.

Within the vast population of Angels, there are eight levels, or "ranks," in a way, if we can make sure the word "importance" never interferes with the word "ranks." (There are no more or less important Angels, no matter what the level or rank.) Angels earn advancement from one level to the next based on their body of experience, and with each new level comes more power. In other words, whether they're

protecting us from harm, saving lives, bringing us messages, performing miracles or simply infusing us with sudden moments of love or joy
or comfort or hope when we least expect them, Angels are eternally
accumulating experiences. The more vast the body of experience, the
higher the level. And the higher the level, the more powerful the Angel.

All eight levels of Angels are charged with being God's mightiest,
most direct link between earth and the Other Side, the messengers,
protectors and miracle workers He sends us. They're physically distinguished from each other at Home by the color of their wings. In as-
cending order, from the least experienced and powerful to the most,
these are the eight levels:

* *Angels* — dusty, gray-white wings
* *Archangels* — pure white wings
* *Cherubim* — white wings with gold tips
* *Seraphim* — white wings with silver tips
* *Virtues* — pale blue wings
* *Dominions* — green wings
* *Thrones* — deep purple wings
* *Principalities* — solid brilliant gold wings

The first seven levels of Angels can take the initiative to intervene
on our behalf in a crisis, available to us in the blink of an eye whether
God sends them or they sense our need on their own. The stunningly
powerful Principalities, on the other hand, come only through a combination of God's command and our very specific call for them. The
Principalities can create miracles, prevent fatalities and turn around
even the most seemingly lost, misguided lives.

In addition to the countless Angels who constantly watch over us
during these brief trips away from Home we hilariously refer to as
"life," we're also assigned our own Angels on the Other Side before we
come here. The more difficult the goals and challenges we've laid out
for ourselves (see "the Chart"), the greater the number or levels of An-

gels who'll be specially designated on our behalf to keep an extra eye out for us. It's also worth mentioning that the more spiritually open, generous and conscious we become, the more added Angels gather around us, drawn like moths to a flame as the light of God's love inside us begins to glow so brightly that we almost sparkle like the Angels themselves.

Apotheosis

On a huge scale, so grand it's virtually useless to the vast majority of us, "apotheosis" means the deification of humankind to the rank of gods. On a much more practical, personal level, it means that as we each continue to explore all aspects of our connection to God, we're on our own step-by-step elevation to the Divine.

I've been doing readings for fifty years. Only in the last ten or so have people been showing genuine concern about whether or not they're on track with their life chart, what their purpose is for being here and if they're fulfilling that purpose. There's a groundswell of inner consciousness going on, a growing Homesickness for our God-center, not a fad as we've seen in past decades, but a heartfelt realization that without an active, fully expressed relationship with our Father, we're not whole.

A client I'll call Martha started her reading the other day by asking about her Life Theme, her purpose for being here. I told her she actually had two: rejection and caretaker.

She was shocked. "Rejection?!" she protested. "I haven't been rejected."

I admit it: Every time a client asks me a question, I give an honest/psychic answer and they immediately argue with me; I find myself wondering why they bothered to come see me. If they'd prefer to answer all their own questions, I could just sit there and nod like an airhead no matter what they say. But let's face it, it's not exactly my style. In Martha's case, I decided to argue back by giving her a few headlines of her life instead of being polite and waiting for her to give them to me.

"You haven't been rejected? You weren't given up by your mother and then placed in an orphanage when you were two years old?" I asked her.

"Well, yes, but . . ."

"And didn't your husband walk out on you and your three children?" Her voice was a little quieter for, "Yes."

"And then a jealous coworker pulled some dirty tricks and got you fired?"

This time she only nodded.

"And none of this strikes you as rejection?"

She shrugged a little, embarrassed. "I honestly never thought of it that way. And things are much better now."

"I know they are," I told her. "Of course they are. Because you've managed to learn from all this and let it make you stronger, instead of weaker and self-pitying. And now you're taking care of your family, especially your elderly adoptive parents, right?"

She nodded again.

"That's called being a caretaker, Martha."

She was genuinely surprised. And this was not a stupid woman. She was just experiencing something that happens to a lot of us: seeing her life through someone else's eyes and really understanding how far she'd come. And in seeing her life through a spiritual psychic's eyes, she also proved to herself that no matter what it takes, no matter how hard it is, even in a life like Martha's in which it looked as if everyone else were pulling the strings, we *will* stay true to the course of our charts, and we *will* follow our Life Themes.

When she tried to argue with me, and when any of you try to argue with me, make no mistake about it, I really do know it's only your conscious mind that's putting up a fight, just like mine does when I get in my own way. But your spirit mind already knows everything I ever tell you. When some combination of it and I manage to penetrate the noise and the stress and the earthly trivia your conscious mind is so preoccupied with, and I see that recognition and connection with your spirit light up in your eyes, it literally sends a thrill through me every time that has nothing to do with me at all. I'm simply witnessing your glimpse of the truth that I pray you'll hold on to, cherish and celebrate—the truth that there is a spirit inside you, a spirit that always was and always will be, created and loved by no less than God Himself.

You are God's child. His direct descendant.

Never let a day go by when you don't let that truth light up in your eyes.

Never let a day go by without your own apotheosis, your own elevation to the Divine.

Apport/Apportation

The spirit world can and does manipulate physical objects here on earth in some marvelous, dramatic ways, often transporting them through space and seemingly impenetrable barriers so that they appear in places we would swear they can't possibly be. That wonderful manipulation is called apport, or apportation.

Sadly, infuriatingly and/or unfairly, the spirit world isn't always given the credit it deserves for apportation. Most often, we frantically search for any earthly explanation, no matter how idiotic, when even a glaring example of apportation occurs—absentmindedness, carelessness, burglars with a sudden attack of conscience, *anything* but the simple truth that the spirit world tries in countless ways to get our attention and let us know they're with us.

A client recently shared a typical, lovely story that illustrates the phenomenon of apportation beautifully. Her father had passed away after a long illness. She and her two brothers meticulously followed every one of the requests in his will when planning his funeral, from the music he specified to the white suit he wanted to wear and, most especially, his beloved mother's one-of-a-kind engraved, hand-carved rosary, which he wanted to be holding as he was buried. She and her brothers each kissed the rosary in his lifeless hands as a last loving farewell at the grave site in the moments before his casket slowly descended to its final resting place.

They weren't sure whether to be frightened or deeply moved when they gathered in the kitchen of the family home for breakfast early the next morning and found that engraved, hand-carved rosary gleaming in the middle of the table where a ray of sunlight could find it through the nearby window.

I'm happy to report that they spent only a few minutes ruling out those earthly explanations I mentioned earlier. Yes, it was definitely the same one-of-a-kind rosary their father had asked to be buried with. No, it wasn't possible that all three of them had forgotten to put it in his casket with him, and then simply imagined kissing it as they said good-bye to him and watched him disappear six feet into the ground with it wrapped around his hands.

Which meant there were only two ways it could have found its way to the middle of the kitchen table that morning.

Either someone dug up their father's grave during the night without being noticed, absconded with the rosary, drove two hours to the family home, crept into the house, left the rosary and crept out again without setting off the elaborate alarm system, or . . .

Their father, from the spirit world, had apported the rosary to that table as proof to his children that he was alive and well.

Now, between those two alternatives, can you honestly say the first explanation is more logical than that gorgeous, surprisingly common wave from a loving spirit called apportation?

And by the way, sometimes earthly explanations are the logical, correct ones. You'll never hear me suggest that every time something turns up in an odd place, or gets misplaced and then found again, it's the spirit world at work. I'm simply saying that when an object shows up somewhere that seems virtually impossible, or that you know with absolute certainty wasn't there when you looked there earlier, just smile to yourself, recognize the probability of an apport and say thank you to that spirit who's asking to be noticed.

Armageddon

The Biblical book of Revelations contains a verse (16:16) that reads, "And they assembled them at the place which is called in Hebrew Armageddon." That's the one and only time the word "Armageddon" appears in the entirety of the Bible. And yet Armageddon has become a dreaded synonym for the final battle between good and evil, Christ and the Antichrist, God and Satan, or all the kings of the earth, that will end the world.

Revelations is a vision of the Apostle John. Few bodies of writing have been analyzed more closely and interpreted in a wider variety of ways, with the result that humankind has been braced for the cataclysmic Armageddon for about 2,000 years now. It was "definitely" World War I, World War II, the Gulf War, 9/11/01, the onset of polio, the onset of AIDS, the Holocaust, the appearance of the Hale-Bopp comet, and, farther back in history, a few total eclipses, earthquakes, tsunamis and volcanic eruptions. I still love the story of the Armageddon that was "definitely" going to end life on earth when the calendar changed from 999 to 1000. At the stroke of midnight, countless panic-stricken people around the world went running out into the streets in uncontrollable hysteria. Wouldn't you love to know how long they stayed out there before they got bored and went home to bed?

(And while we're busy snickering over those poor, unsophisticated fools, let's pause to count how many people we know who squirreled away vast amounts of bottled water and canned goods, built underground shelters, cashed out their bank accounts, bought gas masks and loaded up on first-aid supplies when the calendar changed from 1999 to 2000.)

Don't misunderstand. I'm a big believer in "better safe than sorry."

But every bit as strongly I believe that a life lived in a hard hat, crouched in the corner of a basement, is a life wasted.

With all respect to the Apostle John, I have never read a prophecy (including my own) that's guaranteed to be one hundred percent accurate. God is the only one-hundred-percent-accurate Being, and the rest of us can only listen and interpret as closely and precisely as possible.

I've also never read a prophecy (including my own) that pinpoints the date of the real Armageddon, when/if such a thing exists. Again, if that's something God knows, He's clearly decided there's no benefit in letting us in on it. As some of you might be aware, I've written a whole book of prophecies that take us to the year 2100. After 2100, I don't see a thing. That could mean that in 2100 the earth goes dark. It could just as easily mean that a century is as far ahead as my prophetic gift allows me to see. Your guess is as good as mine, which is inevitably the case when it comes to doomsday prophecies.

And I've most certainly never read a prophecy about an oncoming Armageddon that doesn't offer hope. For better or worse, we're the hope. Whether or not there's an Armageddon isn't up to God, or some imaginary creature with horns and a pitchfork. Defusing the Armageddon prophecy is an absolute option that rests in the hands of humankind, and our willingness to start being actively responsible for this earth and its citizens for whose care we've been entrusted.

According to the Apostle John, later in Revelations (22:1–2), "Then he [an Angel] showed me the river of the water of life, bright as crystal, flowing from the throne of God and of the Lamb through the middle of the street of the city [the new Jerusalem]; also, on either side of the river, the tree of life with its twelve kinds of fruit, yielding its fruit each month. The leaves of the tree were for the healing of the nations."

Crystal rivers, thriving fertile trees, the healing of nations. We can make those things happen, or we can wait for God to come down and do it. But since He's not the one who made this mess we're in, why should He be responsible for cleaning it up?

From the Inca Q'ero shamans:
"Follow your own footsteps
Learn from the rivers,
The trees and the rocks.
Honor the Christ,
the Buddha,
your brothers and sisters.
Honor the Earth Mother and the Great Spirit.
Honor yourself and all of creation.
Look with the eyes of your soul and engage the essential."

From the Aborigines:
"We've got to learn to love one another.
You see, that's really what's going to happen to the earth.
We're going to have tidal waves.
We're going to have earthquakes.
That's coming because we don't consider this land as our Mother.
We've taken away the balance, and we're not putting it back."

From author, metaphysicist and prophet Sir Arthur Conan Doyle:

"Mankind can be saved by returning to its spiritual values."

And probably no one put it more plainly, less poetically and more eloquently than the brilliant Sir Winston Churchill:

"If you go on with this nuclear arms race, all you are going to do is make the rubble bounce."

So yes, 2,000 years ago the concept of Armageddon, the last battle, the end of the world, was presented to us, and ever since then we've ignored the rest of the story—that if it comes, it won't be inflicted upon us by God; it will be our own greedy, careless, irresponsible, lazy, ego-driven self-fulfilling prophecy.

This one's from me:

"Armageddon is inevitable only if we let it be."

Astral Catalepsy

You're sound asleep when suddenly you're jarred awake by one or more of the following frightening sensations:

* paralysis
* shortness of breath, often from some oppressive weight on the chest
* being touched by something or someone lewd or menacing, but invisible
* an overwhelming vibration
* being pinned down and prevented from moving by an unseen evil presence
* loud noises, from a buzz or hum to a blaring clamor as if fifty different radio stations are blasting at the same time
* the appearance of strange lights
* a certainty that a threatening entity is sitting on the bed or moving the bedclothes

If any of the experiences on that list have happened to you, please take heart: You're not losing your mind, you're not in any real danger and you're certainly not alone. In fact, cultures around the world have created folklore that dates back hundreds of years to explain these phenomena, from witches to a giant devil to an old hag to a baby ghost. And some UFO enthusiasts attribute it to the results of painful experiments during alien abductions.

In truth, though, the explanation for all of those sensations when they jar you from a sound sleep is an unnerving but fascinating occurrence called astral catalepsy.

The term "astral catalepsy" was coined around 1930 by a researcher named Sylvan Muldoon, who spent much of his life recording the astral trips his spirit took during the night while his body slept. The first of those trips that he was aware of, when he was twelve years old, illustrates beautifully the birth of his intensive study of what he'd heard referred to until then only as "sleep paralysis."

Muldoon's first recorded astral trip during sleep started with his waking up in the middle of the night to find himself unable to move, see or hear, with a painful sense of severe pressure on his head. As his senses and ability to move slowly returned, and the pressure on his head subsided, he realized that he was actually outside his body, floating above his bed and able to look down at himself and watch himself sleep. He was conscious of his spirit being pulled from a horizontal position to a vertical one as it left his body, and of embarking on a very detailed tour of the house in which he, in his spirit form, was able to move with great ease through doors and walls. He also was very aware of trying to shake his parents awake because he was afraid of what was happening to him, but they never seemed to feel him touching them.

And then, when he was above his body again, his spirit was pulled back into a horizontal position, and he experienced the same paralysis, loss of senses and pressure on his head that he'd gone through earlier. After a feeling of being jerked abruptly back into his body, he sat bolt upright in bed in a complete panic, able to remember and immediately write down the whole sequence of events with crystal clarity.

Sylvan Muldoon had an advantage in that experience that few who go through astral catalepsy enjoy—he had full memory of all the events before and after the sleep paralysis occurred, which gave him a context for what had happened to him. Without that context, it's no wonder astral catalepsy feels like such a terrifying assault. So here's the context, and the explanation behind it.

Several times a week, whether we're aware of it or not, our spirits take temporary breaks from our bodies during sleep to go visiting, exploring and simply running free outside the confines of these goofy earthbound vehicles we occupy while we're here. These breaks are as refreshing and nourishing for our spirits as they are for our conscious minds, not to mention a frequent reminder that our spirits can and do thrive as the separate, eternal entities they are, no matter what happens to our mortal bodies. (Also see "Astral Projection" and "Astral Travel.")

The vast majority of the time, our spirits slip into and out of our bodies with the greatest of ease, without disturbing our sleeping conscious minds for a moment. But on rare occasions, depending on the level of sleep the conscious mind happens to be in, it can "catch" the spirit coming or going from the body. And in its less-than-alert state, the conscious mind, realizing the spirit is half in and half out of its body, jumps to an obvious conclusion: The body must be dying. It panics and promptly sends "you're dying!" signals to the body that correspond exactly to many of the sensations of astral catalepsy—the paralysis, the loss of the senses, the inability to breathe or cry out for help; a whole series of physiological and neurological "short circuits." But when the conscious mind realizes that the spirit is safe and sound in the body again and it's not dying after all, the signals stop, the sensations subside and another jarring but ultimately harmless incident is over with.

It's also worth pointing out that the spirit world we're part of when we astrally travel is a whole other dimension than the one we live in here on earth. The spirit world's vibrational frequency is much higher than earth's, not to mention the fact that gravity and other earthly laws of physics don't exist there. So a half-asleep conscious mind catching its spirit literally traveling from one dimension to another, from weightlessness to gravity, could understandably be jolted awake by perceptions of noises (like sonic booms) and oppressive heaviness.

"Understandable" doesn't necessarily make it any less frightening while it's happening, of course, but it's also affirming proof that while we sleep, our spirits are off having beautiful adventures, reunions and Homecomings for our benefit whether we're consciously aware of them or not.

Astral Projection

Astral projection is the simple and surprisingly common process of the spirit taking temporary breaks from the body that houses it. The break might be momentary, and the spirit might stay in close proximity to the body, for the sheer exercise of it. Or it might be a more distant experience in which the spirit projects itself to some specific location, which in the dimension of the spirit realm takes no longer than the blink of an eye.

A client recently told me a story that perfectly illustrates the instantaneous and sometimes unintentional nature of an astral projection experience. She was in a meeting with several other executives at a major communications company in Houston. One moment she was seated in her designated chair at the long oval conference table, glancing with no conscious concern out the bank of windows at the city skyline. The next moment she was in the backseat of an Explorer that was careening wildly off an ice-covered mountain road and crashing down a rocky embankment, landing upside down among a stand of massive pines. She saw her husband behind the wheel, his air bag deployed, the left side of his head covered with blood and the Explorer's driver's window fractured. She saw her brother in the passenger's seat, his air bag deployed as well, unconscious, his head hanging at such an odd angle that she knew his neck was broken. He was pinned in place by the passenger's side of the vehicle, which had crushed in around him against a tree. She vaguely noticed a chaotic array of groceries scattered everywhere around her in the backseat, and the seeming impossibility that in this otherwise awful, grotesque silence, a football game still blared loud and clear on the Explorer's radio.

An instant later she was in the conference room again, so shaken that she excused herself and rushed to her office to call the cabin near Vail, Colorado, where she was joining her husband and brother that weekend for a skiing vacation. She looked at the clock as she waited for someone to answer. It was 3:36 P.M. When no one answered at the cabin, she tried both her husband's and her brother's cell phones, her heart in her throat when neither phone even rang.

In the blurry days and weeks that followed she learned more and more of the details. The Explorer had hit a patch of black ice and careened off the road on a trip back to the cabin from the grocery store in the mountain village a few miles away. A driver coming from the opposite direction witnessed the accident and called 911 at 3:24 P.M. Houston time. My client's husband died instantly of a skull fracture as a result of his head hitting the driver's-side window. Her brother died of a broken neck on the way to the hospital. A paramedic at the scene commented later that there was something jarring about the sound of that football game still blaring away as if nothing had happened.

See what I mean? Astral projection, a spirit trip from a conference room in Houston to a winding mountain road in Colorado, in less time than it takes to say the words. In this case, as much as my client loved her husband, it was her profound spirit connection to her brother, from this and many other lives, that propelled her to his side when she knew he was about to head Home.

A perfect example of how, even here on earth, the laws of time, distance and gravity become irrelevant when the spirit takes over.

So closely related to astral projection that they're almost indistinguishable is the phenomenon of astral travel. But very often, as you're about to see, during astral travel we actually experience the trip itself as well as the destination.

Astral Travel

Few activities sound more
foreign but come more naturally to us than astral travel.
Astral travel is nothing more
than our spirits taking a
break from these cumber-
some, gravity-challenged bodies they're housed in and
taking off to visit whomever
or wherever we want. It was
astral travel that brought us
here from the Other Side,
when our spirits entered their
chosen bodies, and it's astral
travel that will take us Home
again. We're born knowing
how to travel astrally, we
routinely travel astrally while

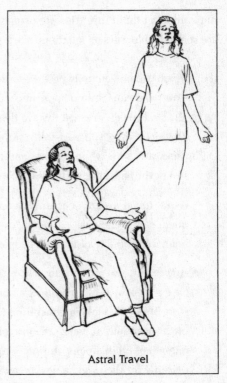

Astral Travel

we sleep (an average of two or three times a week, in fact), astral travel
lies at the core of some of our most vivid and memorable "dreams,"
and we can thank astral travel for the fact that victims of comas and
severely debilitating illnesses are only struggling physiologically, while
their spirits are busily, joyfully dashing from one journey to the next.

There's no limit to the people and places we can visit in our astral
travels. We routinely meet loved ones, both living and departed, from
this life and past lives, as well as dear friends we haven't shared an incarnation with but are very close to back Home. We routinely travel
the globe revisiting places we've loved, we routinely check up on people we miss or are worried about and we routinely go to the Other
Side, that place of places we're most Homesick for of all.

Our most frequent astral trips occur while we're sleeping, so it's not surprising that those trips are usually mistaken for dreams. There are some simple ways to tell them apart, though:

* If you dream you're flying without benefit of an airplane or other external means, it's not a dream. You're traveling astrally. And not all astral travel "dreams" involve flying, by the way. Like everyone else, including you, I astrally travel to the Other Side several times a month while I sleep, and to the best of my knowledge I've never had a dream in which I'm flying by my own power.

* Astral-travel experiences, unlike dreams, unfold in a logical sequence of events, just as waking experiences do, rather than in a haphazard jumble of images, people and locations.

* Any dream you're not only part of but actually view yourself in isn't a dream; it's an astral experience. You've heard story after story of people looking down from the ceiling at themselves during meditation, surgery, unconsciousness or comas. The same phenomenon happens during "dreams" for exactly the same reason—for the time being, you and your body are separate, and there's definitely a certain curious fascination with finding yourself able to observe yourself in action as an "outsider."

Once we've left our bodies, we actually have three speeds of astral travel to choose from. The first speed is the least disorienting—our spirits move at the same pace our bodies do when we're walking. The intermediate speed is fast enough to create the illusion that we're standing still while everything around us is flying past us from front to back. It's often accompanied by the sensation of moving against a roaring wind, which is actually not wind at all but our own rapid forward movement instead. At supernormal speed, our spirits can travel incomprehensible distances faster than our finite minds can imagine, to the point where we might remember our destinations and what we did while we visited, but we have no awareness at all of how we got there and how we got back. If you've ever had an uncannily realistic dream of exploring a distant planet or touring a newly discovered galaxy halfway across the universe, chances are you've experienced astral travel at supernormal speed.

Some of you believe astral travel is possible but not something you can do yourself. Others of you believe astral travel is just another one of those myths we paranormal nutcases hope you're gullible enough to fall for. I'll respectfully leave you to your beliefs, secure in my certainty that one of these days you'll take an astral trip too clear and too powerful to explain away. Then, when someone tells you it was just your imagination, or you're simply crazy, you'll know how the rest of us feel.

Astrology

We know that God didn't create anything haphazard in this universe but instead designed every detail with great deliberation. So it's no wonder we're constantly searching His creation for the key that will break His code and allow us finally to read and interpret His plans for the future of the world, and for us.

And what more obvious place to keep searching than the cosmos— magnificent, unfathomable, filled with mystery and unanswered questions, making us feel so tiny but at the same time so in awe of this eternal infinity in which we have the honor to be included? Why wouldn't we look to the sun, moon and stars, with their perfect, divine order, and suspect that He's written messages among them?

Astrology, of course, is a result of our search for those messages, for understanding His plans and, if we can, get an edge on them. It's an ancient art, consulted by everyone from pharaohs, emperors, kings and presidents to the most common of us, an equal opportunity messenger with something new to say to each of us every day if we insist on watching it that closely. Its best-used intention is to suggest, not dictate, the options and obstacles in our path and our most beneficial responses to them.

Since there are hundreds if not thousands of books on astrology, and its vast popularity precedes us all (this time around), it's hard to imagine that any of you don't know that the astrology chart, aka the zodiac, is made up of twelve sun/natal signs, each with its own ruling planet and each designated by a specific segment of the calendar. Those sun signs are:

ARIES—ruled by Mars—March 21 to April 19
TAURUS—ruled by Venus—April 20 to May 20
GEMINI—ruled by Mercury—May 21 to June 21
CANCER—ruled by the Moon—June 22 to July 22
LEO—ruled by the Sun—July 23 to August 22
VIRGO—ruled by Mercury—August 23 to September 22
LIBRA—ruled by Venus—September 23 to October 23
SCORPIO—ruled by Pluto—October 24 to November 21
SAGITTARIUS—ruled by Jupiter—November 22 to December 21
CAPRICORN—ruled by Saturn—December 22 to January 19
AQUARIUS—ruled by Uranus—January 20 to February 18
PISCES—ruled by Neptune—February 19 to March 20

Every sign is characterized by a set of character/personality traits, tendencies and habits. And if the astrology story ended with our sun signs, we'd be one boring, predictable planet full of people.

Our sun signs, though, are only the beginning of the cosmic influences that are factored in to make up the totality of our charts, and of our unique identities. *Very* simply put:

✳ OUR SUN SIGN, defined by the position of the Sun at the moment of our birth, is our inner self, the "real us," our most basic outlook on life.

✳ OUR ASCENDANT, also called our "rising sign," defined by which sign is rising above the horizon at the moment of our birth, is our core essence, the "spine" of our character.

✳ OUR MOON SIGN, defined by the position of the Moon at the moment of our birth, is kind of a sum total of our personality and emotional makeup.

Again, while we tend to categorize ourselves and each other by our sun signs, which definitely do influence us, it's important to recognize that our ascendants and our moon signs deeply influence our characters and our personalities as well.

But wait. There's more. (And we're still only scratching the surface.) The signs of the zodiac are also divided into categories according to the four basic earth elements.

THE AIR SIGNS, whose orientation tends toward their intellect, are Libra, Gemini and Aquarius.

THE WATER SIGNS, more emotionally oriented, are Cancer, Pisces and Scorpio.

THE EARTH SIGNS, the practical ones among us, are Capricorn, Virgo and Taurus.

THE FIRE SIGNS, with a tendency toward ambition, are Aries, Sagittarius and Leo.

Then there are the "sister signs," six signs away or directly opposite each other on the astrological chart—Libra and Aries, for example. Sister signs tend to complement each other, like twins, even though their ruling elements are different—in this case, for example, one is an air sign and the other is a fire sign. Taurus and Scorpio, Gemini and Sagittarius, Cancer and Capricorn, Leo and Aquarius, and Virgo and Pisces are the other sister signs who tend to balance each other when they get together.

Which is not to imply for a moment that when looking for a partner or spouse you should rush straight into the arms of a sister sign. In fact, I'm not an advocate of anyone choosing or avoiding anyone on the basis of his/her sun sign. Again, the ascendant and the moon sign are too influential over character and personality traits to dismiss so easily.

One of the most fascinating aspects of astrology that you may not be aware of, that will make even more sense to you when you read the section on the Chart, is that we actually predetermine every major, minor and trivial cosmic influence in our individual astrological makeup before our spirit even enters the fetus. When we write the detailed chart for our upcoming lifetime, we specify the exact time, date and location of our birth—also known as the basics on which every astrological identity and progression are calculated.

Finally, either to amuse or annoy you, I'll give an extremely brief thumbnail sketch of each sun sign's most general tendencies. If you find yourself starting to get offended, reread the above sentence about the shortsightedness of dismissing your ascendant and your moon sign, and/or sit down and read this with an Aries—they tend to have a great sense of humor about themselves, and it wouldn't do the rest of us any harm for some of that to rub off.

* ARIES—both impulsive and compulsive; intensely loyal; tend to keep proving the same point over and over and over again until they're convinced of your intelligence; mortally offended if you turn your back on them when they're talking to you; dislike change; need their own space; resist authority

* TAURUS—when ascendant and moon sign are also Taurus, aka a "triple Taurus," I'm sorry, but boring; chronically act dense for attention; verbalization patterns tend to be either poetic or overly verbose; stubborn; slow to forgive; artistic; care deeply about ecology and neatness; not family oriented but very protective of loved ones; sentimental about birthdays, anniversaries, etc.

* GEMINI—avid talkers; cautious about forming friendships; self-conscious; very concerned with learning; changeable and multi-faceted; fun; easygoing yet fickle and difficult to keep grounded

* CANCER—home-loving and protective; frugal; maudlin and martyred; given to excess; great animal lovers; intensely selective; prone to moodiness but admirably fight it; easily hurt; will tell the same story eighty-five times and leave out the punch line eighty-five times

* LEO—great determination; insecure with loud barks; strong fidelity; heartbroken if hurt but enraged if someone they love is hurt; hate to lie, hate liars more; not fond of hard work but yearn for material wealth; hate to lose; too often let others form their opinion of themselves; more psychic about events than about people

* VIRGO—promiscuous, with usually prim exterior; organized and meticulous; good with people; obsessive about colors, finishing what they start, making lists; hypersensitive; able to be deeply, faithfully in love with two or three people at once; better supporters than front-runners in an organization; dislike change; permissive but inconsistent parents

* LIBRA (my sign)—natural-born mediators; tend to jump from subject to subject when talking; affectionate; magnanimous but paradoxically secretive; bad tempers; resent unsolicited advice; exceptional love of beauty; empathic, but see illness and self-pity as weakness; despise ingratitude; honest to a fault; equal balance of male and female sides

* SCORPIO—guided by their genitals but very goal oriented; not prone to verbalize their thoughts; want to change the world; cover all their bases, personally and professionally; take charge, but slow to battle; innately secure; loners; approach life with their own set of truths; natural stamina; great teachers

* SAGITTARIUS—very analytical; love mind-involved issues; in constant need of validation; anxiety-ridden; quick-witted; love to postulate no matter what the subject; need space and freedom but extremely faithful; softhearted but capable of being vindictive; blunt; highly intellectualized

* CAPRICORN—strongest sign of the zodiac (argue all you like); intellectualized emotion; love obstacles; analytical to a fault; brilliant retentive memories; won't tolerate phobias in themselves; great humanitarians; not vindictive; flexible to others' opinions; fastidious about clothing and neatness; comfortable with set patterns

* AQUARIUS—natural-born teachers; more comfortable with groups than with one-on-one relationships; love to dance, love water and the ocean; introverted while extroverted, as if always containing a hidden compartment; slow to anger but furious when they get there; romantic; very ingenious; hate injustice

* PISCES—the most intently metaphysical sign of the zodiac; thrive on compliments, but not empty flattery; deeply sensitive to slights and insults and rarely suffer in silence when offended; need romance, not just sex, in relationships; avid readers, students and note-takers; stubborn but flexible if they see they're wrong; great secret-keepers; despise prejudice and bigotry in any form; quick to defend others who are being treated unfairly

Atlantis

Once upon a time, 11,000 years ago, according to Plato, there was a continent in the middle of the Atlantic Ocean called Atlantis. Its population was very wealthy, sophisticated and powerful, thriving through a vast array of natural resources, extensive commerce with

Europe and Africa and weather so uniquely nurturing that Atlanteans enjoyed not one but two annual harvests of the widest imaginable variety of crops. The animal kingdom flourished on Atlantis as well in this peaceful, beautiful island nation.

The first king of Atlantis was Atlas, eldest son of the sea god Poseidon and mortal Cleito. A gold statue of Poseidon in a chariot drawn by winged horses gilded the most central hill of the continent, where Cleito raised Atlas and his many brothers. The hill was surrounded by concentric circles of land and water, placed there by Poseidon to protect and provide for his beloved family.

Beyond the farthest circle of water from the hill stood the city of Atlantis, where most of the population of the continent lived. Hundreds of miles of plains surrounded the city, and to the north of the plains, mountains rose.

Slowly but surely the idyllic lives of the Atlanteans became insidiously infected with the corruption of greed, lust and an insatiable hunger for power. Zeus, the mighty god of the sky, looked angrily down at the moral wasteland Atlantis had become and summoned the other gods to exact an appropriate punishment for this ungrateful nation who'd been given so much.

And that punishment was so vast, so violent and so all-consuming that in one massive spasm of attacks from the sky, the sea and all of nature, the continent of Atlantis, all its wealth, all its wisdom, all its beauty and all its people were swallowed whole by the ocean, where they lie to this day in their watery tomb.

Plato told that story in his dialogues *Timaeus* and *Critias* around 350 B.C. It was, to the best of anyone's knowledge, the first written reference to a continent called Atlantis. And ever since, the debate has raged on: Was it fiction or nonfiction?

One of literally thousands of philosophers and prophets who stated with great authority that Atlantis was and will be again a very real continent was Madame Helena Blavatsky. In her book called *The*

Secret Doctrine, written in 1888, she predicted that both Atlantis and its Indian Ocean counterpart Lemuria will reappear, and added, "The elevated ridge in the Atlantic basin, 9,000 feet in height, which runs from a point near the British Islands, first slopes toward South America, then shifts almost at right angles to proceed in a south-easterly line toward the African coast. . . . This ridge is a remnant of an Atlantic continent. . . . Could it be traced further, it would establish the reality of a submarine horseshoe junction with a former continent in the Indian Ocean. . . . An impenetrable veil of secrecy was thrown over the occult and religious mysteries taught [on Atlantis], after the submersion of the last remnant of the Atlantean race, some 12,000 years ago."

Which anyone could say, let's face it, given the limited number of ways to prove them wrong in 1888. But more than one hundred years later, in March of 1996, *Discover* magazine published and described a series of satellite photographs that seemed to confirm the geographic imagery Madame Blavatsky couldn't possibly have witnessed herself:

"The Midatlantic Ridge snakes down the center of that ocean . . . off Greenland to the latitude of Cape Horn. . . . Under South Africa, the Southwest Indian Ridge shoots into the Indian Ocean like a fizzling rocket, or perhaps like the trail of some giant and cartoonish deep-sea mole."

If she were right about the geography, as many others have been, wouldn't it be silly not to at least keep an open mind to the possibility that maybe she was right about the reality of Atlantis as well, and the likelihood of both Atlantis and Lemuria emerging from their respective oceans again someday?

For the record, I couldn't agree with her more. We will see Atlantis and Lemuria rise into existence again. In fact, it's a promise, before the end of this century.

Aura

Your aura is the Life Force, also called the "etheric substance," that emanates from within you and surrounds your body like a subtle oval cloud of varying density. Some think of it as being made of energy. Others think of it as being made of electricity. I think: Use any word that helps you picture a projected power field that those around you undeniably sense and respond to, whether they're consciously aware of it or not, and some are even able to see.

Every aura contains all the colors of the rainbow, but the dominant outer colors vary depending on our physical and emotional health. Red indicates extreme anger, for example. Black is a sign of physical illness. Grief and depression show up as a murky yellow-green. A dark entity (see the section on the Dark Side) or an unhealthy ego (one with a chronically abusive sense of entitlement) will be the brown-black color of mud. Green implies health, and blue is a transmission of heightened awareness. Any of these colors are capable of "spiking," looking very much like a sunspot flaring up from the surface of the sun, when the root cause of the color has a sudden surge of strength or, if it's illness, grief or depression, a sudden downward spiral.

One commonly ignored fact is that, except when you're dealing with dark entities, there are three core bands of constant color and strength at the base of every aura. A band of white, the emanation of the Holy Spirit within us, is closest to the body. Next is gold, the innate dignity of our divine birthright. The third is purple, the glow of the sacred lineage of our spirit. These three inseparable core bands have a total thickness of no more than four to five inches. So to those of you who are able to see auras, please remember that the flares of color you're probably "reading" are temporary physical or emotional conditions. If you want to see a person's true character, look to see if bands of white, gold and purple form the aura's foundation.

Another fact that none of us probably recognize as often as we should is that we can make an active decision to project our core auras when we enter a room full of people, which is the most positive force field we can possibly offer. We know we can project our negative auras. We've all done it, whether we meant to or not, and we've all experienced it: Someone who's in an angry, violent, self-pitying or deeply depressed mood walks into a perfectly comfortable group and, without saying or doing a thing, reduces the group to an equally moody bunch of human thunderclouds. It's such a common phenomenon that we rarely go to a party of more than ten or twelve people without actually expecting at least one bucket of cold water to come walking in sooner or later. But a projected negative aura by any other name can still ruin a good time.

Projecting our core positive aura is as simple as forming the image. The bands of white, gold and purple, when combined and projected, form a bright, almost fluorescent glow of dusty mauve with a tinge of gold. As you enter a room in which you want to try this for yourself, simply picture the room being bathed in a golden mauve that's flowing from you as if you had turned on a strong, free-flowing tap.

One word of caution, though: Don't get discouraged if your effort isn't a success each and every time. What with this being earth and all, a negative aura has a range of about 150–200 feet when it's projected, compared to a positive aura, whose projected range averages thirty to forty feet. If you doubt that, just watch the next time a happy person arrives at a party or workplace, closely followed by an unhappy person, and see which one of them affects the crowd more. My money's on the unhappy person every time. It's unfortunate but true, which is why you'll find a section on Tools of Protection later in this book.

It's not just us humans on this earth who are blessed with auras. Every living thing has one, because every living thing is partly composed of energy, or a Life Force, and therefore every living thing emanates that Life Force from within itself. We'll discuss that at greater length in the section on Kirlian photography, a method by which auras are captured on film. For now, the truth to be focused on and cherished is that these universal auras we have in common all come from the same Source, which means that we have the honor of a divine connection with all living things. What an immediate, stunning difference we'd make in this world if we'd just catch on to the simple, obvious fact that by abusing the life around us we're abusing ourselves, but by nurturing it, we finally begin to thrive again.

Axis Mundi

"Axis mundi" is an ancient term, thousands of years old and of debatable origin, that refers to the pivot around which the earth or the entire cosmos revolves. It's the center of existence or, as I once heard it referred to, "God's navel," which really crystallized the image for me.

Axis mundi is more concept than fact, obviously, and purely a matter of culture and belief systems. Some would argue that if there is an axis mundi, it's Jerusalem, or Bethlehem. Others would swear it's Mecca, or the Vatican, or the Great Pyramids, or Stonehenge. Still others insist the axis mundi would be a purely natural phenomenon, particularly a variation on the symbolic Tree of Life, with branches reaching toward heaven and roots penetrating the core of the earth. And then, of course, there are those who think it's just plain egocentric to limit the search for the axis mundi to our little planet and instead believe it's probably the sun or the Milky Way or some distant galaxy we don't even know exists yet.

I frankly don't know or care what the real axis mundi is, or even if there is such a thing. I just happen to love the idea of it, and the age-old worldwide theories and legends about it.

Azna

There is duality in every living aspect of this infinite universe, and that includes its Creator. There is a Father God, omnipotent, perfect, all-loving and all-knowing.

And there is a Mother God. Her name is Azna. She is the counterpart of the Father, worshipped as His equal and His complement for more than twenty thousand years.

The Father God is the intellect of creation, the constant, unchanging Unmoved Mover.

Azna, the Mother God, is the emotion. She can move, nurture, intervene and interfere. Earth is the most emotionally driven of the inhabited planets, so the relationship between Azna and earth is espe-

Azna, the Mother God

cially close as She takes form from time to time to create miracles. Witnesses at Lourdes, Fatima and Guadalupe called her the Blessed Mother when She appeared to them; by whatever name She's called, the Mother God is the harmonizer, the active helper, the keeper of life. Her dominion is all living things on earth, from which the cherished image of Mother Nature was inspired. She's been called the Lady of Lotus by Buddhists, as well as Ashara, Theodora, Sophie and Isis in faiths and cultures throughout the world for centuries upon centuries.

Without the all-knowing, all-perfect intellect of the Father God, we would be pure emotion. Without Azna, we would be pure intellect, without the instinctive empathy that tells even the most unconditional eternal love when a hand needs to be held or a comforting hug offered.

Azna has been worshipped, by many names and in many cultures, since at least as far back as the ancient Greeks, who called her Gaea, the Mother Goddess who brought forth the sky, the mountains and the sea. In approximately 415 B.C. Plato wrote of her, calling her Ge. The Romans revered her by the name of Terra Mater, or the Mother of Earth.

And then along came Christianity, and Western religion in general, which, for all its magnificence, seemed determined from the beginning to become a patriarchy, starting with Eve, the first woman, but of course created second, from Adam's rib, as if she were simply an extension of him. Eve's primary legacy seems to be the introduction of sin into the paradise of the Garden of Eden. (If you think Eve was shocking, by the way, read the section on Lilith, who, according to Jewish mythology, was Adam's first wife but was kicked out of the Garden for refusing to be submissive to him.) In a patriarchal religion, there was no use for a Mother God, even as a complement to the Father, a natural part of the Godhead in a creation that everywhere else you look is a duality . . . created, as the Bible reminds us, in His image.

I can't resist adding an observation by Joseph Campbell, the most extraordinary teacher/mythologist of the twentieth century. There's a Babylonian myth in which the goddess Tiamat is killed by the god Marduk. Marduk then blows Tiamat's body to smithereens and, voilà, the universe is created. Joseph Campbell's review of this particular myth, which sums up millennia of religious and mythological attitudes toward Azna, by her many names and titles, reads:

> "There was no need to cut her up and make the universe out of her, because she was already the universe. But the male-oriented myth takes over, and *he* becomes—apparently—the creator."

So She is not a fad, a New Age or feminist invention, or an alternative to the Father God. She is simply what She always has been and always will be—His motion, His emotion, the perfection that complements His perfection.

Whether you believe in Her or not, include Her in your prayers from time to time. Thank Her for Her part in your creation if you choose, and ask for some small gesture from Her just out of curiosity—an unexpected flower, a call from an old friend you haven't heard from in a very long time, something that will definitely catch your attention, but be specific. Your belief in Her is not a condition of Her generosity.

Like her counterpart, the other half of the Godhead who is the Father God, Azna adores you, and your spirit's greatest happiness is Her joy.

B

Banshee

The ancient legend of the banshee is centered in the mists of Ireland. The word "banshee" originates from a Celtic word that means "woman of the fairy," and by varying accounts, banshees appear in the form of tiny, bent old hags with wild white hair, or of towering, slender young women with flowing long white hair. What banshees are most noted for, though, is their piercing, unearthly wail, said to break glass for miles around, alerting families to the death of a relative.

I love quaint cultural myths, don't you?

It was 1978, and I was on my first trip to Ireland. Everything about it enchanted me, and everything about it still does, by the way. It had been a long trip, with several personal-appearance stops along the way, and while my then-husband had no trouble falling asleep right after dinner, I was still in some other time zone on some kind of adrenaline overload and decided to leave the hotel and go for a calming evening walk.

I know you don't have to be psychic to feel an almost reverent sense of history in countries as ancient and as passionate toward their ancestry as Ireland. I was so preoccupied with the almost palpable images of the Celts and the Vikings and the farmers and the poor famine

45

victims that I barely noticed the small shops closing for the night, the thick fog rolling in and the scenery around me becoming more rural.

What shocked me back to reality was a sound I'll never forget in this lifetime. It was the most deafening, tortured, unearthly scream I ever hope to hear, so sharp it felt as if it penetrated me to the pit of my stomach. I looked around, frantic, trying to pinpoint where it was coming from, but the fog diffused it into a million sound bites so that it seemed to be coming from everywhere. For a split second I thought it must be someone in agonizing pain, but I've heard the pain of child-birth and the pain of horrible death, and they paled in comparison.

It's an understatement to say that I don't scare easily. I've seen, heard, felt and experienced far too much since the day I was born to be frightened by much of anything. But I have no trouble admitting that that awful scream in the fog on that night in Ireland terrified me. I'm not even sure my feet touched the ground as I ran back to the ho-tel, and before I knew it I was in my room, crying and still trembling, waking my husband to tell him what had happened.

Both sides of his family were Irish, for as many generations back as anyone had bothered to trace. He barely sat up and only half opened his eyes as I gasped out the details of what had happened. When I fin-ished he mumbled, almost bored, "You probably heard the banshee," and went right back to sleep.

"Thank you," I thought, glaring at the back of his head. "Thank you very much, you've been very helpful, that explains everything."

He slept like a baby all night long. I couldn't even get my eyes to close. A banshee? Obviously I'd heard of them, without it ever occur-ring to me that there might actually be such a thing, and I still wasn't convinced. That horrifying scream was still echoing in my ears, but I knew there had to be a more logical explanation than, "You probably heard the banshee."

The next morning I was just sitting down for breakfast in the small restaurant bar when I heard the barman say to one of the locals at the next table, "Did you hear Mrs. O'Flaherty died last night?"

"No. Poor thing. What happened?"

"Heart attack, her son said. Very sudden," the barman told him. "Eighty-three years old, bless her heart."

I was eavesdropping on this with increasing interest. Finally my curiosity got the best of me, and I leaned toward them.

"Excuse me, I couldn't help overhearing," I said. "This woman who passed away . . . do you happen to know where she lived?"

The Irish in general are friendly and happy to chat. Irish barmen elevate it to an art form. "Mrs. O'Flaherty? Not even a mile from here, just on the edge of town. Lovely house, too. Her great-grandfather built it . . ."

I'm sure it was an interesting story, but at the moment I had something much more pressing on my mind. "By any chance, did her son mention what time she died?"

"He did, in fact. He was on the phone with her when it happened, how's that for a shock? The stroke of 9:30, he said."

9:30. I'd looked at the clock shortly after getting back to my hotel room the night before. It had read a minute or two past 10:00.

I swear to you, I really, really tried to piece all this together and make logical sense of it, based on everything I knew as a psychic, as a college graduate and as a devout researcher. If banshees really existed, fine, but what were they, where did they come from, and where did they fit into the realm of the spirit world? And if they didn't exist, that still left the question of the source of that unimaginable, unspeakable, soul-shattering scream.

So I did what I always do when my best efforts have left too many holes in the story—I summoned my ultimate reliable source. And as always my Spirit Guide Francine came to the rescue.

According to Francine, the shrill keening of the banshee that's been echoing through the Irish countryside for hundreds and hundreds of years is actually a lightning-in-a-bottle collaboration between earthly physics and the spirit world. As a spirit leaves its body on earth, it changes dimensions, traveling in a brilliant flash from our lower frequency to the much faster, much more high-pitched frequency of the Other Side. It often sends strong telepathic signals to loved ones as it goes, to alert them and bid them a temporary farewell, and those signals have to change dimensions too, to reach their intended receivers on earth. Powerful telepathic energy, changing frequencies at blinding speed, is enough to cause the effect of a shrill scream all by itself, which is sometimes even audible to the human ear. But add the factor of the truly extraordinary Irish fog, which fills the air with enough moisture to conduct and amplify that energy, and it's no wonder the legend of the banshee will always haunt that beautiful, mystical land.

Bi-Location

You'll see references to the words "bi-locate" and "bi-location" throughout this book. It's simply an ability, common to all residents of the spirit world, to be, literally and not just figuratively, in two places at once. With rare exceptions (see the section on Doppelgängers, for example), this skill is limited to the spirit world for the most part (for the time being) and doesn't lend itself to earthly gravity.

I should add that, while I don't claim to have what you'd call a rapt interest in or talent for the sciences (and somewhere in my garage I still have the report cards to prove it), I do understand that the ongoing development of quantum physics is making phenomena like bi-location look less and less like something only we goofy woo-woo people believe in. One of the basic principles of quantum physics goes like this: It's possible to go from Point A to Point C without necessarily going through Point B. Going from one location to another with the space in between becoming irrelevant is called a "quantum leap." Just the beginning of so many earthly absolutes we were taught as fact that are being thrown out the window as minds continue to open up. And if you have any further questions about quantum physics and/or the quantum leap, there's no need to ask me; you can take it up with Einstein.

Bleed-Through

A bleed-through is an event in which two separate times or dimensions come together with such intense spiritual force that for a brief time they meet, blend and become one.

My first experience with a bleed-through is probably one of the clearest examples I can offer, not to mention one of the most unforgettable incidents my church congregation and I have ever shared.

I was conducting a trance session one night, in which my Spirit Guide Francine was speaking through me to a large group, telling the story of Christ's crucifixion at Golgotha in Jerusalem. There were fifty or sixty tape recorders running, but except for Francine, using my voice, the room was absolutely silent—the slightest noise can break my trance. Francine and I can't both inhabit my body at the same time, so I never have any awareness or memory of what she says. But from what I was told, and from hearing the tape later myself, it was a very wrenching, emotional evening, with Francine making the crucifixion of Christ so real and so intensely personal that everyone there felt as if they were weeping at the foot of the cross themselves.

My phone started ringing off the hook early the next morning. Six of the people who had taped the session the night before, none of whom had talked to each other, were anxious to play their tapes for me, wondering if I could hear what they thought they were hearing or if maybe they were just imagining things.

They weren't imagining things. I could hear exactly what they were hearing, and I didn't let any of them tell me ahead of time what I was listening for. It was unmistakable, shocking and impossible to miss: On six of the tapes made that night, sometimes almost drowning out Francine's riveting narrative of Christ's crucifixion, was the heartbreaking sound of people wailing and sobbing in unbearable grief. On the forty-some other tapes made that same night, which I listened to later, there was nothing but what everyone present was aware of hearing—Francine's voice, and complete, absolute silence.

I have no way of proving that the group that attended that trance session was transported to Jesus's cross 2,000 years ago on Golgotha. But thanks to six simple tape recorders, I do have proof of a bleed-through: two completely separate times and places, united by a common spiritual bond so divinely powerful that it transcended every dimension and earthly law of time and space that would seem to make it impossible.

The Boogeyman

I know. It seems like an odd, silly word to include in a book of paranormal terms. But I'm guessing every single one of you resonates to it. If you were sitting in front of me at a lecture I'd ask you to raise your hands if you were told when you were a child that if you didn't behave, or especially if you didn't settle down and go to sleep, the boogeyman would get you. And I would see the whole roomful of hands go up. You might not remember who told you that—if it wasn't a parent or perverse sibling, it was an aunt or uncle or grandparent or babysitter or cousin. No one ever explained who this boogeyman was, where he came from, what he looked like, where he might be hiding or what exactly "get you" entailed. And you didn't ask. You especially didn't ask where he was hiding, because you already knew: He was either under your bed, just waiting for you to dangle your hand or foot over the side of the bed, or he was in that dark hell that by day looked so deceptively like an innocent closet. So there you'd lie, heart pounding, afraid to even close your eyes, let alone fall asleep, because at the inevitable moment when the boogeyman leapt out at you, you wanted to be ready to run. And sure enough, the next morning, the same person who gave you that parting shot about the boogeyman would be the first one to scold you for being tired and cranky.

I'm not the first person to point out how idiotic it is to frighten our children with threats of monsters as our lazy excuse for discipline, but I'd love to be the last. I'd love to think we could finally get it through our thick heads that instilling a sense of peace, safety and security about the dark might be healthier than instilling fear.

We might think being afraid of the dark is "natural," but a more appropriate way of putting it might be "primitive," or "uninformed." True enough, the caveman had to be on the lookout for nocturnal beasts who might eat him or his family. That's fair. But the mythology that came later, that gave birth to vampires, and werewolves, and monsters who created darkness by eating the sun, and the incubi and succubi and baby-eating goblins who were rumored to run rampant through your home while you slept, is no more "natural" and no more productive than the ever-present, age-old boogeyman.

What I think would be a truly wonderful replacement for any form of the boogeyman talk that goes on with your children at bedtime would be positive, supportive, educational conversations about beings that really might show up in their rooms in the dark—the spirits, the ghosts, the Angels, their Spirit Guides. You could teach them who those people really are, where they came from, the differences between them and why ghosts need our help when the rest of them don't. You could explain how marvelous it is that these beings are able to come visit, because it means we live forever. In fact, since children, along with animals, are the most psychic creatures on earth, they'll probably see and hear some things you don't, and remember some things from the Other Side and even their past lives that you've forgotten, so it could be a wonderful time for them to educate you too.

Another show of hands—how many of you who've told your children about the boogeyman, or some other scary story when they went to bed, read the suggestion of telling them about the spirit world instead and thought, "That would be crazy"?

Several, I'll bet.

And isn't being more comfortable with boogeyman stories than spirit stories even crazier?

As long as we're on the subject of sleeping children, we might as well spend a moment talking about night terrors. They're those events a child experiences that go beyond nightmares, when they wake up screaming and their eyes look glassy and unfocused and it takes several moments to "bring them back."

Believe it or not, almost without exception, night terrors are caused by your child either recalling or revisiting some horrifying trauma from a past life, which again, I promise you, children still remember when they're very young, especially while they sleep.

Which is why I believe so strongly in talking to children while they sleep. Don't worry about their not understanding what you say. Their conscious vocabulary may be limited, but the spirit you're talking to through the subconscious is ageless and as fluent as you are.

The peace and healing you can give a child during sleep really will help make the night terrors vanish once and for all. You don't have to believe me. Just try it every night for a couple of weeks. It can't hurt, it takes only a minute or two, and if I'm right, how can it possibly not be worth it? Just move close enough that she/he can hear your voice without being awakened by it, and then say your most comfortable version of the following:

"My child, may you keep all the joy and wisdom your past lives have given you, and may all sorrow, fear, illness and negativity from those past lives be released and dissolved for all time into the white light of the Holy Spirit."

And as you're tiptoeing out of your child's room, remember to take the boogeyman with you, and feed him to the monster who ate the sun.

C

Cell Memory

Cell memory is the total body of knowledge our spirit minds have gathered during all our past lives, infused and reacted to by every cell in the body the moment we "take up residence" in the fetus. It's the key to resolving countless health problems, phobias, chronic pains and unmotivated, outdated small-mindedness once we understand the process that creates it.

The basic steps of cell memory go like this:

* Our bodies are made up of billions of interacting cells.

* Each of those cells is a living, breathing, feeling organism, receiving and responding very literally to the information it receives from the subconscious mind. Under hypnosis, for example, when the subconscious mind is in charge, if we're told that the hypnotist's finger is actually a burning candle, and that finger touches our arm, the cells of our arm will form a blister, exactly as they're programmed to do when they come in contact with a flame.

* It's in the subconscious that our spirit minds live—safe, sound and eternally intact, no matter how healthy or unhealthy our conscious minds might be.

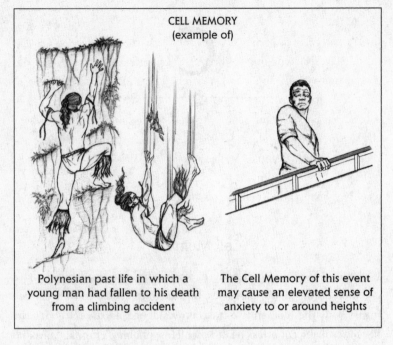

CELL MEMORY
(example of)

Polynesian past life in which a young man had fallen to his death from a climbing accident	The Cell Memory of this event may cause an elevated sense of anxiety to or around heights

Our spirit minds remember every moment we've experienced, in this life and every other life we've lived since we were created.

The instant our spirit minds enter our physical bodies for a new incarnation, they're flooded with the familiarity of being in a body, and all those memories and sensations come rushing back. (If you've ever returned to a place that holds powerful memories for you and been stirred both physically and emotionally from the jolt of the present colliding with the past, you've been through a minuscule version of what our spirits feel when they find themselves in a body again.) As with all the other information in our subconscious minds, our billions of cells are simultaneously infused with those same spirit memories and sensations and respond to them as their reality until our spirits leave our bodies again and head Home.

Our cells, literal as they are, continue to react physiologically to all the memories from this life and previous ones that our spirit minds infuse them with, whether our conscious minds are aware of those memories or not.

And so, by accessing those cell memories and understanding that they're part of lives and deaths we've already moved on from, we can rid ourselves of long-buried illnesses, phobias, pain and trauma and give ourselves a "clean slate" to work with in the incarnation we're in the midst of now.

As a certified master hypnotist, I've helped countless thousands of clients unearth and release their cell memories through past-life regressions. A few examples should clarify how cell memory can manifest itself in our present lives and how literally life-altering it can be when we finally put a cell memory in the distant past where it most certainly belongs:

* A man who'd suffered indigestion and chronic stomach spasms all his adult life for reasons doctors couldn't seem to diagnose was permanently cured during the regression in which he discovered he'd died of stomach cancer in a past life at the same age his indigestion and spasms had started.

* For as long as she could remember, a woman had been terrified of turning forty. She'd always assumed it had something to do with her biological clock. Instead, thanks to a single past-life regression, she discovered she'd died in two past lives at the age of forty, having nothing to do with the age she'll be when she dies in this one. (I still get a Christmas card from her every year, and she just turned seventy-two.)

* A four-year-old boy became inexplicably panic-stricken every time his mother prepared to take a shower. Since children are among the easiest regressive hypnosis subjects in the world, it was easy for him and me to uncover the tragic fact that in his previous life he'd been put through the horror of seeing his beloved mother die in the showers of Auschwitz before his own life ended there too. It took a few sessions to convince him of the concept of "that was then, this is now," but we got him there, and it was worth every minute.

✳ And then there's one of my all-time favorite cell memory stories, one of the experiences that made me a committed believer and disciple. Molly, age ten, had received a heart transplant from a seventeen-year-old stabbing victim named David. Months after the transplant, when the police had few clues and no suspects in David's murder, Molly began having nightmares about a dark figure in a ski mask lying in wait for her with a knife. Through hypnosis, Molly was able to separate from her fear, remove the dark figure's ski mask and identify the face of a young man named Martin—not a face or a name she knew, but, it turned out, a longtime acquaintance of David's. The police were notified, and Martin was brought in for questioning. He ultimately confessed to the murder, all thanks to David's cell memory, transplanted and infused throughout the body of a girl who had the courage to tell the truth that only David's spirit could possibly have known.

That's just a glimpse of the power of cell memory. More than that, it's yet another glimpse into God's promise to us that our lives really are eternal.

Chakras

It's not news to any of you, I know, that our physical bodies are energy containers, possessors of a Life Force so powerful that we can emanate it and have it felt by those around us. We can walk into a room and, without offering any visible or audible cues at all, project love, anger, confidence, fear and a whole kaleidoscope of other emotions that the people in that room will react to as surely as if we were wearing a neon sign announcing how we feel. We can conduct our strength and vitality through our hands and, with simple touch, make a sick loved one stronger and healthier. We can even change the size, shape and color of the energy field we're creating by changing our mood, diet, physical fitness and general well-being, and have those changes

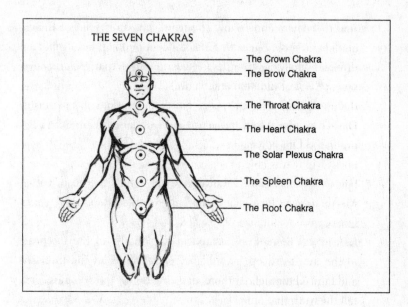

THE SEVEN CHAKRAS

The Crown Chakra
The Brow Chakra
The Throat Chakra
The Heart Chakra
The Solar Plexus Chakra
The Spleen Chakra
The Root Chakra

documented by Kirlian photography, which captures on film the actual energy patterns that radiate from every living thing on earth.

It's in the aura of our radiated energy, or Life Force, that our chakras are found. They're basically the vortexes, or energy centers, of our Life Force. There are seven chakras, each of them corresponding to a major endocrine gland in the body and each of them controlling specific physical areas and functions. Stress, present and future illness, depression, circulatory blockages, ovarian cysts and countless other health problems can be counted on to manifest themselves in the chakras at the same moment or even before they manifest themselves in the body itself. The chakra in charge of the affected area of the body will appear darker, murkier, duller and less "alive" than the rest of the aura. And the good news is, cleansing, unblocking and restoring energy to that chakra can actually heal the physical problem the chakra was reacting to.

I always smile a little when I read some skeptical critique debating the existence and effectiveness of chakras and find them referred to as a New Age fad/concept/scam. At the very least chakras date back to the earliest Hindus and Buddhists, which means they predate

Christianity, Judaism and Islam. The word "chakra" itself is Sanskrit for "vortex" or "wheel." Agree with the concept or don't, but I think it's fair to give credit where it's due and acknowledge that chakras have withstood the test of time remarkably well.

As I describe the seven chakras and their locations, try picturing them an inch or two away from your body, contained within the aura of your radiated Life Force.

* THE CROWN CHAKRA—Located at the top of the head, corresponds to the pineal gland; in charge of the brain and nervous system

* THE BROW CHAKRA—Located in the middle of the forehead where the "third eye" would be, corresponds to the pituitary gland; in charge of the forehead, including the temples, and carotid system

* THE THROAT CHAKRA—Located at the base of the throat, corresponds to the thyroid gland; in charge of the throat, neck and brachial systems

* THE HEART CHAKRA—Located in the center of the chest, corresponds to the thymus gland; in charge of the heart, circulatory and cardiac systems, lungs and total chest area

* THE SOLAR PLEXUS CHAKRA—Located halfway between the navel and the bottom of the breastbone, corresponds to the pancreas; a major power center, in charge of the stomach, intestines, liver, eyes, skin and muscular system

* THE SPLEEN CHAKRA—Located in the center of the abdomen, corresponds to the gonads; in charge of the reproductive system and lumbar area

* THE ROOT CHAKRA—Located midway between the sex organs and the anus, corresponds to the adrenal glands; in charge of the skeletal (including the teeth), bladder and lymph systems, spinal cord, sciatic nerve and all other components of the sacral plexus, legs, feet, ankles and sense of smell

There seem to be as many attributes assigned to each chakra as there are cultures who subscribe to them for effective spiritual and physical healing. Depending on your sources, the chakras have their own colors, their own earth elements (fire, air, water and earth), their own stone (quartz, amethyst, obsidian, tigereye, etc.), even their own specific number of lotus petals. There are secondary chakras, minor chakras and mini chakras. The methods of cleansing and unblocking the chakras are even more varied—crystals, music, several different yoga disciplines, the laying on of stones, the application of special oils or herbs, beams of appropriately colored light concentrated on the chakra in question, etc., etc., etc.

The endless number of available approaches to the chakras is a study in good news/bad news. On one hand, it makes it virtually impossible to run out of variations to explore. On the other hand, I've had countless clients tell me that they've never pursued the subject of chakras at all because they were so overwhelmed and confused by the mountain of often conflicting information they found themselves up against, just trying to get an idea of the basics. It's nobody's fault. In fact, it's a testament to the popularity and acknowledged potential of chakras throughout the world. But I can easily understand feeling bombarded in a simple search for "what are chakras and what do I do about them?"

I'm sure that any number of the age-old approaches to cleansing, unblocking and restoring health to your chakras are wonderful. I'm not about to claim I've tried even a fraction of them. But I can recommend the quick, easy method I use every morning in those moments before I get out of bed. I simply picture each of my chakras, starting at the top of my head and working my way down my body, and then, one at a time, envision them glowing first with a laser beam of green light, because green is the color of healing, and then with the white light of the Holy Spirit, for protection, purity and a grateful acknowledgment of my God center. It's relaxing, it's exhilarating and it takes less than five minutes. And I feel safe in promising that whether you believe me or not, if you try it every morning for one short month, you'll be astonished at the improvement in your general health, well-being and appreciative re-connection between your body and your divine Life Force.

Channel/Channeling

You'll find both these words in various places throughout the book, and al-though I'm sure most of you know what they mean, I just want to clarify:

A channel is a medium (one who's able to communicate with the spirit world) who receives spirit communication by going into an al-tered state of consciousness, usually a meditation or a trance, and al-lows the spirit to literally speak through them. The communicating spirit never possesses, replaces or eliminates the spirit of the channel. Instead, the channel simply withdraws or steps aside temporarily and acts as nothing more than a tube through which the communicat-ing spirit can speak directly, without the middleman of the medium. This is exactly what I do when I let my Spirit Guide Francine use my voice for lectures and sermons. And because I use a trance rather than meditation when I channel Francine, I'm what's called a "trance channeler."

Still a little perplexed by the terminology? When you read the sec-tion entitled "Medium," you'll see my best effort at making the distinc-tions among a psychic, a medium and a channel.

The Chart

Make no mistake, earth is not our Home. The Other Side is our Home. We had joyful, busy lives there before we came here, and we'll return to those lives when we leave here. That's a promise. Not from me. From God, who gave us eternal spirits as part of our birthright the moment He created us.

We make these brief trips to earth to learn the hard way, through firsthand experience, for the growth and progress of our souls on their eternal journey. It's a whole different education than we could ever hope for on the Other Side, because on the Other Side, everything is infused with God's perfection. And as my Spirit Guide Francine has rhetorically asked me a million times, "What have you learned when times were good?"

So we choose to come here, as rarely or as often as we feel the need, and we choose what we're interested in learning and working on this time around. And just as we would never head off to college without deciding which college would serve us best, what courses we'll need, where we should live and with whom and countless other details to give ourselves the best odds up front of what we want to accomplish, we wouldn't dream of coming to earth unprepared.

And so before we come here, we write our chart. It's an understatement to call them "detailed." From the broad strokes to the most trivial moments, we leave nothing to chance in pursuit of our goals.

I don't know anyone, including myself, who can imagine having deliberately chosen some of the unpleasantness, ugliness and tragedy in his/her life. But let me just remind you, and myself, again: We write our charts in preparation for coming to a very rough boarding school, so the charts themselves are bound to be filled with difficult challenges and lessons learned the hard way. If what we were in search of was a happy, carefree, perfect life, we'd stay Home.

And then there's the blissful euphoria that is our constant state of mind on the Other Side, including when we're with our chosen Spirit Guide writing our chart. We're fearless, we're utterly confident, we're our most loving selves and we're surrounded by nothing but unconditional love twenty-four hours a day, seven days a week (or we would be, if there were such a thing as time on the Other Side). There's nothing we feel unequipped to handle, nothing we're reluctant to take on in our hunger for spiritual growth. Writing our chart in that state of mind is a little like going to the grocery store on an empty stomach— it's not exactly a recipe for restraint. However challenging your life is, I promise you were in the process of planning something even rougher for yourself until your Spirit Guide, who's lived on earth at least once and hasn't forgotten what it's like, persuaded you into doing something a little more realistic.

Our charts include our intended purpose, aka our Life Theme; our most difficult obstacle, aka our Option Line; our plans for how and when to return to the Other Side, aka our Exit Points; and the animal spirit we bring along to join our Spirit Guide and our Angels in watching over us throughout our time on earth, aka our Totem. Those are the generalities, the engines that will keep us moving forward. We then begin the painstaking task of choosing each and every fine point of the journey. To name just a few:

* We choose our parents, siblings and every other family member.
* We choose every aspect of our physical appearance, from hair, skin and eye color to body type to height to weight, including major and minor gains and losses, to any distinctive markings, peculiarities and disfigurement.
* We choose our exact place, time and date of birth, which means that we choose all the details of our astrological chart.
* We choose our friends, our lovers, our spouses, our children, our bosses and coworkers, our casual acquaintances, even our pets.
* We choose the enemies, no matter how well disguised, we'll meet along the way, and the sociopaths, aka the Dark Side.
* We choose the cities, the neighborhoods and the houses we'll live in.
* We choose our preferences, our weaknesses, our flaws, our sense of humor or lack of one, our skills and talents and our areas of incompetence.
* We choose every minor injury and major illness we'll experience.
* We choose our hobbies, our interests, our passions and the quirks that no one else knows about but us.

And so on, and so on, and so on, including every important and trivial moment of the lifetime that lies ahead.

One of the most common fallacies about the chart when the concept of them first comes up is that we arrive on earth with no free will. Actually, we come here with countless choices surrounding every detail. If it's in your chart to catch a cold when you're four years old, it's up to you whether you'll stay in bed and get over it or let it develop into pneumonia. If your chart clearly states that you're invited to a friend's birthday party when you're twenty, you can choose to be rude and ignore the invitation, properly decline with a phone call or note, go to the party and be miserable or go and have a wonderful time. When a Dark Entity (see "the Dark Side") shows up as dictated in your chart, it's your choice whether to walk away, get involved and let it destroy you or get involved and learn to keep your distance next time. A charted life is absolutely a life full of options, and proof that our lives aren't measured by what we're confronted with, but by how we deal with what we're confronted with.

Clairaudience

As clairvoyance is the ability to see things that originate in another dimension, clairaudience is the ability to hear them. It's not the silent communication of telepathy or infused knowledge; it's the definite earthly audio-perception of actual sounds and words that come from anywhere else but here. "Clairaudience" is a French word that means "clear hearing." I have to assume that whoever coined it never experienced the high-frequency, chirping, hyperspeed sound of voices from the Other Side that takes every ounce of concentration to understand. Clear isn't one of the adjectives that leaps to mind.

If you've seen John Edward or me or any other legitimate medium giving specific names and details about audience members' deceased loved ones that we'd have no possible way of knowing, you've seen clairaudience in action. On rare occasions information might come telepathically, but, at least speaking for myself, the vast majority of the time it's out loud, in my ear, piercing and somewhat distorted. You have no idea how often in fifty-plus years I've had to force myself to just open my mouth and repeat what I think I've heard, even when I was sure it couldn't possibly be right and I was about to make a complete idiot of myself. It's not easy, especially on national television, when you're someone like I am whose life's work is one hundred percent dependent on credibility. But part of my vow to God about these gifts He's given me is that as long as He sees fit to let the spirit world communicate through me, I won't question it, I won't edit, I won't try to interpret or make sense of it and I certainly won't take credit for it. I'll just listen closely, stay out of the way and let it come.

Sitting alone with clients in the privacy of my office and saying things like, "You have a worm farm" and "Your wife's pet name for you was 'Wooshie' " is tough. Finding out that things like that were exactly correct has been known to amaze me more than it amazed my clients. But I was talking to a bereaved couple on TV not long ago whose son had died very suddenly. They were in agony as they told me the whole heartbreaking story, and I was concentrating as best I could. But at the same time, I had an urgent chirping voice in my ear, that I thought was male, yelling the same word over and over and over and over again, like a chant at seventy-eight rpm. Those poor parents were grief-stricken. I had no choice but to interrupt them to say, "He keeps talking about balloons. He wants me to say 'balloons' to you." If I'd been wrong, and cut them off to interject something as silly and irrelevant as "balloons," I'm not sure I'd have blamed them if they'd walked out on me. I don't mind telling you, I was relieved when they asked me to repeat it and then smiled as the husband announced with a little awe in his voice, "I used to work in a balloon factory."

Now, here are a couple of facts about clairaudience I want you to remember for future reference:

 * It's not something that happens only to us weird, woo-woo psychics. It happens to normal people all over the world every single

day, few of whom asked for it or expected it. So if you've been reading along thinking, "Wow, I'm glad I'm not as crazy as Sylvia Browne and won't ever have to hear voices like that," don't say I didn't warn you.

* The more you explore your spirituality and invest your time and energy in your God-given genetic place in the spirit world, the more likely you are to experience clairaudience and other forms of contact from Home. Stay open to it, welcome it and most definitely educate yourself about it so that if and when it happens, you'll be grateful rather than terrified.

* No voice from the Other Side will *ever* say something angry, mean or threatening, or that encourages you to do anything harmful or destructive to yourself or anyone else. I say this as someone who has infinite respect for my many friends and colleagues in the mental health community: If you hear voices and they're dark in any way, *please* get to a reputable, licensed therapist right away and let him/her help you, or call my office and we'll be happy to refer you to an experienced professional.

I can't resist adding a P.S. with Lindsay's permission. Lindsay Harrison, my friend and cowriter on several of my books (this is our eighth together), will be the first to tell you she's got no more psychic ability than any other normal person. She's been by my side too many thousands of times to doubt the experiences in these books, and as I've heard her tell many people when they ask her if I'm for real, there's no amount of money that could persuade her to write something she doesn't believe. (And as stubborn and Midwestern as she is, I know she's not kidding.) But it's been a running joke with us for years that while clients and audiences all over the world, everywhere I go, hear spirits without always even understanding what they are, she knows exactly what they are, knows they're around all the time when we're together and has yet to hear a thing. . . .

With the one exception of a year ago when she called me early one morning and breathlessly announced, "I heard a spirit voice."

Something woke her up in the middle of the night, so there was no doubt that she was wide awake when it happened. It was exactly as high-pitched and chirpy and hyperfast as she's been describing on paper all these years. It said "Lindsay" once. That was all. Nothing more. There wasn't an actual thunderclap of rapport that occasionally happens when a spirit crosses dimensions, but she felt a strong percussive hit in the air of her bedroom. She knew it was a woman, and I knew it was her Spirit Guide, whose name is Rachel. She understood exactly what it was, so it didn't really frighten her, but her heart was still pounding hours later when she picked up the phone to tell me about it.

She takes the position that if it can happen to her, it can happen to anyone, and she accuses me of rubbing off on her. You may have heard Montel Williams say the same thing twenty or thirty thousand times in the last fourteen years of our appearances together.

The truth is, it's not me. It's the spirits on the Other Side, who simply recognize a welcome mat when they see one.

Clairsentience

Clairsentience is the ability to receive a silent thought, message or projected emotion, from nearby or from other dimensions, and experience it as an actual physical and emotional sensation. If a clairsentient is doing a reading for a grief-stricken client, for example, she'll literally take on the agonizing emotional pain of grief her client is going through. If she is tuning in to a missing child whose leg is broken, she'll feel a very real pain in her own correlating leg. If she's focused on a murder victim, she'll feel specific physical pain relative to the victim's wounds, as well as the terror, rage, betrayal or other powerful psychic agony the victim went through in the last moments of life.

In other words, clairsentience is essentially empathy in hyperdrive, a total surrender of objectivity, and those who practice it can easily become drained and overexposed, not to mention ill or deeply depressed: When you make yourself available not just to receive but absorb from the people and spirits around you, filtering out anything potentially harmful or dark becomes almost impossible. And the strongly developed clairsentients I've known have also had a difficult time being able to discern absorbed physical and emotional sensations from their own, so that, for example, they're never quite sure if they have the flu or are just picking up symptoms from someone around them.

Probably more than any other psychic gift, clairsentience requires an enormous amount of discipline and every Tool of Protection in the arsenal (see "Tools of Protection").

Clairvoyance

Clairvoyance is the ability to see beings, objects or information that originate from some other dimension. Whether they're spirits from the Other Side, objects from the past that no longer exist in the present or visions of future events, clairvoyants have what's sometimes called "second sight," which allows their eyes to perceive a wider range of input and frequencies than normal.

My first indisputable sign that I was psychic was a clairvoyant experience, and believe me, I wasn't thrilled about it. I was five years old, the whole family was gathered around the dinner table and I suddenly noticed that both of my great-grandmothers' faces seemed to be melting. I don't mean their makeup needed freshening, I mean it was as if their faces were made of hot candle wax and had started running right down the front of their heads. As if that weren't shocking enough, everyone else at the table acted as if this were the most normal thing in the world for these women's faces to do every once in a while, and it finally sank in that maybe I was the only one seeing this. When both of them passed away within the next two weeks, I privately sobbed out a confession to my brilliantly psychic Grandma Ada that I'd somehow killed my great-grandmothers by making their faces melt; I was really sorry and I wouldn't do it again. The logic of a five-year-old. Thus came my first lessons from Grandma Ada in General Psychics and Clairvoyance 101, and without her guidance throughout my childhood I don't doubt for a moment that I would have gone insane (or, as I can hear some of you suggesting, insan*er*).

Clairvoyance is what allows someone to see and accurately describe what spirits from Home are around you, where a missing child or murder victim can be found, the final moments in a murder victim's life whether it was ten minutes or ten years ago, or the person you're going to marry three years from now. Remember, clairvoyant visions originate in other dimensions, and earth is the only dimension where we have this inane concept called "time." Everywhere else there's nothing but now, so past, present and future aren't necessarily factored into a vision. It's a matter of skill and training to learn which is which, so that, for example, you don't end up predicting a plane crash that happened ten hours ago that you simply haven't heard about yet, or send police looking for a bright blue house that was painted white or torn down earlier that week.

The gift of clairvoyance isn't even slightly limited to us freak-show psychics, as millions of you already know. You're seeing things you either don't want to see or don't understand, and/or your children are seeing them and becoming confused or frightened. In the meantime, by the way, skeptics are having a high old time claiming there's no such thing as clairvoyance to begin with. To those skeptics I say, "You're more than entitled to your beliefs, and thanks for sharing. Now, excuse us, we're busy."

To the rest of you, who know you're having clairvoyant experiences and aren't any more interested in debating it than I am, I want to share an important lesson Grandma Ada taught me after that first hideous face-running vision. I was terrified by the idea of spending my life being a sitting duck for any random, violent, grotesque images that happened along whether I was strong enough to handle them or not. I still remember telling Grandma Ada that I didn't want to see any of these things, I didn't want to be psychic, I just wanted it all to go away and be a normal five-year-old.

She explained that my psychic gifts, my gift of clairvoyance and any information that comes as a result of those gifts have the same Source—they're from God. Which means they're to be honored, respected and used for His work or not at all. And since He gave them to me for a reason, He was the first place I should turn for any help and guidance I might need. "Ask and it shall be given."

So, with a little coaching from Grandma Ada, I gave Him my word that I would devote these gifts to His best purpose, if He would please send only clairvoyant images I could do something about. If I have to see a plane go down, show me enough information to let me warn the right people. If I have to see a house in flames, give me a town, an address, something to help me make sure no one's inside when it burns, or tell me how the fire can be prevented in the first place. Don't show me a diseased heart without telling me whose it is and what needs to be done, or a sinking ship without a location where rescuers can find it.

I prayed and prayed and prayed for useful clairvoyance or none at all, and it worked. As I said, if you, a loved one or especially a child you're close to has been given the gift of clairvoyance, by all means learn as I did from my Grandma Ada: Thank God for the gift, honor it, devote it to Him and pray to be given only visions you can work with to further His divine purpose.

Cocooning

Some spirits, even when long illnesses would seem to give them plenty of time to make peace with dying, have a very rough transition to the Other Side. The traditional reviewing of our life at the Scanning Machine and Orientation process most of us will experience when we first arrive back Home can't offer these especially troubled spirits the intensive care they need. When that intensive care is called for, the spirits on the Other Side are brilliantly trained to provide a quiet, loving procedure called cocooning.

During cocooning, the spirit is put into a healing twilight sleep, and receives constant care and a steady infusion of God's peaceful, empowering love. The spirit is cocooned for as long as it takes for it to be healthy and whole again, and it awakens exhilarated, joyful about being Home again.

My daddy and I, for example, had an extraordinary bond from the day I was born. When he died after many months of devastating illness, he arrived on the Other Side highly agitated from the grief of being separated from me, almost as if he took on both his grief and mine in the hope of sparing me the pain of losing him. He was lovingly cocooned through his withdrawal. I, in the meantime, was stuck here, trying literally to work my way through my emptiness without him, faced with the irony of seeing everyone else's deceased loved ones but my own—I watched, I waited, I listened, I prayed, I begged, I sobbed, but Daddy was nowhere to be seen. Finally, after eight months that seemed like forever, I detected an unmistakable hint of his favorite cherry blend pipe tobacco in a corner of the room and turned to see him watching me, peaceful and smiling.

"Daddy!" I cried. "What took you so long?"

His reply was completely earnest. "What do you mean? I just left."

Never forget, it's only here on earth that we're obsessed with time. In the context of eternity on the Other Side, eight months, eight years or even eight decades is the blink of an eye.

If you suspect deceased loved ones might not have been emotionally prepared to go Home, or you don't sense them around you as quickly as you're yearning for, please try to be patient, and don't worry. They're most likely being cocooned, they're in safe, sacred Hands, and they'll be around you again very soon, as peaceful, happy and glowing with health as you've prayed they'd be, just like Daddy was and is, thank God.

Coincidence

You've experienced enough coincidences to know how they go. You've been thinking about someone for no apparent reason, and suddenly they call, or you run into them, for the first time in ages. You're planning a trip to a place you've never been before, and suddenly you're almost inundated by news about that place, people who just happen to be from that place, and people who just returned from a vacation to that place. A song has been running through your head that you can't get rid of, and suddenly you turn on the radio at the exact moment when that very song is playing.

Because we don't understand their significance, we rarely give much thought to these fairly common experiences. After all, they're just coincidences. But they really have a far greater magnificence than we give them credit for.

As you'll read in the definition of the Chart, we don't come to earth for another incarnation without writing a highly detailed blueprint on the Other Side of the lifetime we're about to undertake, to make sure we have the best chance of achieving everything we're here to accomplish. Included in our charts are little flagged events—not necessarily significant, just highlighted—like simple distance markers along a lengthy stretch of highway.

One way we find ourselves recognizing one of those flagged events in our charts can be found in the definition of Déjà Vu.

Another is in the experience of coincidence.

What a coincidence boils down to is a) having a thought, and b) seeing it manifest itself shortly after the thought has occurred. To put it more accurately, in the context of charts, we foresee one of those flagged events we wrote shortly before that event occurs. Which means that, for an instant or two, we have a fleeting but crystal-clear memory of that chart we wrote while we were on the Other Side, preparing to come here.

Which means that those experiences we tend to shrug off dismissively as just coincidences are really nothing less than proof, played out right before our eyes, that we were very much alive before we were born into this current lifetime, just as we'll be very much alive when we leave it again.

So pause to say thank you for your coincidences, large and small. They're all snapshots of your immortality, and confirmation that you and your chart are in perfect synch.

Control

You might easily run across references to "a control" or "my control" as you explore the vast library of books available on the general subject of spirituality. "Control" is simply another name for "Spirit Guide." Renowned spiritualist and medium Arthur Ford (1896–1971) channeled his control, whose name was Fletcher, throughout his life, just as I channel my Spirit Guide Francine. Eileen Garrett (1893–1970), another wonderfully gifted medium and author of the best-selling book *Many Voices*, referred to Spirit Guides as controls as well.

As long as you acknowledge and make full use of your handpicked advisor from the Other Side, I'm sure it doesn't matter what you call him/her. I've just always felt that "control" was too strong a word for that role in our lives and that "Spirit Guide" was more descriptive— after all, the *control* over our decisions is always ours, and the best they can do, when and if we listen to them, is *guide* us.

Small technicalities like "control" versus "Spirit Guide" aside, I have nothing but the deepest admiration for Arthur Ford, Eileen Garrett and countless other brave pioneers in the paranormal field who blazed a path for the rest of us at a time when the world was even more judgmental than it is now. In fact, there's a quote from the preface of Eileen Garrett's autobiography that I keep on hand and reread when I need a spiritual shot in the arm:

"I have a gift, a capacity—a delusion, if you will—which is called 'psychic.' I do not care what it may be called, for living with and utilizing this psychic capacity long ago inured me to a variety of epithets—ranging from expressions almost of reverence, through doubt and pity, to open vituperation. In short, I have been called many things, from a charlatan to a miracle woman. I am, at least, neither of these."

The Cosmic Other Side

Life never ends. What is living now always was and always will be, so there is no such thing as the end on any inhabited planet. The reason is exactly what God promised at the moment He created us: The Other Side of every inhabited planet, which embraces every living thing, is eternal.

As inhabited planets become more spiritually advanced and less separate from each other, and especially when their environments no longer support life, their Other Sides begin blending with the great infinite universal Other Side. If the earth were destroyed tomorrow, we and our Other Side would join the spirits whose planets have already completed their natural cycles, who are living the same blissful, sacred lives that wait for us beyond the stars, where our cosmic Home beyond Home always thrives.

The cosmic Other Side is as identical a reflection of the universe as our Other Side is of earth. It's populated by incarnated spirits and Spirit Guides and messiahs from abandoned planets in every galaxy. It has its own legion of Angels and its own venerated Council. The residents of the cosmic Other Side are the most highly advanced in the universe. And someday, about a hundred years from now if we keep working toward making earth an uninhabitable planet, we'll be right there among them.

The Council

The Council, also known as the Elders or the Master Teachers, is its own phylum of eighteen highly advanced male and female spirits who essentially act as God's voice on the Other Side. They are the exception to the rule of everyone at Home being thirty years old. As an emblem of their revered wisdom, the men wear identical white-silver beards, and the women have long straight white-silver hair. Their faces are extraordinarily beautiful, mature but perfectly unlined, and both the men and the women dress in flowing floor-length robes. Like the phylum of Angels, the eighteen Council members never incarnate, and their sacred titles are appointed for eternity.

The Council presides in a vast white marble room in the Hall of Justice, at a gleaming white marble U-shaped table. A legion of gold-winged Principalities stand sentinel behind them as a proud, silent testament to their importance. The Council is not a governing body, since government and laws are unnecessary on the Other Side. But because the wisdom of the Council membership is as infinite as their love for us, they're entrusted by God with responsibilities that profoundly affect both life at Home and our lives here on earth.

I've often said it shocks me that I actually was sober when I wrote my chart for this lifetime, and I'm sure many of you relate. My theory is that we must feel so invincible on the Other Side that sometimes we choose some bigger obstacles to confront on earth than our goals really require. One obstacle I obviously insisted on in my chart was someone I trusted defrauding and betraying me, jeopardizing my career and the credibility I've worked a lifetime to earn. I was devastated and scared to death. My Spirit Guide Francine kept promising I wasn't just going to be okay. I was going to come out of that horrible experience stronger, wiser and better than ever. I didn't believe one word of that, and I was sure I'd finally written something into my chart that would pull me under and keep me there. As it turned out,

Francine was true to her word as always. I did come out stronger, wiser and better than ever by the time it was over. But I didn't know until later how far she'd gone to keep her promise. It seems that while I was slogging my way through endless legal battles, Francine was lobbying the Council to modify my chart. She never asked that the crisis be erased or that I be spared the consequences of my own poor judgment, but she successfully convinced the eighteen venerable Master Teachers to spare my life's work and me from being permanently compromised.

So take it from me, the Council is so powerful that they actually can intervene in our charts midemergency when they know the outcome will be devoted to God's greatest good.

But then, few residents of the Other Side are more intimately familiar with our life charts than the Council, because it's to them that we present the rough drafts for their divine guidance as one of our final steps before leaving Home to come here. They talk us through every detail of the boot camp we've set up for ourselves, asking questions, advocating modifications, pointing out ways we can maximize the value of the lessons we're intent on learning and areas in which we might be setting ourselves up for more pain than some lessons are worth.

Once we've finally arrived at a chart that satisfies both our goals and the Council's loving, protective wisdom, we're sent away with one final sacred blessing from these eighteen transcendent beings: It's the Council's responsibility, based on the difficulty of the incarnation we've just charted for ourselves, to assign the specific Angels who will watch over and protect us until we're safely Home again. That's not to say we can't call for extra help along the way when the need arises. God's entire legion of Angels is always paying attention and is ready to rush to our side, although the most powerful of them, the Principalities, will arrive only when we're in need of a miracle and we summon them specifically. But there are few moments we treasure more as we leave the Other Side, headed for this cold, rough earth, than the sight of those eighteen divine, beautiful beings rising from their massive white marble dais to present us with the chosen Angels who'll spend our lifetime right beside us, on the Council's loving orders.

Covens

A coven is a gathering of witches, Wiccans or warlocks, usually thirteen, for the purpose of worshipping Mother Earth, learning and deepening the appreciation for the rites, history, spirituality, theology, mythology and traditions of witchcraft, and casting spells that will benefit nature and its ecological balance.

The traditional number of thirteen attendees is thought to be an homage to the thirteen lunar months of the year, i.e., the thirteen occurrences per year of the full moon. One of those thirteen members is always a leader, usually a High Priestess with extensive training in ritual, customs, leadership, magic, psychic development and theology, as well as a reputation for integrity and respect in the community in which the coven exists. There's a tendency to imagine covens as isolated little groups, living in mysterious camps, staying to themselves, rarely interacting with anyone but each other, performing ceremonies of God only knows what unspeakable evil. In truth, with very few exceptions, members of a coven have jobs, homes, friends and lives in which their beliefs are at the center but not to the exclusion of everything else.

Neither practitioners of witchcraft nor members of individual covens will be found marching up and down the streets recruiting, proselytizing and touring in missionary groups. Being part of an ancient belief system that in almost every corner of the world has been accused of virtually every unspeakable evil, blamed for virtually every unspeakable atrocity and executed just for being suspected of being one of "them," it's understandable that the Wiccan community has no interest in rounding up volunteers and prefers to be selective, particularly about their covens.

Becoming a witch or warlock has nothing to do with buying a pointed hat and a cape and painting a pentagram on your face. In many ways it's very much like becoming a Christian, or becoming a Muslim. Witchcraft is a religion—not a mainstream one, but a religion nonetheless. Contrary to popular belief, classic Wicca is no more involved with Satanism or a worship of evil than Christians, Jews, Muslims, Buddhists and Hindus are. Wiccans pray to the Goddess, to Mother Nature, find divinity in all living things, concern themselves with ecology and with nurturing the planet. They're repelled by such concepts as controlling or harming other people, or casting spells intended to alter another person's free will. Their rituals, which are highly secretive for the same reason the majority of the religion itself is secretive, are aimed at favorable weather, the fertility of the earth, the purity of air and water, the successful growth of crops and the overall well-being of the resources we've been given, that we rely on for our existence. So to become a Wiccan begins with an initial openness to those concepts and beliefs, and then learning and studying the history, practices and everything else you can find about witchcraft to see if it's a belief you can sincerely embrace and commit to. Again, it's not unlike a desire to become a Christian—believing in Christ as the son of God is a great start, but imagine how limited your definition of "Christian" would be if you never took the time to read the Bible.

Joining a coven isn't as easy as filling out an application and sending in your ten-dollar fee. In fact, most covens refuse initiation fees, and they keep themselves private enough that it's up to you to find your way to them and express an interest in being part of the group. It will be up to them, not you, whether or not to accept you, based on their perception of your sincerity, your ability to fit in with the rest of the group and your ability to contribute spiritually to the rest of the group.

For more on this subject, see the section on Witchcraft, Witches and Warlocks.

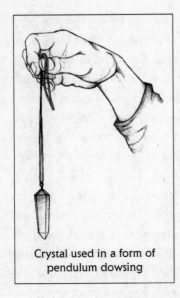

Crystal used in a form of pendulum dowsing

Crystals and Gems

Frankly, I think it's unfortunate that the use and wearing of crystals and other beneficial stones became such an overdone New Age fad that it became a little off-putting to much of mainstream society. Crystals and gemstones really can be of subtle, very real help to our physical and emotional well-being—as long as we don't get as carried away as a friend of mine who, at the height of all the New Age hype, wore so many crystals to cure her chronic neck injury that she actually exacerbated the problem.

There's a logic to the effect crystals have on us, a logic that's been honored for thousands and thousands of years. Crystals, and other natural gems, are formed in the earth, over countless millennia. The energy they've absorbed during their formation is rich, ancient and potent, and their atoms are arranged with geometric precision. As a result, the potent energy they emit has a geometric precision about it as well, a consistent vibrational pattern capable of balancing human energy, which, let's face it, is anything but consistent. And then, as you'll read in the section on Devas, there's the Life Force present in every natural element on this planet, concentrated into powerful, magnetically charged sources of potential healing.

Because we humans are deeply connected to colors, and even emit a wide variety of them in our auras, the colors of various crystalline stones have been discovered, over thousands of years of study and observation, to have specific benefits on the human body and even target specific chakras, which you'll find discussed in their own section. To name just a few:

amber—targets the spleen chakra—calms nerves

amethyst—targets both the throat chakra and the brow chakra—enhances inner peace and spirituality, helps battle addictions

aquamarine—targets the heart chakra—enhances strength and a sense of control in fearful situations

citrine—targets the spleen chakra—detoxifies the body, cleanses the aura

diamond—targets the crown chakra—attracts love, harmony and abundance

emerald—targets the heart chakra—promotes general healing, deepens the significance of and the ability to remember dreams

garnet—targets the root chakra and the heart chakra—inspires imagination and balances energy

gold—targets the solar plexus chakra—purifies, heals, lends masculine energy

jade—targets the heart chakra—calming for the eyes, promotes longevity

lapis lazuli—targets the brow chakra—stimulates the thyroid, increases general perception

malachite—targets the heart chakra—known as "the lucky money stone," also eases asthma

moonstone—targets the spleen chakra—known as "the lucky love stone," also promotes emotional balance

onyx—targets the root chakra—promotes healing during the grief process

peridot—targets the heart chakra—stimulates emotional growth and new opportunities

quartz—targets any and all of the chakras—can be programmed for a variety of purposes

ruby—targets the heart chakra—stimulates circulation, can also inadvertently create anger in others by disrupting their field of energy

sapphire—targets the throat and brow chakras—highly spiritual, also helps achieve goals

silver—targets any and all the chakras—great energy conductor, lends feminine energy

tanzanite—targets the brow chakra—stimulates spiritual insights

turquoise—targets the throat chakra—beneficial to the upper respiratory system

Also worth mentioning as a closing word of caution: There is a myth that opals bring bad luck. They don't. Nothing does, unless you believe it does. But opals do intensify both positive and negative emotions. So they really are worth avoiding if you're going through grief, or if you're prone to chronic depression.

Cults

If you haven't read the definition of the Dark Side yet, please take the time to do so before you read this.

There. Thank you. Now: Cults are a convenient, insidious way for dark entities to seduce and destroy the God-centered light of white entities as a group, as opposed to the time-consuming inconvenience of extinguishing them one at a time. Sadly, white entities who are on a sincere, well-intentioned spiritual search are usually the most vulnerable and the most receptive to a talented dark entity with the right jargon. Spirits whose commitment to God is utterly sincere can't imagine anyone else faking something so precious and sacred. But dark entities can fake anything that attracts your attention, gains your trust and gives them control over you. If the key to your trust is a commitment to God, they'll memorize the Bible if they have to and recite it beautifully, without meaning a single, solitary word.

I know that a few of you who are reading this are, right this minute, giving serious thought to joining a "group" or "sect" or "mission" (they're never honest enough to call themselves a "cult") with a very charismatic, devout leader at its core (two of the most frequently used adjectives to describe Jim Jones of the People's Temple and David Koresh of the Branch Davidians, by the way).

I've worked with a lot of families, psychologists, legitimate members of the clergy and the FBI on the problem of cults and their victims, and I voluntarily participated in my share of deprogramming sessions until deprogramming became illegal. ("Freedom of religion" I revere. I'm just not clear on how groups who promote suicide, isolation, involuntary servitude, tax evasion, child endangerment, child molestation and sometimes even child sacrifice qualify as religions.) I feel qualified to offer a word of expert advice to those of you who are weighing the decision to join, relocate with and/or donate your worldly possessions to a religious group of any kind: "DON'T!"

In case that doesn't persuade you, and it won't, I do ask you from the bottom of my heart to see if any of the following rings a bell:

* Almost without exception, the head of the group requires that you offer obedient recognition of them as your God-center. You're dependent on the leader for your proximity to God; they have a superior closeness to God and God listens to your prayers only if you speak through them.

Every word of that is a lie. I don't care what particular religion you practice; you are and will always be your own God-center. You and He are part of each other, Father and child, eternally inseparable, your spirit and His interlocked. There is no greater closeness than yours and His, no one He loves more and no one's voice He'd rather hear than yours.

* Almost without exception, sooner rather than later, your leader will insist that the group renounce family and friends (aka "non-believers"), relocate and isolate itself from the rest of society. Nonbelievers, they'll assure you, are liars who've been sent by the

devil to plant doubt in your mind about your faith, your group's unique and exclusive mission and of course your leader's credibility as a great prophet and/or messiah. As for the rest of society, they'll be denounced as Godless heretics with Godless arbitrary laws who are out to destroy the great good work that God Himself has personally commanded the leader to accomplish.

The truth is, there's only one reason a cult leader, or any other scam artist, for that matter, wants to isolate you from family, friends and society in general: because neither they nor their rhetoric bears up under scrutiny from outsiders. If they were legitimate, they'd be as eager as every great prophet, healer and messiah in history to move among the masses, spreading the word of God far and wide, helping and healing those in need along the way, seeing to it that this world is better for their having been here. Only dark entities insist on dark, furtive isolation. And as for those "arbitrary laws" they're usually so indignant about—those usually involve paying taxes, neither abusing nor molesting children, limiting weapons to those who are legally registered (these particular God-fearing pacifists seem to hate weapons but stockpile them "just in case") and never detaining people against their will. (Ask anyone who's realized they made a mistake and tried to leave a cult. The word "escape" always comes up, assuming they live long enough to talk about it.)

* Almost without exception, one of the first demands the leader will make on a new member is to renounce his earthly goods, which definitely includes his bank accounts. "Blessed are the poor" will probably be quoted as part of the incentive, along with the "money is the root of all evil" cliché, with some rhetoric about the nobility of sacrifice and poverty thrown in.

The truth is, stripped of all their money and possessions, the group will now be completely dependent on their leader, who manages never to be held accountable for where all that money and all those possessions went. Let's see. The group has renounced society, so we know nothing's being donated to reputable charities, or the good of mankind in general. And cults aren't exactly known for their luxurious lifestyles, so the money isn't being spent on them. A popular claim is that the money is "for God," but I'd love to hear exactly what possible use God has for money. My best guess is that the leader, who's so fond of quoting "blessed are the poor," has secretly decided that being blessed isn't really all it's cracked up to be anyway, and he's stashing away every dime he can get his hands on.

If, after considering those issues and a whole lot more, you still decide that following some group or mission or charismatic leader is what you're destined to do, I truly wish you Godspeed. Just one final request, though—don't drag your children into it! If what you're signing up for is really a worthwhile, God-centered pursuit, they can join you when they're old enough to make their own decisions—if you have the right to choose, fair is fair; they should have that same right someday too. In the meantime, stop and think: You know that the parents who joined the People's Temple and the Branch Davidians didn't start out believing that they were condemning their helpless children to a death sentence. Your life is yours to do with as you please. But every child deserves a chance to grow up safe and secure and cared for, so please don't visit your risks on them.

Curses

I hope you didn't turn to this word expecting to find a list of effective curses with which to inflict misery on those people in your life who need to be taught a lesson.

I don't have any.

Because there aren't any.

Because curses aren't real.

Curses are nothing but a way of controlling you and/or separating you from your money through fear and the inevitability that not every-thing in your life will always go perfectly. All you need to be vulnerable to the threat of a curse is a little bad luck and a sincere desire to get to the bottom of it and put a stop to it. Those who claim to be able to tell you where a curse is coming from and what to do about it call them-selves many things, from psychics to mediums to fortune-tellers to spiritualists, but they all have one thing in common: They're liars.

Here's the truth: Only one person in this world can put a curse on you, and that person is *you*. No one else has that power unless you give it to them.

I'm living proof that curses are meaningless without your permis-sion. I've helped law enforcement authorities all over the world put dozens of these despicable curse doctors out of business, so it's a safe bet that if curses were real, I'd either be bedridden or dead by now.

There are cultures whose belief in curses is ancient, deeply in-grained and as alive today as it ever was, and I mean them no disre-spect in my outrage against the curse business. In fact, a great deal of my outrage is on their behalf, knowing as I do that their beliefs are be-ing exploited and they're being frightened and tricked into handing over hard-earned money to get rid of something that never existed in the first place.

And what a coincidence that the only way to get rid of every curse, no matter what it is or who's behind it, is money. Not prayer. Not more regular attendance at church. Not more active volunteer work at a lo-cal charity to help balance your karma. Money. Or, to be fair, it might be your car, or your jewelry, or your house, or anything you own that can be *converted* into money. And once you're either cleaned out or starting to get suspicious, what do you know, the curse will probably vanish, along with the fortune-teller and your cash.

A lot of these scam artists don't get prosecuted because their vic-tims are too embarrassed by their own gullible stupidity to come forward and file complaints. I promise you, a lot of very bright, sophisticated people have been taken in and, in some cases, lost their life savings to the curse business, so please don't get embarrassed. Get mad!

First of all, remember that these lowlifes, some of whom are *very* skillful, by the way, already have an edge on you the minute you walk through the door: If things were going well, you wouldn't be there.

I don't care how educated, practical and grounded you are. When you're going through a rough time, you're weaker and more vulnerable than usual. So if someone says, with the right amount of conviction, "I know what's wrong and I can fix it," let's face it, you want to believe them. On your best day the mere suggestion of the word "curse" would send you right back out the door again, probably laughing as you go. On your worst day, because you're human and temporarily unsure of yourself, it's no surprise that at the suggestion of that same word a small voice might penetrate your usual skepticism and say, "What if she's right?"

If you still look skeptical about a curse, you'll usually be treated to a convincing sleight-of-hand performance that will "prove" it once and for all. And then, inevitably, the certainty that there's a curse involved will both increase the fee and require more sessions. If the fortune-teller is a small-time fraud and plans to stick around for a while, you'll probably be sold two dollars' worth of candles for eighty dollars and a small vial of holy tap water to tide you over until your next appointment.

If she's after a bigger, quicker take, she'll probably discover that the curse has taken up residence in your jewelry, your car or, most often, the largest quantity of cash you can get your hands on. There's only one solution, of course—to rid yourself of the curse, you have to rid yourself of the possession in question and give it to the fortune-teller (although if it's genuinely cursed, why does she want it?). Whether that's what it looks like or not, whether she pretends to set fire to it, throw it in a river or hand it to a stranger on the subway, the minute your possessions leave your hands and your eyesight, she's got them, and you'll never see them again.

No matter what variations and disguises and smoke screens and deceits the curse doctors of this world devise, there are three simple truths that can save you a lot of money and even more pain.

1) Anyone who tries to turn your fears against you to make you even more afraid and vulnerable is out to control you, not to help you.
2) There is *never* a reason why a reading with any psychic, medium, fortune-teller or spiritualist should cost you one penny more than the price you agreed to pay at the beginning.
3) The moment you hear any reference to a "curse," "hex," "evil eye," "dark cloud" or any other term implying you've been targeted for damnation, leave immediately and call your district attorney, or me, or both of us.

Please, on your own behalf and on behalf of future victims who might be even less able to afford it than you—if you've been scammed by anyone you've turned to for any form of psychic or spiritual help, turn them in! You may feel stupid, embarrassed or gullible, but remember, that's exactly what these deadbeat frauds are counting on, and your silence is their only hope of staying in business.

D

The Dark Side

The Dark Side is that segment of the spirit world made up of those who've rejected God and His laws of humanity, integrity, compassion and nonjudgmental love. Those who occupy the Dark Side will be called "dark entities" for this discussion. Their polar opposites, those who embrace and revere God and the white light of the Holy Spirit, will be called "white entities." Please don't even let it enter your mind that "dark" and "white" have anything to do with race or skin color. The mere suggestion of any such thing is offensive.

God didn't create the insidious, evil negativity that rules the world of the Dark Side. What He created is spirits endowed with free will. And some spirits used that free will to turn their backs on their Creator and pursue lives unencumbered by responsibility to anyone but themselves. Their choice, not God's. And there's no horned, pitchfork-carrying god who presides over the Dark Side from his throne in hell. For that matter, there is no hell. But dark entities are their own masters, too narcissistic to believe in a being superior to them, and they bring up Satan and other mythical devils only when they're facing consequences they don't like and need someone else to blame.

The Dark Side exists in both human and spirit form, just as we white entities do. In human form, they look exactly like the rest of us.

(Don't forget, if it weren't for the choices they'd made, they would *be* the rest of us.) They might be a family member, a lover or spouse, a next-door neighbor, a coworker, a supposed friend. In spirit form, their negative energy can deeply affect everything from mechanical and electrical devices to our mental health without our even realizing what's happening. But whether they're in human form or spirit form, the entities of the Dark Side all share the same basic qualities:

* They have no conscience, no genuine remorse and no sense of responsibility for their actions. They take all the credit and none of the blame for everything that happens around them, and self-justification is their first and only response to criticism.

* In psychiatric terms, they're true sociopaths. They mimic human behavior brilliantly without ever really feeling it. They can simulate extraordinary charm, sensitivity, empathy, love, regret, even devout piety if they can use it to their advantage to gain our trust. Once the act has worked, as it often does, they promptly drop it, having no further use for it and frankly finding it to be too much work. We white entities, because our emotions and faith are genuine, have trouble imagining that we've been witnessing a performance. So we stay around, trying desperately to resuscitate that wonderful person we're sure is in there because we saw them with our own eyes, unable to grasp that that wonderful person never really existed in the first place.

* As far as the Dark Side is concerned, we white entities are nothing but a collection of walking mirrors. If their reflections through our eyes are flattering, we're valuable to them. But the minute we catch on that we've been looking at a mask, and they no longer like the way they look in our mirror, they'll react in one of two ways—they'll get as far away from us as possible, or they'll repeat the performance that won our approval in the first place in the hope of winning it again.

* Dark entities live by their own self-serving rules, which change at their convenience and don't necessarily apply to anyone else around them. In their minds, their behavior is always acceptable, but they might become outraged or deeply wounded if someone else aims that same behavior at them. The result is that the white entities close to them are kept constantly off balance, which gives the dark entity that much more power.

* The goal of the dark entity isn't to turn a white entity dark. They know that can't be done. Their goal is to extinguish the white entity's light, since darkness can't exist where there's light. They don't necessarily try to destroy the white entity physically. More often they'll simply create as much emotional turbulence, self-doubt, guilt and depression as possible in as many white entities as they can seduce into trusting them.

* Dark entities rarely enjoy each other's company—with no light to extinguish, no flattering reflection to gaze into and no control to be gained over someone with the same bag of tricks, what possibly would be the point? Instead, they deliberately seek us out. And at least once in our lives, we're likely to seek them out too. It has nothing to do with being stupid. It has to do with taking our spiritual responsibilities seriously and believing it's our moral responsibility to reach out to someone we perceive to be lost, in trouble or misunderstood.

Now, about this myth of being able to help a dark entity. It's against our humanitarian instincts to turn our back on a child of God who needs us. But I promise, when it's the Dark Side you're up against, you're wasting your time. A dark entity can't be turned white, any more than a white entity can be turned dark. You can't appeal to a conscience that doesn't exist; you can't inspire genuine remorse in someone who takes no responsibility for his actions; and you can't ignite sincere love in someone who loves God Himself only on an as-needed basis. I say this as both a spiritual psychic and as a person who's learned the hard way: If there's a dark entity in your life, in Jesus' own words, "Shake off the dust from your feet."

No discussion of who dark entities are would be complete without making it clear who they *aren't*. Not all murderers and other violent criminals are dark entities. Not everyone who's ever hurt you is a dark entity. Not everyone who's ill-tempered or hard to get along with is a dark entity. Not everyone you don't like, or who doesn't like you, is a dark entity. There are white entities I don't like. There are white entities who don't like me. This isn't about labeling people, or passing judgment, or worst of all, becoming a spiritual snob, which can be just as repellent as the Dark Side itself. It's simply about learning how and why we need to pay close attention to who is in our lives. True, we wrote every one of those people into our charts before we came here. But we wrote in some of them to teach us the wisdom of knowing when to walk away—the one area in which the Dark Side can be of use to us, for a change.

Déjà Vu

Déjà vu is an experience most of us have from time to time, and it's easy to think of it as nothing more than an interesting momentary diversion. What it really is, though, is a fleeting glimpse into our other lives, on earth and on the Other Side.

There are two kinds of déjà vu. The first occurs when you visit a certain house, city, road, foreign country or some other place you've never been before and suddenly realize it seems very familiar. Sometimes you even find you know your way around. It happened to me on my first trip to Kenya. It so immediately felt like home from the moment I stepped off the plane that I actually was telling my guide where the geographical highlights were before he could tell me, and I knew it had nothing to do with my being psychic. What it did have to do with, and what each of us is experiencing when we feel intense familiarity with an unfamiliar place, is our spirit's memories of a past life. We absolutely have been to that supposedly strange place before; it was just in another body, in another time. And when the spirit memories buried in the subconscious are stirred so deeply by sights from a whole other incarnation that those memories emerge into the conscious mind, that "unexplainable familiarity" kind of déjà vu is created—more accurately, powerful, miraculous glimpses into the eternity of our souls.

That same kind of déjà vu applies to people as well, by the way. We all know people who seem familiar the moment we meet them, strangers we feel we've known all our lives. And other people you know you're supposed to feel a special closeness to, like some family members, for example, you somehow never feel a connection with no matter how hard you try. I'll bet if you take a long look at every significant person in your life and ask yourself, without judgment, "Have I known this person in a past life?" you'll be surprised at how easily you can answer yes or no. If the answer is yes, by the way, don't feel obligated to form a connection with them this time around. That person may have been the bane of your previous existence. Or he may have been nice enough before, but he has chosen to come back this time as a complete jerk. You don't have to act on past-life familiarity, or place lesser importance on those with whom you don't feel it. Just notice it when it happens and recognize it as another window into your eternity.

The second kind of déjà vu is so common, subtle and seemingly trivial that we rarely give it more than a passing thought. It consists of a moment in which every detail, from what you're doing to whom you're doing it with to your surroundings to what you're wearing and thinking and feeling, is so familiar that you're absolutely sure you're reliving an exact duplicate of a moment from your past. It never lasts more than a few seconds, and it is never a significant event. It's invariably as trivial as, "Once before I was in a room just like this, on a sofa just like this, watching a TV that was at the same place that one is, reaching for the phone just like I am right now . . ." The moment is always gone again in less time than it took us to notice it. So it's not that surprising that we fail to realize how amazing, affirming and magical those déjà vu moments really are. To understand them fully, we need to fully understand charts.

As you'll read in the section on Charts, before we come here from the Other Side, we very specifically map out the incarnation we're about to undertake. We also include in those charts a few tiny, trivial details here and there, just some meaningless little vignettes along the way to let us know we are on the right track. And from time to time those meaningless vignettes occur in the form of déjà vu. Because they strike a chord of such sudden, total familiarity, we logically assume we must be inexplicably duplicating a moment we've lived before in this life. We're not. What we're doing when déjà vu occurs is experiencing a spirit memory of a tiny, trivial, familiar detail from the chart we created on the Other Side before we were born. Déjà vu is our spirit resonating so profoundly with the realization, "I remember the chart I wrote" that it echoes from our subconscious, where the spirit mind exists, to our conscious mind. For that instant, both our subconscious and conscious minds are receiving an affirmation, in the form of déjà vu, that we are in perfect synch with our chart. Even more than that, they're getting a glimpse at our eternal lives on the Other Side, as our spirit remembers, acknowledges and yearns for Home.

Devas

The definition of devas I've always been taught, and that I happen to love, is that they're the Life Forces pulsing through nature, or, if it communicates the same idea to you, natural spirits.

To clarify a couple of things first, though: When I say "natural spirits," I'm by no means implying that we humans ever reincarnate as a tree or a flower or a bee or a coral reef. We don't switch species from one lifetime to the next. And as you'll read in the discussion of psychometry, I don't believe that spirits can occupy inanimate objects.

Nor do living things in nature have evolving, wisdom-acquiring souls on journeys toward perfection. But they're alive with the same energy, the same Life Force, that literally gives us life, without which our bodies would be of no more use than our cars are without us inside them to turn on the ignition and make them move. The Life Force in us and all of nature comes from the same Source and creates a sacred connection between us, and it also creates a vast, sensitive, feeling world population in which we humans are actually a minority.

What's wonderful is that the devas are more aware of this connection than most of humankind tends to be, and they're available to be our allies if we just call on them when the need arises. If you think that's a preposterous idea, it might help to know that the age-old tradition of knocking on wood for luck originated in an ancient belief in summoning the spirits in trees for help and protection. (And I'm not superstitious, but I admit it, I knock on wood from time to time, even when I try to stop myself.)

I have a client who was diagnosed with liver cancer. By the time I met him he'd been declared completely cured, and I asked him how he did it. Well, for one thing, he'd tirelessly pursued the best available medical help, *which nothing ever can or should replace*! For another thing, and he unnecessarily blushed when he told me this, he'd made it a habit to give pep talks to the devas in his liver every morning while he drove to work. Can he or I prove that talking to his devas made a difference? Of course not. Can anyone prove it didn't?

Other clients, and several reputable scholars too, by the way, expand the deva/Life Force proposition to everything that exists, both living and inanimate. I don't have a shred of proof to the contrary, so if that belief makes sense to you, by all means put it to the same use those clients have. One, who's afraid to fly, never boards a plane without asking the plane's devas for a safe trip. Another misplaced a very valuable bracelet, and after frantic hours of tearing her house apart became desperate enough to ask the bracelet devas to please bring it out of hiding. It appeared within minutes, in plain sight in the middle of her bedroom floor, where she'd already looked fifty times and couldn't possibly have missed it.

Again, devas are all around us, whatever the specifics of where they live. They're yours to scoff at, dismiss and ignore. Or, if you like, you can include them in your life, in times of crisis or just for a passing knock on wood, and frankly, I'll be surprised if they don't make a difference.

Dharma and Karma

The word "dharma" originated in the ancient language of Sanskrit. It's a principal element of the great religions of Buddhism and Hinduism, and at its most basic, it means "protection." But what makes dharma so compelling is that it's a proactive concept. Protecting ourselves from unhappiness is no one else's responsibility but ours, and it's accomplished not by physical force but by living within our own inner laws of righteousness, peace and tolerance. Dharma dictates absolute honor for all living things and the land that nourishes them, and the belief that until each of us finds our own inner peace, there aren't enough marches, protests and demonstrations in the world to achieve peace among the nations on earth.

There are no specific rules in living according to dharma, other than not causing harm to any human, animal or the land itself. Instead, it's based on the idealistic premise that humankind ultimately will rise to its own innate, sacred goodness when shown the way to its spiritual path.

My Spirit Guide Francine points out that there's a Universal Dharma, and since our universe was created by God, it's not surprising that its dharma is the same righteousness, peace and tolerance we possess within ourselves. When we live outside the bounds of our own divine dharma, we're naturally out of synch with the universe and pay the price in the form of stress, misery and bitterness, regardless of how much wealth and supposed success we might accumulate.

Karma is a sister of dharma in that it offers a road map outlining amazingly simple directions to a peaceful, fulfilling life of goodness. Karma is another universal law that really does boil down to all those sayings you've heard before: "What goes around comes around," "What ye sow, so shall ye reap," and "You get back what you give." In this life or the next one, it's a guarantee that your karma will catch up with you, good or bad. Actually, a friend of mine insists it takes five years for bad karma to catch up with someone who has it coming, on the condition that you not interfere or lift a finger to try to speed it up in any way. Don't waste one moment of your time and energy on revenge or causing someone even minor trouble or wishing them the worst possible luck. Sure, it's tempting, but his theory is, they don't deserve the compliment of any more of your attention, even if it's negative. And besides, if you retaliate or wish awful things on someone, "who wants *that* karma?" Mentally and emotionally, he's the healthiest person I've ever met, so I've been enjoying watching his five-year theory play out, and I don't have a single disagreement with it so far.

There are a couple of finer points of karma that are often misunderstood and need to be cleared up. One is that motives are a major factor when it comes to reaping what we've sown. We've all hurt people in our lives, and I'll bet thirty to forty percent of my clients every single week spend part of our time together trying to work through the guilt they're consumed with over that one issue. In addition to asking if they've done everything they can to take responsibility for the pain they've caused and to make things right again, my other inevitable question relates to karma: "Did you deliberately hurt that person, or was it inadvertent?" Genuinely inadvertent harm—harm you had no reason to believe you would cause by your actions—doesn't equate to the dark karmic clouds that are guaranteed by the harm you were well aware you might be causing but didn't let stop you. The reverse is equally true, by the way. If you live your life with little or no regard for other people but have developed a talent for shifting the blame or creating inventive excuses when it looks as if there might be consequences, don't be too quick to relax. There's no such thing as getting away with it when it comes to karma. It will all catch up with you. It just will. As the saying goes, it's not a threat; it's a promise.

Also, remember that when we plan our upcoming lifetimes, we write the chart for those lifetimes according to the spiritual learning and growth we want to accomplish. Nothing is inflicted on us. Whatever we go through in any given incarnation, it's because we chose it ahead of time. It's how we handle the best and worst of what we chose that determines our success.

So imagine the advance courage, determination and divine aspiration it takes for a spirit to write a chart that includes physical or mental challenges, poverty, hunger, abandonment and other forms of severe deprivation and genuine emotional abuse. It's an honor to live among these exceptional spirits, it's our privilege when we're able to help them and it's incalculable how much we can learn from them. And yet, one of the most commonly misunderstood concepts about karma is that instead of being the elevated souls they are, these people are mistakenly perceived as obviously being punished for all sorts of heinous crimes against humanity in past lives. Please believe me, exactly the opposite is true. The tougher the chart, the finer the soul who wrote it.

In essence, then, a simple formula for those of us, myself included, who never stop trying to deepen our spiritual consciousness is to learn every day through our karma while living every day by our dharma.

Discarnate

This is a word that seems to come up often in my clients' readings and seems to confuse them more than it needs to. In case you're going through the same frustration:

"Incarnate" means "occupying a body," or "living within flesh." So "Christ incarnate," for example, is simply a reference to Jesus, the man, when He walked on earth. "Carnate" is a synonym. Catholicism states that when Jesus was born "the Word became carnate," meaning the Word, or God, in this case, had taken human form.

Discarnate is the opposite—existing outside of a body, or exclusive of flesh, which could perfectly describe a spirit or ghost.

Divination

Since the beginning of time, humankind has looked everywhere for answers to questions that seemed beyond their reach and control. And everywhere isn't an overstatement. It's as if for as long as we've occupied this planet, we've been sure that God has hidden all those answers in plain sight, in some object, or configuration of objects, if we could just find them and learn to interpret them.

Divination is the use of objects and/or omens in the hope of finding those elusive answers. Self-professed fortune-tellers, mediums, healers, shamans, psychics, exorcists, soothsayers, priests and witches in every culture of every country of every continent on earth have devised more divining arts than I can possibly list here, but some of them are too fascinating to ignore. I don't doubt for a moment, by the way, that every one of these practices has its share of earnest, well-meaning practitioners. I also don't doubt that, like anyone else who uses people's fear and trust as an opportunity to rob them blind, some of them belong behind bars.

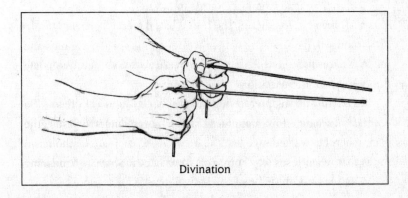

Divination

* *Alchemy*—at its most ancient roots, a divining and healing practice in which an elusive substance called the "philosopher's stone" transformed common base metals into gold and silver
* *Aleuromancy*—divination through the use of fortune cookies
* *Astragyromancy*—the rolling of special dice whose facets contain letters and numbers
* *Botanomancy*—seeking signs and omens in the varying patterns of burning twigs, leaves and branches
* *Capnomancy*—reading messages in rising smoke
* *Ceraunoscopy*—divining answers in thunder and lightning storms
* *Daphnomancy*—hearing messages in the crackling of specially selected branches (usually laurel) tossed onto an open fire
* *Dowsing*—the practice of locating water or precious stones and minerals through the use of a forked stick called a "divining rod"
* *Gyromancy*—a long, tedious process, a distant relative of the Ouija board, in which the client walks around a lettered circle to the point of dizziness, and prophecies are spelled out from the letters on which the dizzy client begins to stumble
* *Ichthyomancy*—fortune-telling through the movements of live fish
* *Metoposcopy*—unearthing the truth about a person's character and destiny by reading the lines in the forehead
* *Molybdomancy*—divining meaning from the sputters and hisses of molten lead when it's poured into water
* *Myomancy*—predicting the future based on the behavior of mice and rats
* *Necromancy*—predicting the future through communication with spirits of the dead
* *Oneiromancy*—interpreting the prophecies found in dreams
* *Ophiomancy*—finding omens in the movements and behavior of serpents
* *Phrenology*—reading messages found in the shape, irregularities and bumps of the head

* *Rhapsodomancy*—randomly opening a sacred book or a book of poetry and divining meaning from a passage found there
* *Spodomancy*—predicting the future by reading images in the cinders of a freshly extinguished fire
* *Tasseography*—reading of tea leaves

Doppelgänger

This is an amazing phenomenon, almost like the ghost of a living person. "Doppelgänger" is a German word meaning "double goer." It's thought by some to be a separate shadow identity that every person has, that can be seen only by the originator. Others believe a doppelgänger can be seen by anyone who knows the originator, so that as much confusion and mistaken identity as possible can result. Still others believe that a doppelgänger appears only as an omen, when the originator is about to die.

Please don't let me confuse you—doppelgängers are not synonymous with astral projection or astral travel. During an astral experience, the spirit leaves the body for various adventures, but the body stays where it is and certainly never seems to appear anywhere else. When a doppelgänger is involved, the body—the living, breathing, very much alive body—literally seems to bi-locate, or be in two places at once.

There was a time when I thought this was one of the silliest ghost stories I'd ever heard, and/or one of the poorest excuses for an alibi in the history of the legal system.

Then, as usually happens when I'm especially vocal about my disbelief in something, I came face-to-face with my own doppelgänger.

It was the late 1960s. My children were very young. I was wearing a God-awful flowery nightdress with big red roses all over it that my mother had given me. And when I say God-awful, I mean it was unforgettably hideous. I woke up in the middle of the night so hot I was sweating (don't bother doing the math, I'll tell you myself: I was much too young for hot flashes), and there was no chance I was going back to sleep until I found out why my bedroom was sweltering. Step 1, obviously—check the thermostat.

You need to know that I'm not one of those people I sometimes envy, who can scuff around only half-awake after they get out of bed and go right back to sleep if they feel like it. When I'm up, I'm up, as wide awake as if it's the middle of the day and I've had three cups of coffee. So right up front we can rule out the theory that I must have been dreaming.

I marched downstairs and found the thermostat set at about 80°. I cranked it back down to a temperature more suitable for human beings than for rare hybrid orchids, promising silently in the process to hunt down and destroy whatever sadist in the house had been playing with the thermostat, then turned to start up the stairs again.

Instead, I just stood there gaping at the bottom of the stairs, because, impossibly, there I was, coming down the stairs, in that grotesque, ridiculous nightdress.

My mind felt as if it were short-circuiting as I tried to fathom what was going on, but I was so stunned I couldn't even figure out which one "I" actually was. I had just flashed on a theory that somehow I was the one on the stairs, not the one who was watching, when—well, the only way I know to describe it is that I slammed into myself at the thermostat.

You know I didn't get another wink of sleep that night, and I was camped out at the library doors the next morning when they opened. (This was long before computers, obviously, when we still used libraries to research things.) I read, I studied, I talked to every colleague I knew who could shed some light on the subject. That's how I learned about doppelgängers, and that's how I also learned, to my relief, that while they're not exactly common, they're not unheard of either. I was even in some fairly interesting company, as a matter of fact. Apparently Guy de Maupassant, whose novels and short stories I'd read in college as a literature major, had his doppelgänger sitting at a table with him dictating, toward the end of his life. And Percy Bysshe Shelley, one of my favorite classical poets, ran into his doppelgänger one day near the

Mediterranean Sea. His doppelgänger did nothing more than point toward the sea. That was all. And it was in the Mediterranean Sea that Shelley drowned, less than a year after his doppelgänger appeared.

I can't give you an absolutely authoritative explanation for doppelgängers, but I can give you a very well-educated probability: Our spirits, in their most natural forms in the spirit world, are able to be in two places at once, or bi-locate, as easily as you and I are able to breathe. And just because they're temporarily inhabiting bodies doesn't mean our spirits lose all their memories and skills. I believe that doppelgängers are rare but real events, not necessarily monumental at all if they can concern themselves with thermostats, in which the spirit gets restless, feels like stretching its muscles, or simply reverts to what comes naturally for a moment and decides to bi-locate. And then, when it either catches itself in the act and says "oops" or has done what it set out to accomplish, it returns to itself again inside the body, limited to uni-locating as before, until it's back in the spirit world and free of all the restraints and inconveniences it tolerates on earth for the sake of its eternal journey.

Dowsing

Dowsing is a form of divination (relying on an object to harness paranormal or supernatural energy) that's been used for thousands and thousands of years to search for everything from underground water and minerals to buried treasure. In the most common form of dowsing, the dowser employs a stick or rod—sometimes forked, sometimes L-shaped—called a dowsing rod or divining rod and walks across the area in question until the rod points downward, indicating that the sought-after resource has been located. (Some dowsers prefer using two rods and know they've got a hit when the two rods cross each other.)

While skeptics toward dowsing are almost as numerous as dowsers themselves, it's worth taking a moment to thank God that it's developed into a fairly well-intentioned pursuit, legitimate or not, after a history of some pretty horrifying abuses. Ancient dowsers, particularly in Egypt, Syria and Babylonia, were known to use their "skill" to determine the true wishes of the gods (including who might be a candidate for being banished or sacrificed) and for reaching verdicts and sentences in trials. (The use of divining rods in trials wasn't officially outlawed until the early 1700s, in fact.) There was a lot of very clandestine dowsing when the Middle Ages came along and the idea spread that dowsing was somehow Satanic. But it was the ever down-to-earth Germans who couldn't be bothered with all this talk of the will of the gods, or Satanism, or the justice system and, sometime in the 1400s, focused their dowsing energy on a search for metals and other underground resources. That potential caught on and eventually spread worldwide, and there are still very active dowsing societies in every part of the globe today, none of them focused on malicious or destructive purposes, to the best of my knowledge.

The most popular divining rods, whether they're forked or L-shaped, seem to be made of either brass, steel or twigs. Dowsers who prefer brass or steel claim that a metal rod will respond to their target's magnetic field, and a nonconductive material of some kind is wrapped around the rod's handle to keep the dowser's own electromagnetic energy from interfering with the signals. Twig enthusiasts, on the other hand, argue that only a natural divining rod can respond to the natural elements that are typically the objects of the search.

And then there's the variation called "map dowsing," in which the dowser stands over a map of the area in question with a pendulum, letting the pendulum hone in on the target location. Map dowsing is particularly popular among avid dowsers in searches for missing persons.

The explanations for why dowsing works, and/or why it doesn't, are countless, but they all generally revolve around the question of whether or not the dowser is manipulating the movement of the rod. It's more than a little fascinating that those who dismiss dowsers as frauds use the argument that *of course* the dowser is manipulating the movement of the rod, ergo dowsing is bogus. Those who passionately embrace dowsers as legitimate use the argument that *of course* the dowser is manipulating the movement of the rod, ergo dowsing is valid. In other words, dowsers insist that it's a combination of their own electromagnetic sensitivity to the object of their search, the involuntary hand movements that sensitivity creates, and the resulting amplified movement of the rod that make dowsing successful. Skeptics take the position that any manipulation on the part of the dowser invalidates the whole process. And on and on it's gone, and continues to go today, which means that, if nothing else, there's enough substance to the subject of dowsing to keep debates about its credibility raging for more millennia than we can count.

Dreams

We spend one-third of our lives sleeping. It's a brilliant part of God's plan, since sleep opens up a world of ways to nourish, inform and expand our souls. During sleep, obviously, our conscious minds take a break and allow our subconscious minds, where our spirit minds live, to take over. And one of the ways the subconscious expresses itself while we sleep is in dreams.

There are hundreds of theories on dream interpretation, and countless brilliant minds have done countless studies of dreams. It speaks volumes about their complexity, and the mysteries hidden inside them, that in spite of all that, dreams seem to keep as many secrets from us as they ever did.

The frequency, timing and cycles of dreaming are connected to the structure of sleep itself. There are two basic stages of sleep: REM, which stands for "rapid eye movement" and is the lightest stage of sleep, and Non-REM, which is the deeper sleep when our muscle responses become almost nonexistent. It's during REM sleep that we dream, and it's when we're awakened during or immediately after REM sleep that we're most likely to remember our dreams.

The Non-REM stage accounts for about seventy-five percent of our sleep, leaving twenty-five percent for REM sleep. And while we sleep, our brain waves fluctuate in approximately ninety-minute cycles. Brain waves have been charted into distinct levels for those ninety-minute cycles:

Beta Level: We're wide awake, active and alert.

Alpha Level: We're awake but relaxed, and our eyes are closed.

Theta Level: We're very sleepy or in the process of falling asleep, and usually in the REM stage.

Delta Level: We're very deeply asleep and in the Non-REM stage.

Once we reach the Delta level of the cycle, the order simply reverses, and our sleep becomes progressively lighter again. When we wake up feeling rested and refreshed, it's very likely that these ninety-minute cycles have been allowed to progress on their own without interference or interruption.

The same parts of the brain that control our sleep cycles also inhibit our other motor activities. That explains why, in the relatively light sleep of REM, when we're still asleep but vaguely aware of our surroundings, we'll occasionally have those frustrating dreams in which we want to run but our legs refuse to move—it's a blend of the situation in the dream and the normal, sleep-induced inhibition of body motions.

I've read, studied, researched and taught dream interpretation, and I wrote my own *Book of Dreams*. In my strong opinion, there are five categories of dreams:

* Release Dreams, in which your subconscious mind takes the opportunity to let off emotional steam your conscious mind hasn't dealt with. They are also helpful guides to unfinished business that needs your attention.

* Wish Dreams, which are exactly what they sound like—sometimes, as the lovely song says, a dream really is a wish your heart makes

when you're fast asleep. If we don't make the mistake of taking wish dreams too literally, they can throw a valuable spotlight on wishes you may not have even put into words yet. Sexual dreams, for example, aren't necessarily about sexual desire at all, or about some deeply buried attraction to the partner in your dream— they're usually a wish for more intimacy in your life, which doesn't have to be physical at all. A dream about a new house doesn't mean you should wake up the next morning and call a Realtor—it can mean there's something about yourself (*you* are where you live, after all, regardless of what house you occupy) that you're longing to change. A dream about giving birth definitely is not a cue to get pregnant—that new life you're giving birth to could be yours, some good idea you are about to bring into fruition or some new spiritual depth in yourself you're starting to unearth. In other words, always look at the overview rather than the specifics of wish dreams—you will be surprised how much you can learn about yourself and what you're really wishing for.

* Prophetic Dreams, which are simply dreams that predict some future moment, conversation or event. You don't have to be psychic when you're awake for the spirit mind to show off amazing psychic powers while you're sleeping. And take it from me, the reverse is true, too—I'm not remotely psychic when I dream. If you suspect that you tend to dream prophetically, try this for a month: Write down every dream you can remember that you think might have been a glimpse into the future, put it away and don't look at it until that month has passed. It will be easily apparent whether or not your dreams are truly prophetic, bearing in mind that "truly prophetic" doesn't just mean seeing into the future, it means doing it accurately.

* Information or Problem-Solving Dreams, which explain why and how you can go to sleep completely perplexed about a situation or an unresolved issue and wake up knowing exactly what to do.

The dreams themselves may not even appear to bear any resemblance to what's troubling you, but with the spirit mind being so adept at symbolism, it will get the point and pass along the translation to the conscious mind.

* Astral Visits, which technically aren't dreams. Have you ever had a dream about a visit to a departed loved one, or to someone or someplace on earth, at Home or anywhere in the universe, that seemed to be very real and, unlike most dreams, proceeded in a logical order from beginning to end? There's a strong probability that if you have, it was your spirit making an actual visit to that loved one, thanks to the magic of astral travel. (You can read the definition of Astral Travel under its own listing.) It's simply worth mentioning here because of the frequency with which astral visits are confused with dreams. Remember, just because it happened while you were sleeping doesn't mean it was a dream. *If it seemed exceptionally real and proceeded in a logical order from beginning to end, you can rest assured it was an astral visit.*

Dreaming is as essential to us as breathing. Whether we remember our dreams or not, whether we understand what they mean or not, they're a release valve, the mind's way of protecting and preserving some sense of balance in a waking world that often seems to offer very little balance at all.

Sleep researcher William C. Dement once said, "Dreaming permits each and every one of us to be quietly and safely insane every night of our lives." Perfectly put, and thank God for it.

E

Earthbound

An earthbound is simply another name for a ghost or a spirit that has left its physical body but is unable or unwilling to enter the tunnel and head Home, and as a result stays bound to the earth instead.

One of the most bittersweet earthbound stories I've heard was sent

An earthbound entity either doesn't know or doesn't accept that it is no longer in life

by a man named Noah, a successful building contractor in Toronto. Noah grew up in a house in the Maryland woods in which an eight-year-old boy named Richard had died a decade earlier from a two-story fall down a laundry chute while trying to escape his abusive, alcoholic father. Richard was still an active presence in the house throughout Noah's childhood.

"I used to play with him and spend hours talking to him, and because he had long hair I apparently thought he was a girl, until he told me he was a boy and his name was Richard. To this day I wish I could remember what Richard and I talked about. Most memorable, though, was a day when some of my cousins were visiting. They were playing in the backyard and looked over and thought they saw me standing at the back door watching them. They called to 'me' to come join them, but 'I' just smiled and waved. At that moment my uncle happened to come out the back door from inside the house and walked right through what they thought was me. They all started screaming, scared to death. Richard instantly disappeared from the doorway, and my uncle just stood there staring at my cousins, wondering what all the screaming was about.

"I know how crazy all this sounds, but I'm a sane, normal, hardworking Christian guy from a sane, normal, hardworking Christian family. I've got nothing to gain from making up ghost stories, I guess I just wanted to say on Richard's behalf to everyone who thinks ghosts are imaginary or evil—I lived with one who was very real and as sweet and harmless as could be, just a little boy who should never have died in the first place."

Now, Richard was an earthbound who not only had no idea he'd died when he hit the cement basement floor at the bottom of that laundry chute; he'd also ironically been trying to stay safe by continuing to hide in the basement from a father who'd long since committed suicide. He ventured out only when he heard the odd, irresistible sound of children laughing and playing in a house where there'd never been anything but dark rage, and for that particular little boy who didn't know he was dead, there was no reason to pay attention to the tunnel even if he did happen to notice it—being part of a happy family *was* paradise.

As it turned out, Richard's primary attachment was to Noah, and when Noah left home for college, Richard did start noticing and becoming curious about the tunnel. He was retrieved by some watchful spirits from the Other Side and joyfully reunited with his mother, who'd died when he was three.

Like I said, it's a bittersweet story. On one hand, I applaud anyone who has compassion for an earthbound's difficult, confused situation. On the other hand, no matter how happy, comfortable and content an earthbound seems to be, it pales in comparison to the perfect bliss that waits for them on the Other Side where they belong, and where we need to help them find their way if we possibly can.

Ectoplasm

According to the dictionary, ectoplasm is "the outer relatively rigid granule-free layer of the cytoplasm usually held to be a gel reversibly convertible to a sol." And cytoplasm, of course, is "the organized complex of inorganic and organic substances external to the nuclear membrane of a cell and including the cytosol and membrane-bound organelles."

I've read that more times than I can count, and I'm tempted to write to the author of those definitions and say, "If you didn't want me to know what ectoplasm is, why didn't you just say so?"

For our purposes, ectoplasm is thought to be the tangible residue of energy that's transmitted between a psychic/medium and a ghost. One theory is that when ectoplasm is present during or after an encounter between a medium and an earthbound, it's actually emanated by the medium—in other words, the Life Force or etheric substance (which you'll find discussed at length in its own section) of the medium congeals on the skin as it tries to lend enough power to the ghost to help it fully materialize. Another theory is that ectoplasm originates in the earthbound and is the manifestation of the ghost's own etheric substance caught between dimensions as the ghost itself happens to be.

Like everything else in the paranormal world, there are great debates about whether or not ectoplasm even exists.

I say, yes, it does.

I was investigating a haunting at the Brookdale Lodge in northern California for a TV show the exquisite Henry Winkler was producing. At one point I came upon a very unhappy man it turned out no one else could see. He found me and my very presence intrusive, and the sum total of our conversation went like this:

"What's your name?" I asked.

"Judge," he finally muttered.

"Your *name* is Judge?" I was trying to be chatty, but when a ghost is in no mood to talk, there's no one more stubborn or sullen. "Or you *are* a judge? Or you think I'm here to judge you? I give up, what does 'judge' mean?"

"Judge," he muttered again, with a slight sneer.

That was it. He was done with me, and by now the feeling was mutual.

Many hours later, after other encounters with earthbounds that were much more successful, my staff and I were headed for the door when something made me look down at myself. To this day I have no idea what that something was, because I didn't feel anything. But there, covering the whole front of my blouse, was a white sticky substance. It was thick, it was odorless and it was disgusting. My staff gathered around to gape at it, as mystified as I was about what it was, when it had appeared and where it could possibly have come from. I hadn't eaten anything. I hadn't had anything to drink. If I'd brushed up against anyone or anything that was covered with whatever this was, there's no way I wouldn't have noticed.

Finally my right-hand man Michael put into words what I'm sure the rest of us were thinking: "Don't look now, but I think you've been slimed."

For those of you who didn't see the movie *Ghostbusters*, being "slimed" means finding yourself drenched with ectoplasm from a ghostly encounter.

Now, I'm hardly an authority after only one experience with ectoplasm, but I felt then as I feel now, considering the list of "suspects" at the Brookdale Lodge that day, Judge was forceful enough and aggressive enough that his etheric substance, congealed into ectoplasm, emanated strongly enough from him that it projected itself . . . in this case, onto a perfectly good silk blouse, thank you.

Everyone who witnessed it that day, including me, has tried and failed to come up with a logical explanation. I spent a day among ghosts, one angry one in particular, and left with my blouse covered with slime. It was real. Several people saw it, touched it, grimaced over it and will still confirm today that it was nothing I'd done to myself.

So, yes. In my opinion, there is absolutely such a thing as ectoplasm.

Elementals

The theory behind the ancient myth of the existence of elementals goes like this. The earth is made up of four elements: Fire, Water, Earth and Air. Earth and Water are believed to be female-energy elements. Fire and Air are thought of as male-energy elements.

Inhabiting each of these elements are spirits of nature called Elementals. They're impossible to describe, since they don't have a form or appearance of their own. But if they care to they can take the shape of animals or humans and walk among us, soulless and deceitful, seducing unsuspecting genuine humans for the purpose of conceiving and bearing children. Julius Caesar and Hercules were among those rumored to be the offspring of Elementals. (Now, there's a tough rumor to dispel.)

Elementals' primary claim to fame, though, seems to be as forces of nature who can trigger volcanoes, tsunamis, earthquakes, catastrophic storms and unexplainable patterns and directions of ocean currents. Released from within the earth by volcanoes and earthquakes, some Elementals, according to legend, can even attach themselves to us like little formless negative energy barnacles. Once their presence has been established, we can be cleansed of them through the use of either a mild electrical current or through literally scraping them off with piano wire.

For the record, there's not one thing about Elementals, including their existence, that I happen to believe.

Elves

An elf is commonly thought to be a tiny imaginary being, kind of like a male fairy, who loves to play mischievous tricks on humans and, on a far more serious note, exchange their own babies for human babies they steal from cribs during the night. They seem to have originated in German mythology, as diminutive minor gods of nature, with life spans that lasted hundreds of years.

When the popularity of mythological elves spread to northern Europe, they became a bit more specialized. Some became highly skilled blacksmiths, while others evolved into beautiful women with the ability to dance with a man until he's in such a frenzy that he drops dead. (Those same female dancing elves, if seen from behind, are discovered to be hollow, by the way.) There were the elves in the fairy tale *The Shoemaker and the Elves* by the Brothers Grimm, in which elves were naked, twelve inches tall and enjoyed working on shoes. There was an especially kind, compassionate strain of elves who loved children and would appear at their bedsides to comfort them when they were about to die.

Great Britain and North America decided it would be quaint to recruit mythological elves to the North Pole to be little gift wrappers and toy makers for the equally mythological Santa Claus. Northern Europe, still preferring its own legends, kept their elves local and traditionally left out bowls of porridge for them on Christmas Eve to bribe them into leaving gifts rather than playing tricks.

All of which is as charming and colorful as can be, but the fact is, elves are not imaginary at all. They're among the fascinating population of the Underworld, which you'll find discussed at length in its own section.

Essence

The word "essence" comes up frequently in writings about the paranormal. I just wanted to clear up what it really means:

"Essence" is simply the "I am," those attributes without which that specific object, substance or being would not exist.

I especially like an explanation by philosopher George Santayana, that the essence of a being is simply everything about it, separate and apart from the question of its existence.

There's a school of thought that the essences of a being can't be divided without destroying the being itself. A human being, for example, is made up of two indivisible essences: the body and the soul. The body by itself is not a human being. The soul by itself is not a human being. Only those two essences, uniquely interwoven, can form this creature we call a human being.

Philosophers all the way back to Socrates and Aristotle have actually had some unbelievably complex arguments about whether or not a thing's existence is part of its essence. My eyes roll back in my head after reading about three pages of these arguments. But the one thing about which there seems to be very little disagreement is the one thing I understand perfectly and couldn't agree with more: In all the unimaginably infinite universe, there is only one Being who is an essence unto Himself, because only in God are His essence and His existence identical.

Etheric Substance

The etheric substance is that God-given energy that permeates and emanates from every space in the universe and every space within each of us. In various places throughout this book you'll find that energy is referred to as a "Life Force," which is simply a more common and more descriptive synonym of the etheric substance that gives us life and eternally connects us to each other, to every living thing, to every corner of the cosmos and to our Creator.

Science tells us that the vast, infinite universe is filled with ether, and that it's this ether, or etheric substance, that unites all universes, from the unimaginable heavens to the tiniest of molecules that make up our physical bodies and everything else in the physical world. The etheric substance is what scientists call "pure space." It's the cause and the source of all existence, the medium by which God infuses His breath. It's finer, lighter and more delicate than light waves, but at the same time it's indestructible. It's our most finely tuned receiver and our most powerful transmitter. We emanate it in the form of auras, and we internalize it in the form of our faith in God and our absolute knowledge that we're a part of the Divine and He is a part of us.

Etheric substance. Energy. Life Force. Use whichever synonym communicates the Breath of Creation to you, and resonates in your soul.

There's a beautiful description of etheric substance and its relation to the body during death that I think illustrates the whole etheric substance/Life Force concept perfectly. From "Vishnu's Intro to the Sixth Dialogue":

"Let us gaze upon the thought opposite to life: the fear of the word 'death,' which holds all of mankind in a grimy grip of despair. Death! There is no death! It is but a transition . . . a chemical screen, a strainer or a finely woven sieve through which the perpetual process of mother nature gradually brings forth a recycling, a process to a new degree of vibrating within a higher frequency. . . . Think of death as this fine chemical screen, where the refined etheric substance escapes to its true place. That which is left as the house of clay is only the debris of the negative processes that have not been strained through that finely woven sieve . . . The death of the body is but the expression of those negative conditions that defeat the very mainstream of life, the thoughts of greed and hate and selfishness, yet death calls upon each one as an individual to weigh upon a great cosmic scale the justice and the right that was expressed by his individual spirit in the past life. Again I repeat, and again I wish to install within the spirit of mankind, that there is no death. It is but a wondrous transition, part of a gradual climb to the House of Infinity."

Exit Points

When we write our life charts on the Other Side for an upcoming incarnation, we're well aware what a grueling challenge life on earth can be. So we never complete our charts without building in five possible escape routes, or five different ways and means to declare ourselves finished here and head Home.

These five self-devised bailout scenarios are called Exit Points. Exit Points are circumstances we prearrange that can result in the end of this incarnation if we choose to take advantage of them. Writing five of them into our charts doesn't mean we have to stick around for the fifth one. We might decide when our first Exit Point comes along, or second, or fourth, that we've accomplished all we need to on this trip. And we don't necessarily space them out evenly when we create them. We might write in two Exit Points for the same year, for example, and then have twenty or thirty years to wait until our next one comes along.

The most obvious Exit Points include critical illnesses and surgeries, potentially fatal accidents and any other events that could have resulted in death but didn't—not because of luck, because we simply chose not to take that particular Exit Point. Other Exit Points, though, are so subtle that we might not even be able to recognize them: deciding for no reason to drive a different route than usual to work; trivial delays that keep us from leaving the house on time; a last-minute change in travel plans; canceling a commitment because we suddenly just don't feel like it. Countless incidents that seem utterly meaningless could easily be a subconscious memory of an Exit Point that we wrote into our chart but decided not to take advantage of after all.

Another way that memories of our Exit Points sometimes surface is in the form of recurring dreams. Pay close attention to any recurring dreams about an unfamiliar but very specific person, place or situation that makes you feel uneasy. If that dream ends up manifesting itself in real life, it might mean the dream was prophetic. But just as often, it's the memory of an Exit Point you know is on its way, and you're about to have a choice to make.

It's also occasionally possible to become aware of an unchosen Exit Point while recovering from that potential Exit Point. I once did regressive hypnosis on a client who was still in traction from a motorcycle accident. He had no conscious memory of the accident at all. But under hypnosis he clearly remembered making a very deliberate decision to veer off the road and down an embankment. He found out later, from a paramedic on the scene, that he'd veered just in time to avoid a head-on collision with a truck that had lost its brakes and was hurtling toward him in the wrong lane.

He also remembered that just as he was regaining consciousness at the bottom of the embankment, a voice (his Spirit Guide) whispered, "That was number four." He'd never heard of Exit Points and asked me what "number four" could have meant. When I explained it to him, he smiled as if a whole lot of other questions had just been answered at the same time and simply replied, "I know that's the truth."

Five choices, ours to make, of when and how to go Home. That is the truth. And I hope you find it as empowering as I do.

Extraterrestrials

We are not the only inhabited planet in the universe. True, the other planets in our tiny solar system are uninhabited. But concluding we can apply that status to the rest of an infinite universe is like sitting in the only house on a secluded island and assuming ours must be the only house on Earth because we can't see any other houses through our front window.

That's not to imply that I believe in little green men. I don't pretend to know what all the beings on all the other inhabited planets look like. But since we earthlings are beings on an inhabited planet, and we're not little green men, I'm open to all possibilities, including their looking a lot like us.

There are many brilliant people who are as convinced there's no other life in the universe as I'm convinced there is. They say, "Show me proof." I say, "You go first." The minute I see photos of every square foot of every planet of every solar system in every galaxy clearly showing nothing but moonscapes in a universe so vast our best telescopes have seen only a fraction of it, I'll be happy to rethink my position. Until then, I'll continue to be sure that we're not just privileged members of a global community but members of a universal community as well.

The residents of other solar systems are God's children, just as we are. They have the same journeys of the spirit that we do, the same options of reincarnation and the same sacred, joyful lives on the Other Side—not our Other Side, but their own, as identical to their planets as ours is to Earth. In other words, rather than sharing our

Other Side with us, every inhabited planet throughout the universe has a divine Home of its own, each one blessed with the same help from its Other Side that we're blessed with from ours. Other planets' inhabitants have their own Spirit Guides, just as we do, their own legions of Angels, their own Council, their own sacred messiahs and, beyond any doubt, the same God who created us all.

Within the next quarter century, we'll begin communicating openly with the life-forms with whom we share this universe. And that's a fact worth celebrating. We on Earth are essentially newcomers to the cosmos, and our understanding of our relationship with God and His infinite creation are in their infancy by comparison. We have more to learn from our brothers and sisters on other planets than we can begin to conceive of, so we might as well disarm our missiles and prepare to welcome extraterrestrials, embrace them and start listening.

It shouldn't be too much of an adjustment, actually, since they've already been here for countless millennia and are here among us now. They've been arriving from Andromeda, and the Pleiades and galaxies we've never conceived of on earth. They've traveled freely for millions of years on the highways of the Bermuda Triangle and the Great Pyramids and the other atmospheric envelopes that are a basic part of their knowledge. They were welcome here once, and the time will come when they will be again. In the meantime, for those of them who are with us now, it's no one's business but theirs to reveal themselves when they're ready, so let's respect their privacy and leave it at that, like the considerate hosts we'll want them to be for us someday.

Fairies

I know I'm about to erase any lingering public faith in my mental stability with this little section, but facts are facts, so it can't be helped.

I've always loved the idea of fairies. I'm sure everyone who's clapped to bring Tinkerbell back to life, or grew up with a Celtic background or in the British Isles, or simply heard the folklore has always quietly believed that if you looked very quickly in exactly the right places in exactly the right light, you just might see one of these tiny gossamer-winged creatures.

From what I could piece together through various myths and legends I heard as a child, fairies, invariably beautiful as they were, could be either good or bad. They could heroically save the day, clean your house, fly ahead of you as your faithful scout or steal your baby. (I said I loved the idea of them. I didn't say I had a firm grasp on the concept.) My Grandma Ada, as practical and grounded as she was brilliantly psychic, was as casually sure of the existence of fairies as you and I are of the existence of carrots and bath towels. When I was a child she regaled me with countless stories of the fairies she used to see outside her family home near Hamburg, Germany. I was delighted by every story she ever told, so I wasn't about to discourage her by admitting that a lawn full of fairies sounded darling, but I wasn't buying a single word she said.

As I got older I began to realize, thanks to lots of travel and research, that Grandma Ada wasn't the only intelligent person who believed in fairies. I always believe there's an explanation for everything, and I don't rest until I've figured out what it is. So I was actually relieved and a little proud of myself when I arrived at the brainstorm that fairies were obviously a form of tulpa—creatures conceived of in the mind, who gain such wide acceptance that they take physical form.

Thank God *that* was settled once and for all.

And then, it was off to Ireland.

The Irish love to tell stories, and the local airport workers were no exception. From the moment we landed until we climbed into the hotel transport with our luggage, they were excitedly tripping over each other to make sure each new arrival heard about the recently rerouted runways, but there was constant bad luck because they kept running into fairy mounds and having to re-reroute them or something. To this day I have no idea what they were talking about; I just remember chuckling to myself over what a great time they were having telling it, and how funny it was to see all these grown men in such a superstitious snit about the inevitable bad luck of fairy mounds. Living proof of what fools superstitions make of people, the poor things.

We'd planned to devote a few days to being shamelessly clichéd tourists, so we started with the most shameless (and wonderful) clichéd tourist activity we could find, a horse-and-buggy ride around the Ring of Kerry. Even our driver was a cliché—tan plaid coat, oversized newsboy cap, an ancient face that looked like a map of Ireland, with a brogue and smile that made him a dead ringer for Barry Fitzgerald in *Going My Way*.

I couldn't take my eyes off the incredible landscape, lush and rich, in more shades of green than I even knew existed, and I was kind of lost in my own private botanical heaven when we came around a bend and I looked ahead to see a gorgeous oleander, so gigantic and healthy it almost looked surreal.

And there, near its base, in a small patch of sunlight, I swear to God, sat a fairy.

She was slightly less than a foot tall. She had blond hair tied into a bun on top of her head. She had on a shimmering green dress, and her translucent gossamer wings were moving a little in a passing breeze. Her head was tilted slightly back, as if she were enjoying the feel of the sun on her delicate, beautiful face.

I can count on one hand the times in my life when I've been rendered speechless. This was one of those times. I couldn't even catch my breath, and my mind was short-circuiting—"It's a mirage, I'm not seeing this, maybe it's jet lag, this is ridiculous, I know perfectly well she's not real, all I have to do is blink; that's what I'll do, and she'll go away."

I blinked. She was still there. She knew I was staring at her, and she didn't mind a bit; she just looked back at me, not defiant, not shy, nothing more than a silent, "I know you see me, and I see you."

I'm sure I didn't move, or breathe again, until we went around another curve in the road and lost sight of her. I finally managed to collect myself enough to tap the driver on the shoulder and announce in a clenched voice, "Dear God, I think I just saw a fairy."

He didn't even find it worth turning his head for. "So ye did, miss. They live all over this area."

"Are you serious?!" I didn't mean to shriek quite as loudly as I did.

Now he turned, smiled and quietly replied, "I saw her too."

Make of it what you will. As for me, I've said so many times in my life and career I'm even tired of hearing myself say it: Until I've seen or experienced something for myself, I don't believe it.

I believe in fairies.

Fakirs

The word "fakir" had its beginnings in Islam, but it now includes specific orders of yogis, Sufis and East Indians as well, who embrace the belief that poverty and deprivation are essential for a true closeness to God. Fakirs are typically reclusive street beggars who panhandle for their basic sustenance while chanting religious scriptures. Their initiation into this fiercely devout order is said to include the denial of food and sleep, teaching them to transcend physical discomfort through the brute strength of their spirituality. The clichéd image of the fakir, in fact, is that of a painfully slender man wearing nothing but a loincloth either lying on a bed of nails or walking barefoot on hot coals. I once heard of a fakir who sat with his arm raised in the air for eleven years, as an homage to his passion for God and his own God-center far and above the ease of his own lifetime.

Father God

Father God is the omnipotent, perfect, all-loving and all-knowing Creator who, with Azna, the Mother God, forms the holiest, most sacred Godhead. He is the intellect of the universe, the constant, the Unmoved Mover, just as Azna is the emotion, the nurturer, the traveling Force of the Godhead.

The sign of Father God, Om

In the Old Testament of the Bible, He is the Creator, the Lawmaker, the Protector, the All-Merciful and the All-Just, rewarding the obedient and punishing those who do not obey Him.

In the New Testament, He gave the world His incarnated son, Jesus Christ, who, instead of the Old Testament's "eye for an eye, tooth for a tooth" mentality, presented God's commandment, "Thou shalt not kill."

In Islam He is Allah, not a "father" at all, which is an offensively presumptuous concept in the Muslim faith. Allah is the only true, permanent reality, the only uncreated presence in the universe. According to the Qur'an, "He begetteth not nor was begotten. And to Him has never been one equal." He sees all things and knows all things, and He is never to be depicted in any form, since He is greater than can ever be described, and an earthly depiction could lead to idol worship.

To the Hindus He is Brahman, the supreme divine entity who is both at one with the universe and transcends it. He exists as three separate identities: Brahma, the Creator, who perpetually creates new realities; Vishnu, the Preserver, protector and preserver of the Creator, who travels to earth when eternal order is threatened; and Shiva, the Destroyer.

He is the Buddha, the Great Spirit, the Supreme Being, the Alpha and the Omega, the Beginning and the End.

And by whatever name we call Him, whatever the earthly details of our faith, there will be a time on the Other Side—brief, beyond divinity, beyond sanctity—when, on some High Holy Day, God will manifest Himself, for no longer than a heartbeat or two. The manifestation of the intellect of the Godhead is more like a brilliant, flashing arc of electricity, an Image so highly charged it's neither distinct nor describable. My Spirit Guide Francine, who is not an emotional woman, has tried on rare occasions to express the hallowed awe of a manifestation of the Face of God, but her voice catches, and she finally concludes that no word exists on earth to describe it because we on earth have never experienced anything we can compare it to. A glimpse of His physical presence is a privilege eternally reserved for the rarest, most sacrosanct moments on the Other Side, and all our earthly names and adjectives for him will be so clearly inadequate that we'll finally see the foolishness of ever having fought over them.

G

Ghosts

We all know that when our bodies die, our spirits go right on surviving. The vast majority of spirits proceed straight through the proverbial tunnel to the white light of God's infinite, perfect, eternal love on the Other Side.

Some spirits, though, for a variety of very personal reasons, either see the tunnel and reject it or refuse to acknowledge it at all, which leaves them stranded here, outside of their bodies, caught between the lower vibrational level we exist in on earth and the much higher-frequency vibrational level of Home.

Like millions of others, I've had a near-death experience, to the point where I was almost to the end of the tunnel before I was pulled back into my body by a friend's voice demanding that I not leave yet because I had too much left to do. And one of countless details we near-death veterans agree on is that not for a moment, even while hurtling through that indescribably sacred tunnel, did we have the slightest sensation of being dead. Free, joyful, robust, invincible, peaceful, infused with love, yes. Dead, no. Ghosts, who've left their bodies but missed the tunnel, are deprived of all those other wonderful sensations and left with just one: "dead, no." They're clueless that, in earthly terms, they've died, and they don't even have the transcended spirits' advantage of a dramatic change of scenery. They're exactly where they were an hour, a day or a week ago, very much alive as far as they're concerned. Nothing has changed from their perspective except for the sudden, inexplicable fact that no one seems to be able to see or hear them because they've changed frequencies without knowing it. People who've experienced hauntings complain about how ornery and irritable ghosts seem to be. Try having everyone around you suddenly start treating you as if you don't exist and see if it doesn't make you a little cranky.

While the details vary dramatically from one ghost to the next, the two most common reasons why they inadvertently or deliberately miss the opportunity to go Home boil down to passion (which can be either love or hate) and fear. Some stay behind to care for a child they adore, or to wait for a lover to come home, or to protect their cherished home from intruders. Others stay behind to seek revenge on real or imagined enemies (which never works, by the way, so don't spend one minute worrying about that). Still others are so afraid God will find them undeserving of His loving welcome Home that they remain earthbound rather than face Him.

Fortunately, mostly for them but for us as well, let's face it, there is no such thing as a ghost who's eternally trapped here on earth. Thanks to an enormous and constantly growing amount of human sensitivity, a lot of ghosts are directed to the tunnel and the Other Side by people who recognize them and understand that there's really great compassion in saying, "You're dead. Go Home." But the spirits on the Other Side are far more aware of earthbound souls than we are, and they perform their own constant interventions for as long as it takes until each ghost has celebrated the joyful reunion that's waiting for him on the other end of that tunnel.

If you sense or you've actually seen that you're sharing your home with a presence and you're not sure whether it's a spirit or a ghost, there are a few very simple ways to tell the difference:

* If the presence seems even slightly unhappy, angry, mean-spirited or discontent, there's no question that it's a ghost. Remember, the Other Side is perfect. The spirits there are incapable of unhappiness, anger, meanness and discontent. That's why they call it "heaven."

* If the presence shows any kind of injury, or even a hint of a physical, mental or emotional impairment, it's a ghost. Again, Home means perfection. The instant we arrive there, we leave all pain and illness and wounds and scars behind on this imperfect earth, whereas ghosts remain stuck, imperfections and all.

* When you read the definition of the Other Side, you'll see that it actually exists just three feet above our floor level here on earth, but on a much, much higher vibrational level. When you see a spirit from the Other Side, you'll notice that it seems to be floating above the ground. The truth is, it's simply moving along on the floor level of the Other Side. Ghosts, on the other hand, are likely to shuffle along right down here with us, not floating at all, "earthbound" both literally and figuratively.

* And last, because they really are caught between the low-frequency dimension of earth and the high-frequency dimension of Home, ghosts are easier to hear and see than spirits.

If there's a ghost around you, or around someone you know, try your best to get past your fear and discomfort and arrive as quickly as you can at compassion for a confused soul who has no idea she's dead. And perhaps even more than that, don't lose sight of the single most important and most often overlooked truth about the fact that ghosts exist: Sad and confused as they are, they also offer still more proof that our spirits really do and always will go right on living after our bodies die.

Ghouls

This fairly common subject of low-budget movies and source of scary campfire stories for children around the world actually has its roots in Muslim folklore. Ghouls, it seems, were thought to be evil demons who lurked around graveyards, eating the flesh of corpses and possessing their spirits to prevent them from reaching paradise.

The folklore of ghouls contributed considerably to the inception of Halloween, so for those of you who love that holiday, you may owe a long overdue imaginary thank-you. On All Hallow's Eve, the souls of the deceased were thought to rise from their graves, which would understandably attract ghouls for miles and miles around. Frightened of the ghouls and not wanting to be mistaken for their potential next meal, the villagers would dress up in their best interpretation of what ghouls probably looked like, in a kind of "if you can't beat them, join them" effort. Dressing up as what you're hoping to ward off on October 31 obviously became a simultaneous worldwide practice, covering everything from ghouls, ghosts, witches and vampires to such current favorites as Britney Spears and prominent politicians. Whether or not that's a shift from the original tradition is a matter of interpretation.

There are still tribes in isolated parts of Africa and South America who keep the legend of ghouls alive, but I'm pleased to say that after fifty years of world travel, I have yet to run across a genuine ghoul, or even a poor excuse for one.

Glossolalia

This word almost sounds exactly like what it means: talking in tongues. Talking in tongues is a practice still observed in some Pentacostal religious sects in which a person is elevated to a state of ecstasy that seems to trigger a stream of incomprehensible syllables unrelated to any known language, past or present. Those who practice it seem to be taking their inspiration from Chapter 2, Verse 4, of the Bible's Acts

of the Apostles: "And they were all filled with the Holy Spirit and began to speak in other tongues, as the Spirit gave them utterance."

I founded the Nirvana Foundation for Psychic Research in 1974,
and the phenomenon of glossolalia struck me as a fascinating area to
explore, since frankly I knew very little about it and certainly hadn't
formed an opinion one way or another about its validity. So my fellow
researchers and I devised an experiment. We found ten volunteers
who had experience with talking in tongues. None of them knew each
other; they came from all over the country and we kept them isolated
from one another as, one by one, they let me record them talking in
tongues for several minutes.

I couldn't have been more amazed when we listened to and compared the tapes the next day. I mean no disrespect when I say that
separately, each of these people's litanies sounded like gibberish
played at the wrong speed. But it was unmistakable even the first time
through that these ten total strangers from completely different parts
of the United States were using many of the same identical sounds,
indecipherable words and long, complicated phrases of syllables that
none of us who were hearing it could begin to understand. It was mesmerizing how alike they were.

My Spirit Guide Francine's explanation is that what we'd witnessed was a series of classic cases of cell memory—the whole body
acting in accordance with the spirit mind's past life memories. It
seems that these ten people, and others who practice talking in
tongues, are re-creating a time and place when there were two separate
and distinct languages, one reserved for daily lives and one reserved
for prayer. The languages themselves were destroyed along with their
home continent of Atlantis, which is why they're unrecognizable today.

Glossolalia? Possibly. Especially since the Bible verse, Acts 2:4,
doesn't specify that the "other tongues, as the Spirit gave them utterance" were limited to languages that never existed on this earth. It
might also have been an example of another phenomenon called
xenoglossy, which you'll find discussed in its own section. Whatever it

was, though, it was thrilling to witness, knowing we hadn't manipu-
lated the results or even had a motive to manipulate them—I certainly
had no stake one way or the other in the validity of glossolalia. And if
ten total strangers spontaneously duplicating that many identical syllables, words and phrases was just a coincidence, as far as I'm concerned that would be even more unbelievable—and I mean that word
with all my heart—than glossolalia could ever be.

Gnomes

Gnomes are thought to be small mythical creatures who live underground and can walk as easily through subterranean earth as we humans can walk through air. Some cultures believe that gnomes are
turned to stone by the rays of the sun, while others believe that
gnomes are only gnomes at night but spend their days as toads. Another common legend is that gnomes never emerge from deep within
the earth, where they stand guard over their hoarded buried treasure
and, according to some, even more vast wealth of secret knowledge. The
exact origin of gnome mythology is almost impossible to trace, since
gnomes can be found in the literature of both Europe and Prussia.

Not all stories of these secretive little subterranean creatures are
completely mythical, in fact, as you'll see in the section on the Underworld and read about its First Level.

H

Hall of Justice

The Hall of Justice is one of the triumvirate of magnificent buildings—the Hall of Justice, the Hall of Records and the Hall of Wisdom—that create what could be called the formal entrance to the Other Side, one of the first welcome, familiar sights we see when we return Home. Its architecture is Greco-Roman. Towering pillars stand guard in front of its massive doors. Its dome is white marble. At its entrance stands a magnificent, treasured statue of Azna, the Mother God.

The Hall of Justice is filled with countless rooms in which we spend vast amounts of time once we've made the decision to return to earth, planning every detail of our upcoming incarnation with the help of our Spirit Guide and an Orientation team of our choosing. It's in these rooms filled with white marble tables and benches, resembling pristine classrooms, their walls lined with maps, charts and countless other visual tools, that we write our chart.

In the heart of the Hall of Justice lies a massive, sacred arena. In its center is a gleaming U-shaped table of the whitest white stone, at which the revered eighteen-member Council sits, a legion of gold-winged Principalities standing sentinel behind them. If you've already read the definition of the Council, you'll appreciate the awe the very air in that arena inspires.

Possibly the most memorable, the most cherished and the most yearned-for feature of the Hall of Justice is its endless expanse of Gardens. For as far as the eye can see in any direction from the Hall of Justice itself lies an impeccable, intricately designed wealth of brilliantly colored flowers, sparkling waterfalls and fountains, lush forests of ferns, towering trees of every variety and canopies of Spanish moss, stone pathways, footbridges, meditation benches, unexpected carpets of soft green grass surrounded by crystal streams and hidden by walls of bougainvillea in shades of red, purple and pink we can only approximate here.

It's our memories of the Gardens of the Hall of Justice that give us that deeply resonant sense of comfort when we find ourselves in the presence of natural beauty on earth. Something as simple as a small bush of wild roses or as overwhelming as a national park can create the same pang in our hearts at the most unexpected moments. We don't always understand where that pang comes from, or what to call it. It's easier than you think. It's called Homesickness.

You'll also notice that you often have dreams that are set in a garden location, particularly when your dream involves a reunion with a deceased loved one. The lovely truth is, 99.9 percent of those aren't dreams. The Gardens of the Hall of Justice are one of our spirits' favorite astral travel destinations while we sleep and one of the most popular meeting places for us and those we miss on the Other Side.

Hall of Records

The Hall of Records is another of the three sister buildings waiting for us at the entrance to the Other Side. Like its two companions, it's Greco-Roman in structure, with spectacular columns and a soaring dome. It also happens to be the busiest, most constantly bustling hub of this white marble triumvirate, for the most fascinating reasons.

To get an image of the inside of the Hall of Records, picture an infinite number of aisles, lined on either side with an infinite number of shelves filled with an infinite number of scrolls, books, documents, maps, artwork, blueprints, etc., every shelf kept in perfect order. Now take each of those infinite numbers of aisles, shelves and contents, multiply them by some other infinite number and you have some idea of the scope of the Hall of Records' breathtaking expanse. Its purpose requires every square inch of that expanse, although the laws of physics on the Other Side prevent it from ever being filled to capacity.

The Hall of Records houses every historical and literary work ever written, drawn, drafted, sketched or painted on earth and at Home. That includes precious documents and artwork whose originals have been destroyed here, from those that perished in the burning of the legendary libraries of Alexandria 2,000 years ago to the brilliant tomes swallowed by the sea when the continents of Atlantis and Lemuria were lost.

It also, incredibly, houses every detailed chart of every incarnation of every one of us who's ever lived on this planet. I've lived fifty-four lifetimes, which isn't an unusually high number. That's fifty-four charts just for me, times the earth's population of approximately six billion. (You're welcome to do the math if you like. I get tired just thinking about it.) And each of those charts is impeccably preserved on scrolls, scripted in flawless Aramaic, which is the universal language on the Other Side, and kept in perfect order for us or for anyone else at Home to review, study, research and learn from.

Access to all those charts is one of the reasons the Hall of Records is such a popular center of activity. We can travel astrally to the Hall of Records during sleep, meditation or hypnosis while we're still on earth, and we often do, but we're never given access to our own charts. (It would fall loosely under the category of cheating on a major exam—it's just not done.) Once we're on the Other Side again, though, we can study all our own charts for as long as we like, for context and perspective on the journey of our soul. We can study the charts of loved ones we've left behind on earth, for insights into our interactions with them, good and bad, and to see what lies ahead for them and why. We can study the charts of historical figures we've admired or despised or never understood, or of people still on earth whose impact seems significant, personally or globally, and track the future of that impact. We can even merge with a chart if we choose to, a process that acts almost like a time machine, in which our spirit becomes a literal eyewitness to any event or life it chooses without ever leaving its gleaming infinite aisle in the vast Hall of Records.

As functional and endlessly fascinating as the Hall of Records is to the residents of the Other Side, it's also among the most sacred, because it's within the Hall of Records that the Akashic Records are preserved, the complete written body of God's knowledge, laws and memories.

Hall of Tones

At the moment of our creation, an eternity ago, each of us was given by our Creator our own unique mantra—a word, or a series of syllables—to which our equally unique spirit will resonate throughout our eternal lives. If you think of your spirit as an exquisite, handcrafted, one-of-a-kind musical instrument whose specific sound is yours and yours alone, the mantra you were given when your spirit was created is the tuning fork that keeps your soul in perfect pitch with the God who conceived it.

Every one of our mantras starts with the word "om," a universally spiritual acknowledgment of affirmation and acceptance. "Om" is then most often followed by a tone made up of two syllables. My Spirit Guide Francine tells me that my mantra is "om-shireem." I was so hoping I would feel some flame of recognition deep in my ancient soul when she first said it. The truth is, I would have sworn on a mile-high stack of Bibles that I'd never heard it before. It might just be me, or it might be that for most of us the divine resonance of our mantras gets drowned out by the clamor of our noisy everyday lives on earth.

On the Other Side, though, our mantras are as familiar and as singularly ours as our very identities, and we use them to keep our spirits in tune just as routinely as we keep our bodies in tune while we occupy them here. This isn't to imply that our souls are ever as out of tune or as off-key as these silly, fallible bodies we're lugging around tend to get. Our spirits are always in synch and right on pitch with God when we're at Home. It's simply our joy to keep them that way, by chanting our own unique mantra, that one sound that is no one else's but ours, our gift from God when He created us and our gift to Him every time we utter it.

And it's for the specific purpose of gathering to chant our special, sacred mantras that we assemble whenever we care to in a beautiful building near the entrance to the Other Side but set apart from the far more massive three white marble structures that greet us when we first arrive. It's called the House of Tones, and like all other houses of worship at Home, it's constantly filled, constantly joyful and constantly devoted to a celebration of our love for and genetic link to our Father and Mother.

No matter when we arrive at the Hall of Tones, it's always filled and yet there's always room for more, as many spirits who arrive. And of even greater wonder is the fact that no matter what tone or pitch we choose for the chanting of our mantra, we find that our voice quickly blends with the others in that magnificent Hall, whether there are ten of us or ten thousand, into perfect harmony. Individual sounds find and join each other, over and over, until a thrilling chord evolves, spirits in precise tune with each other and with God at the same time, the very definition of heaven.

Hall of Voices

The Hall of Voices sits to the right of the Hall of Tones: seamless white granite, windows of beveled stained glass, an acoustic miracle inside its golden doors. It exists for only one purpose, a purpose that offers one of the most transcendent, sacred privileges our spirits ever experience.

When you read the definition of Angels, you'll discover that while their communication with us and with each other is very powerful, it's accomplished exclusively through telepathy. Angels never speak. Not a word.

But on the highest of God's true holy days, all the Angels in God's infinite legion, Angels of every wing color and level of power, gather in the Hall of Voices to perform an a cappella concert of soaring hymns celebrating the joyful worship of their Creator. This vast, sacred choir, full of beings whose only sounds are reserved for songs praising God, produce a magnificence unlike any other in the universe, and spirits flock to the Hall of Voices by the millions from every corner of the Other Side to watch and listen in humble awe.

And every few thousand years, an event so holy occurs that the Angels' joy can't be contained by the Hall of Voices, or by the Other Side or by the dimension in which it exists, and it spills into all the dimensions of God's creation, including ours on earth. One of those events was recorded in the Bible, in Luke 2:13–14, which describes those moments immediately following the birth of Jesus: "And suddenly there was with the angel a multitude of the heavenly host praising God and saying, 'Glory to God in the highest, and on earth peace, good will among men.' "

A multitude of the heavenly host, also known as a choir of all God's Angels, gathered for a rare, divine concert in the Hall of Voices.

Hall of Wisdom

The Hall of Wisdom is the centerpiece of the triumvirate of buildings at the entrance to the Other Side. It's the first building we see when we emerge from the tunnel, as intimately associated with Home in our spirit minds as the Eiffel Tower is with Paris.

When you read the section defining that legendary (and very real) tunnel, you'll discover that, contrary to popular myth, it doesn't lower from somewhere above us to embrace us when our bodies die. It actually rises *from* us to transport us Home. And just as "all roads lead to Rome," as the saying goes, all tunnels lead to the Hall of Wisdom. It's the comforting, wonderful truth that no matter where on this earth we happen to be at that moment when we no longer have any use for our bodies and we're ready to leave them behind, we all arrive at the very same place on the Other Side. There's no danger of getting lost or not being able to find each other, however far apart we might be when we "die." The Hall of Wisdom is, just for starters, the Grand Central Terminal of Home.

It's Romanesque in structure, adorned with exquisite statuary, fountains and fragrant flowers in constant brilliant bloom. But its most stunning feature is the infinite expanse of marble steps that surrounds the building and leads to its entrances. These steps are such a treasured part of our spirit memories that they're one of our favorite places to travel astrally, play and make nuisances of ourselves during our first few years in a new incarnation on earth.

The most famous and popular feature of the Hall of Wisdom, once we've stepped inside its massive doors, can be found deep in its heart, in a huge round room surrounded by pillars. We're first taken there on our return Home by our Spirit Guide, who leads us to one of the cool white marble benches and then steps back while we sit down for our amazing, inevitable session at the domed glass Scanning Machine where, as you'll read in that section, our whole life very literally flashes before our eyes.

It's also inside the Hall of Wisdom, once we've finished at the Scanning Machine, that we go through any debriefing and Orientation we might need to help us make a smooth transition from earth back to the Other Side. Our Spirit Guide is joined by trained Orientators, if necessary, who've studied our charts and our incarnations thanks to the Scanning Machine. They're there to help us make sense of anything and everything we're confused, disappointed and troubled about that might prevent us from fully appreciating what we learned and what we taught in that lifetime we've left behind, however badly we might feel we accomplished it. They're also there to ease the transition for those whose deaths were so sudden that they're too confused or annoyed to luxuriate in the joyful peace of Home when they first arrive. If the expert Orientators believe it will be helpful, they'll give a newly arrived spirit the added care of Cocooning them, which, as explained in that definition, is a process involving a healing twilight sleep. And it's the Hall of Wisdom that houses the Cocooning chambers as well.

I'd be surprised if you don't find yourself having occasional "dreams" of vast marble steps, whether or not you're sure where they lead, that are actually astral trips to the most familiar landmark of that place you'll be Homesick for until the day you return. And on that day when you do return Home, and you emerge from the tunnel to find yourself at the foot of the steps of the Hall of Wisdom, I'll be honored if you remember reading this promise that that's exactly what would happen.

Haunting

Cohabiting with one or more earthbounds, which you'll find fully discussed in the section on Ghosts, is a far more common experience than many people realize. I've long since stopped trying to convince closed-minded disbelievers that because God promised us life after death, there are naturally spirits and ghosts around us all the time. It's like politics and religion—nobody's going to change anyone's mind by arguing about it, so why bring it up? I'll just hope to be around to see the looks on their faces when the most vocal of the skeptics find themselves on the receiving end of a good old-fashioned haunting and still try to call me loony.

You'll discover in the "Ghosts" section that there are many reasons earthbounds stay behind instead of heading on to the perfect joy of the Other Side. One of the saddest and least common was illustrated by a ghost I met when I was asked to investigate a haunting at a place called the Slaughter House, which turned out to be a nice, modest home with an unfortunate nickname near San Francisco. The couple who lived there were being terrorized by a presence they truly believed might harm them.

"Why don't they just move?" I asked.

"They can't afford it," was the reply.

Now, that I could relate to. If someone had suggested I move at that point in my life, I couldn't have afforded it either. It struck a sympathetic enough chord in me that I heard myself say, "I'll be there," before I had time to talk myself out of it.

The house really was as modest and innocuous looking as I'd been assured it was, and the anxious owners, whom I'll call John and Mary, were as sweet and normal as they could be. We sat in the living room for a few minutes so that they could give me some idea of what they'd been through. Besides the usual unexplainable noises, footsteps and cold spots, and the occasional sighting of awful faces at the windows, their biggest complaint would have unnerved me too.

"We'll both wake up in the middle of the night to find a man standing over our bed," Mary told me. "He has this wild, insane look of pure hatred in his eyes, as if finding John and me together has outraged him. He even grabbed my arm once. I can still feel his strong, ice-cold hand on my skin."

"And I saw him do it and couldn't do a damned thing about it," John added.

I'd heard all I wanted to hear. I was ready and eager to get to work. I hadn't sensed a single thing in the living room, so I headed into the kitchen. Nothing there either. Into the small separate dining room. Still nothing. And on into the hallway, where, without feeling it coming, I walked into a cold spot. Not just any cold spot, either. This one went right to the bone. I could see my breath, in an un-air-conditioned house in the middle of July.

In every haunting there's a heart, a place from which all the paranormal activity emanates. In this haunting, that heart was the master bedroom. I could feel the highly concentrated energy like a force field the minute I stepped through the doorway. I walked to the bed and sat down. My heart was pounding, from adrenaline, from fear and from the growing awareness that a strong, deeply troubled presence was approaching me.

I first saw him outside the window, looking in at me, not one bit sure if he wanted me there or not. He was very handsome, with thick dark hair. I made eye contact with him and held it to let him know that yes, I could see him perfectly, and no, he couldn't frighten me away. Then I simply said, "Come in."

Suddenly he was standing in front of me, taller and broader than I first thought. He was holding a scythe with a rough wooden handle, its long crescent blade looking old and used but still sharp enough to do serious damage. I refused to react to it, just continued making eye contact with him, and either he respected me for it or he was relieved that finally, after a long, long time, someone wasn't shrieking at him to get away. He gave an almost courtly nod.

"My name is Giovanni," he said. "What's yours?"

I told him, then asked what he was doing there.

He spoke in a clear, quiet voice. "I'm sad because my wife is gone."

The instant those words came out of his mouth I was flooded with a rapid-fire montage of images in what seemed like less than a second. Another bed in this same room. A dark-haired man in the bed, not Giovanni but resembling him. A dark-haired woman in the bed with him. Both of them sleeping. Giovanni, eyes vacant, advancing toward the bed, the scythe raised high above his head.

"Giovanni, did you kill someone?" I asked.

He began to weep. "It was wrong what my brother Anthony did. I brought Maria here from Italy to be my wife, and while I was out in the hot fields they were in here making love. I made them both sorry that they did this to Giovanni."

"After you killed them, what did you do next?"

"I ran away," he confessed. "I hid in the hills for a long time. Then I got very sick and felt very hot, and that's the last thing I remember."

In other words, he ran away with nothing but the blood-covered clothes on his back, disappeared into the cold, damp winter hills near the bay and, without realizing it, died of pneumonia. I broke that news to him, explained to him that he'd trapped himself here on earth and assured him that it was time for him to go on toward the light now so that he could be at peace.

He shook his head, ashamed and frightened. "I can't face God. He'll never forgive me."

"I don't know anything about a god who never forgives, Giovanni. My God is all-loving, all-knowing, all-forgiving and embraces every one of us who holds out our arms to Him." He looked at me, taking this in. It wasn't the first time I'd met an earthbound spirit who was deliberately avoiding the tunnel and the light that would take him Home because he was sure he'd done something unforgivable in God's eyes. It wouldn't be the last, either, and few things break my heart more. There's no question that sooner or later, in some lifetime or other, we have to make things right in our own souls, to balance the books spiritually when we've intentionally wronged someone. But that's because our spirits are genetically programmed ultimately to seek their highest potential and their greatest good. God doesn't see to our eventually making things right. We see to it ourselves, with His guidance, His constant, patient, unwavering, unconditional love and His powerful faith in us.

I spent hours explaining that only by moving on could he free himself from the hell of guilt in which he'd imprisoned himself. At best, he'd join his wife and brother on the Other Side and learn that they'd forgiven him. At worst, he'd come right back to earth in utero and spend a lifetime making amends for the lives he took. Either way was a step toward liberating himself from the awful burden he was carrying. Either way there was hope, while the nonlife he was living now held no hope at all.

Finally, and with some reluctance, Giovanni agreed to go. He looked at me for one more nod of reassurance and said, "You'd better be right." With that, he disappeared. And according to subsequent phone calls and letters from John and Mary, neither he nor any other ghost ever bothered them or set foot in the Slaughter House again.

You'll read under "Ghosts" that telling them they're dead and talking them over, convincing them to step into the tunnel and go toward the light, is the most effective way to get a ghost out of your house. It's also the toughest, because of the many complex agendas that keep them here. If you're living with a ghost, the more you can learn about the history of your house and, of far more importance, the history of the property your house sits on, the better your chances of figuring out the identity of your ghost, what happened to him, what his point of view and agenda might be. As you've just seen in the story of the Slaughter House, "Go to the light" for some ghosts is a more terrifying prospect than the hopeless, lonely, nonexistent existence they're clinging to.

The Holding Place

There are actually three places our spirits can go when they leave our bodies at the end of an incarnation: the blissful perfection of the Other Side, the Godlessness of the Left Door and a kind of anteroom to the Left Door called the Holding Place, which is the real purgatory, a netherworld of confused despair.

I first learned about the Holding Place several years ago, when I astrally traveled there during a fitful night's sleep. I had no idea where I was. I just knew I was surrounded by an endless sea of lost spirits who'd been separated from their faith by the dull, quiet chaos of deep despair. They never said a word, to me or to one another, as they shuffled aimlessly, heads down, eyes lifeless. There were no small children, only young adolescents and older, moving through a silence so thick with hopelessness that it took me days to recover after only a few minutes in their presence.

Again, I had no idea where I was or who these tragic people were, but purely on impulse I began rushing around in a panic, hugging each one of them and saying, "Say you love God. Please, just say you love God and you can get out of here." No one responded, or even looked at me.

In the distance I could vaguely make out the presence of a vast entrance. I couldn't see beyond it, but I didn't want to. The mere sight of it terrified me. I knew in my soul that it was the Left Door, and that no one who chose to go through it could possibly fathom the enormity of the void that waited there. Those tragic spirits around me were too close to it to be safe and too confused to understand the danger they were in.

It was my Spirit Guide Francine who explained the next morning that I'd been to the Holding Place, and confirmed that what leads and holds spirits there, torn between the bliss of the Other Side and the dark chasm of the Left Door, is a tormented, often destructive despair, many of them suicide victims.

It's a cruel myth that everyone who commits suicide is eternally doomed. No one ever writes suicide into their chart, which does make it a broken contract with God. And there are suicides who guarantee themselves a trip through the Left Door—those motivated by cowardice, or self-pity, or revenge, for example, especially if there are children involved in any way.

But suicides caused by mental illness, untreated genetic chemical imbalances or the isolation of paralyzing depression can hardly be compared to acts that are methodically, deliberately calculated for effect. Only some combination of the arrogant and ignorant condemn those who took on special and often invisible challenges in this life.

God? Arrogant and ignorant? I can't even use those words in the same sentence.

There are absolutely some suicides, then, who proceed just as quickly as the rest of us to God's unconditional love and forgiveness on the Other Side.

Others languish in the Holding Place, in need of the spirits at Home and our prayers from earth to pull them away from the looming proximity of the Left Door and rekindle that flame they were created with, that light inside them that will reconnect them to the Light that's waiting to embrace them, that they simply lost track of somewhere along the way.

Host of Heaven

The term "host of heaven" is a phrase used frequently throughout Christianity, Judaism and Islam. Some believe the "host of heaven" is the universe, and particularly the stars, in light of such references as:

> "And beware lest you lift up your eyes to heaven, and when you see the sun and the moon and the stars, all the host of heaven, you be drawn away and worship them and serve them." —*Deuteronomy 4:19*

Others are convinced that the "host of heaven" is God's legion of Angels.

> "I saw the Lord sitting on his throne, and all the host of heaven standing by him on his right hand and on his left." —*1 Kings 22:19*

In ancient times there was thought by many faiths to be a close connection between the stars and the Angels, some believing there was a star in the sky for each Angel in heaven, others embracing the image that the stars were the eyes of the Angels watching over us. So the question of whether the host of heaven is the stars or the Angels is probably a well-intentioned close call.

It's my personal opinion that the host of heaven includes all of God's most advanced beings on the Other Side: the Angels, the Council, the Messiahs and the Guides.

All of which I bring up for only two reasons: Many of my clients and members of my church and my study groups have wondered what the host of heaven refers to; and I'd love for you to remember that when you're going through an especially rough time, calling on the hosts of heaven for help is yet another way of summoning God's best, most invincible army to your side.

Hypnosis

Hypnosis is a procedure by which the conscious mind is suppressed enough that underlying information held in the subconscious and/or the spirit mind can be accessed.

For our purposes in this book, I've focused on a more specific and useful form of this procedure. You'll find that very thorough discussion under "Regressive Hypnosis."

Imitative Magic

Imitative magic has its official origins in ancient times, among primitive cultures. It's still practiced throughout the world today and is most commonly associated with Wicca (witchcraft), many Native American and African tribes and the Australian Aborigines.

The theory behind imitative magic is as uncomplicated as it gets: The magician or practitioner simply acts out the result they're hoping to effect, often but not necessarily in the course of a ceremonial ritual.

To bring rain to drought-stricken land, for example, a native chieftain, to the beat of drums that will attract the gods and goddesses of the earth, might pour an urn of water into the center of a circle.

To ensure a successful hunt, tribal warriors, some wearing heads of wild animals, might act out the hunt in front of the entire tribe, with the hunters ultimately slaying the "animals" and bringing them back to the tribe for food.

To encourage the growth of crops, witches for centuries have ridden broomsticks (which they use to sweep away evil forces) through newly planted fields, jumping as high as they can to give the crops an image of what it is they're supposed to do. (If you've ever wondered where the myth of witches flying on broomsticks came from, now you know.)

The rain dance is a form of imitative magic

All of which makes imitative magic sound quaint and possibly oh, so uncivilized, until you stop to think of the number of ways we've worked imitative magic into our civilized society as well, and frankly, good for us.

As you'll read in the section on ghouls, for example, the annual giddiness of dressing up as monsters, vampires and other scary creatures for Halloween is a form of imitative magic.

Hanging lights on Christmas trees and keeping holiday candles lit throughout the house originate from the imitative magic of bringing back the warmth of the sun to drive away the cold winter.

And a lesson my Grandma Ada drilled into me when I was a child, which I will thank her for eternally and which is an actual motto in an organization or two I can think of, can be summed up by the words, "Act as if." Like so many other families during the Depression, mine was hit very hard, and my father suddenly went from comfortable to struggling.

I was too young to understand fully what "poor" was about, except that it wasn't good. Grandma Ada wouldn't put up for one minute with my behaving like a child who was needy or in any way deprived. "Act as if you have everything you could possibly want," she told me. "Act as if everything's fine, and just you watch, sooner or later, it will be." Denial? Absolutely not. She wasn't telling me everything *was* fine, which would have been a lie. She was telling me to act as if it were. And that was a classic, brilliant use of imitative magic that I still use and endorse to this day. You can ask my staff and my close friends—when one husband drove me into bankruptcy, and the next one left me for someone else and I'm still trying to unravel the chaos he left in his wake, unless I was behind closed doors and could break down in private, I "acted as if" I had the world by the tail. (Have I mentioned often enough that I'm not the least bit psychic about myself?)

The point is, before we snicker too hard or sneer with too much sophisticated superiority at those pagans with their bizarre rituals like whatever that imitative magic nonsense is, we might want to take a look around and see where it might come in handy in our own lives. Because take it from me, it happens to work. I don't have to "act as if" anymore—I really have never been happier.

Imprints

An imprint is an intensely concentrated pocket of energy, a site at which some extremely dramatic event or series of events has taken place with such profound impact that the images and emotions from those events literally become a part of the land and the atmosphere at the site itself. Not only do those images and emotions—grief, reverence, rage, terror, and joy, for example—become self-sustaining over the years, but everyone who experiences the powerful effect of the imprinted images and emotions and strongly reacts also lends even more energy to the imprint and helps perpetuate it. If you've visited Ground Zero in New York and felt a deep sense of grief and loss, or been overcome with reverent awe during a trip to the Holy Land, you've experienced an imprint and strengthened it with your own reaction.

I learned the hard way about imprints and the images and emotions that characterize them on a drive home from a brief vacation in Palm Springs. I've told this story many times, in books and lectures and on television specials, but it continues to be an effective illustration of what an imprint is. Maybe it's because at the time this happened, I had never heard of imprints. Nor had I ever heard the history or the dark, terrifying reputation of a place called Pacheco Pass.

Pacheco Pass is a stretch of Highway 152 in northern California, cutting through the range of mountains between the inland Interstate 5 and the Pacific Coast Highway. My then-husband Dal had decided to try it for the first time as a shortcut from Palm Springs to our home in San Jose. One moment I was gazing idly out the passenger window of the car. An instant later I felt as if I'd been slammed into a wall of anguish that made me so frantic I couldn't even pray my way back to normal because I couldn't remember how.

I heard deafening voices, the sounds of torture and cruel death, a horrible sound track to an awful assault of images: children trapped inside burning covered wagons; Indians, some being beaten, some circling wildly on horseback; Spanish soldiers torching a hanging corpse; Mexicans and Caucasians in mortal combat; black smoke rolling from inside small wooden shacks. I smelled gunpowder and burning flesh. Time seemed suspended, my memories of the rest of the trip are vague at best, and the hollow, doomed feeling that saturated me so suddenly and completely in Pacheco Pass stayed with me for days afterward.

Months of phone calls, interviews and research later, I was much better informed about Pacheco Pass. It and the land around it had been part of the tragic, violent "Trail of Tears," on which Indians were tortured, enslaved and killed by the ruling Spanish empire. Once that empire was overthrown and the slaves were released, the Indians were at war with invading Mexican bandits and later with American settlers swept up in the westward migration of the California gold rush. The more I heard and read, the more I became aware that the images I'd been assaulted with that day were like a compressed montage of the history of the troubled land we'd traveled through.

And I wasn't even close to being the first person who'd found themselves the unwitting victim of Pacheco Pass. Hundreds of people, it turned out, had reported everything from inexplicable feelings of panic and impending death to actually gaining and losing time while driving through that one stretch of road. The California Highway Patrol even confirmed that the number of car accidents, incidents of road rage and suicides was significantly higher in Pacheco Pass than anywhere else in their jurisdiction.

Now that I knew something very real was going on in Pacheco Pass, I was determined to find out what it was and what caused it. That's how I began intensively reading about and personally exploring the earth's vortexes of intensely concentrated energy called imprints.

One of the most fascinating things to me about imprints, beyond the fact that they exist, is how easily they're mistaken for hauntings. Both imprints and hauntings can evoke very dramatic feelings, and imprints often include images that could easily be mistaken for ghosts. The important difference, though, is that the people and animals in an imprint are not earthbound, nor are they even "alive." Think of them as three-dimensional holograms in a movie that never ends, never changes scenes and never releases the participants or the audience from its emotionally charged grip. The actual participants in whatever created the imprint have long since moved on to the Other Side, through the Left Door, to other incarnations or to stay at Home forever. Only their images remain, no matter how real they might look and behave. But the one thing that will always set an imprint image apart from a ghost is that an imprint image will never interact with us, any more than a hologram will.

So next time you visit a site where you know there's been an event, or a series of events, of such profound emotion that the world feels compelled to pay homage, listen closely for long-silent voices, watch for long-absent faces and know that, whether it's the violent agony of Pacheco Pass or Gettysburg, the reverent unspeakable tragedy of Ground Zero or the joyful sanctity of Lourdes, you're in the remarkable presence of an imprint.

Incubus

According to European mythology, the incubus is an evil male spirit who terrorizes women by stealing into their beds at night and having sexual intercourse with them while they sleep. By all accounts, the women don't awaken during these rapes. If they have any memory of the attack at all, they'll remember it as a dream. And if the rape should result in a pregnancy, the child of an incubus father and a human mother is destined to possess evil supernatural powers.

All of which is mesmerizing, colorful and great tabloid fodder. It's also a complete and total myth. There is no such thing as an incubus, or even a form of ghost that by any stretch of the imagination would ever behave like an incubus.

In a minority of cases, the incubus was a means of shifting blame for a sexual encounter the woman was too overwhelmed with guilt, shame or helplessness to cope with in the context of reality, so instead she literally created the monster of an incubus to explain her inability to defend herself. Tragically, and not coincidentally, incest and rape were rarely if ever mentioned, let alone punished, in the days when imaginary incubi were at their most prevalent in the dark European countrysides, and blame for any inappropriate sexual behavior was far more likely to fall on the woman than on the man. It's hardly a surprise that a mythical demon was psychologically easier to conjure up than a man she'd have to face again and again and for whom there would never be consequences even if she did speak up.

In the vast majority of cases, though—and I do mean the *vast majority*—the incubus was medieval Europe's logical explanation for the frightening experience of astral catalepsy. You'll read a full explanation of astral catalepsy in its own section, but in brief and at its most basic, it's the conscious mind catching the spirit returning to the body after an astral trip during sleep. Sensations of astral catalepsy range from panic, to something heavy pinning you to the bed, to some form of lewd molestation, to a horribly evil presence, to an inability to scream or move or breathe, to a deafening array of unearthly noises. All ultimately harmless, as you'll discover in the astral catalepsy section, but also understandably mistaken for a demon rapist called an incubus if you have no idea what else could be happening.

Infused Knowledge

Infused knowledge is a fascinating phenomenon in which information is directly transferred from one mind to another with no involvement at all from the five physical senses. But unlike other mind-to-mind communication, like telepathy, for example, the receiver is given information he had no knowledge of before, without having any conscious awareness of where it came from.

For example, you go to sleep one night with a problem weighing on your mind, and you wake up the next morning knowing the solution lies in a book you've never heard of called *How to Solve Your Problem*. We've all had problems solved while we slept, and the vast majority of the time it's just a matter of your mind finally being relaxed enough to think clearly. What sets the above example apart as infused knowledge is the subconscious suggestion of a book whose existence is complete news to you, that you've been made aware of by a source you couldn't name or even guess at if your life depended on it.

Infused knowledge is one of the most common ways that the spirit world on the Other Side communicates with our spirit minds here on earth, which are always wide awake and available in our subconscious minds. Our subconscious minds are obviously most accessible when our cluttered conscious minds are as far out of the way as possible—while we sleep, under hypnosis, during meditation or sometimes when we're simply very tired. And there are those whose subconscious minds are just naturally more readily available to infused knowledge from the Other Side, awake or asleep, an innate gift they possess whether they're aware of it or not.

It's particularly through those gifted minds that researchers, scientists and inventors on the Other Side share the results of their work, resulting in some of earth's greatest medical breakthroughs, inventions and other contributions to humankind. I'm sure you've noticed how often brilliant minds on opposite sides of the globe seem to arrive at virtually identical important discoveries almost simultaneously. It's not a coincidence. It's simply because spirits on the Other Side, through infused knowledge, have successfully delivered information to the minds in this world who have the wisdom, dedication, expertise and talent to act on that information and make it a reality.

This collaboration between earth and Home is a completely interdependent partnership, with equal credit belonging to both teams. Researchers on the Other Side need their colleagues here to put practical form and function to the results of their research, and those colleagues need some divine inspiration from the Other Side to help overcome earth's increasingly enormous obstacles. Without the silent miracle of infused knowledge, that God-made collaboration could never take place.

When I make predictions, as I routinely do on television and as I did in my book *Prophecy*, I can't even calculate how much of that prophetic information comes to me through infused knowledge from the Other Side, particularly in the areas of medicine and technology. It's an understatement to say that I don't have a college degree in either of those subjects, and it's not unusual for me to have to race to a dictionary after I'm given news about the future of medicine and technology, because I've heard words I can't begin to spell, let alone define.

Based on my own experience and decades of research on the subject of infused knowledge, I've come to two conclusions about it: Its source is invariably God-centered, coming from Home as it does, and therefore worth your most rapt attention; and on those occasions when you're blessed with receiving it, you owe it to its source to remember and/or pass it along with the most impeccable accuracy you can offer. Performing your own editorial work on infused knowledge really does give new meaning to the question, "Who do you think you are?"

J

Jackals

In real life, the jackal is a relative of the wild dog, almost if not completely exclusive to the African continent. In ancient Egypt, though, the jackal was Anubis, god of mummification, usually portrayed with the head of a jackal and the body of a man. The elevation of the jackal from notorious scavenger to god has an interesting logic behind it. Jackals were known to accomplish some of their most destructive scavenging in cemeteries, digging through tombs and graves. The Egyptians, determined to protect their deceased after burial, began constructing more elaborate grave sites and deified the jackal god Anubis to stand guard and deter any lowly common jackals who dared to approach.

Anubis's protective presence at the side of the deceased inspired his subsequent promotion to keeping watch over the embalming process, so that he could also protect the body of the deceased from decaying. His ascension among the Egyptian gods elevated him to the rank of Guardian of the Underworld and Keeper of the Scales of Truth. The Scales of Truth were owned by Ma'at, the Goddess of Truth. According to mythology, the heart of the deceased would be placed on one side of the Scales, and an ostrich feather from Ma'at's hair would be placed on the other. If the heart, where Egyptians believed the soul dwelled, was so heavy with sin that it outweighed the feather, the deceased was doomed to eternal death. If the heart and the feather weighed the same, the deceased was promised eternal life. It was Anubis, the jackal god, who held the Scales of Truth while the judgment was made and Anubis, Guardian of the Underworld, who was implored for protection from the fate of eternal death.

If you've been to Egypt for any length of time, you've probably seen the many drawings of Anubis on the inner walls of the pyramids, ancient sentries for the deceased against the ravages of wild creatures and decay and a death that never ends. Fictional as he is, I find him mesmerizing and have trouble taking my eyes off of those drawings of him every time I go there.

It has nothing to do with a temptation to join in the deification of jackals or to build a small shrine in my home to Anubis. It has to do, for one thing, with my certainty that, like so many of you, I spent a lifetime or two in ancient Egypt and still resonate with my spirit's memories of it.

But it also has to do with the quiet proof those drawings of Anubis offer, and the mythology that surrounds him and all the other mythological beings throughout the world. For all these millennia, since the first moment the first human footstep imprinted itself on this earth, we've known, and we've needed to express, that there's a Force far, far greater than we are, who created order and options and consequences, and that we're not in this unimaginable vastness alone.

K

Karma

You'll find karma discussed in full in the listing with its sister concept, dharma.

In brief, though, it's derived from a word meaning "balance of experience." It's not a theory; it's a law in God's cyclical universe guaranteeing that, as the Bible puts it, "what ye sow, so shall ye reap," or, in more contemporary words, "you get back what you give."

Kindred Soul

When you read the definition of soul mates, you'll discover that it's an almost guaranteed exercise in futility racing around in search of yours, since you and your soul mate are highly unlikely even to be on earth at the same time. A few of you who've cherished the dream of finding your soul mate might be momentarily disappointed, and you'll wonder who in the world you can dream of meeting instead.

The answer is, dream of meeting your kindred soul—or, more precisely, your kindred *souls*, since unlike soul mates, there are many of them, and they're every bit as significant in their own way.

Kindred souls are spirits you've known in one or more past lives. It's that simple. I'm sure you've experienced the occasional feeling of instant familiarity, good or bad, that happens on being introduced to a complete stranger—instead of saying, "Nice to meet you," you have to restrain an impulse to say, "Oh, there you are. It's about time you showed up."

Sometimes that instant familiarity is the springboard for another earthly relationship as friends, lovers and spouses, family members or business associates. Other times it should be the springboard for you to run like the wind, as far away as your legs will carry you. I have a client who married a man she was sure she recognized from a past life. She was right—in a past life he was her drunken, tyrannical, abusive father. As his wife in this life she's still trying desperately to win his approval, and he's still using her as his own private dictatorship while the rest of the world treats him with the disregard he deserves. On her behalf, and on behalf of any of you who are locked in a struggle with a kindred soul with whom your past life experiences were probably difficult, a bit of advice: It's almost a guarantee that you charted that person into this lifetime to learn to dispose of his power over you. That's not "turn the tables on" or "get revenge for." That's "dispose of." Walk away. The ultimate dismissal isn't continued attention; it's apathy. Keep engaging that person in any way in this lifetime and you can count on having to deal with him again next time around. It's up to you how many incarnations you intend to waste on someone who very probably isn't worth another moment of your time.

On the other hand, there can be great joy in recognizing and reconnecting with loving, positive kindred souls, no matter what role you've charted for them in this lifetime. It's not just that small unexpected flame in your spirit you feel when a stranger seems oddly familiar. It's not just the rare luxury of getting to skip that "awkward get-acquainted phase" because somehow you know you took care of that several decades or centuries ago. It's the reminder, too often lost in the translation, that every time we meet a kindred soul from some past life, we're shaking hands with absolute proof of our own eternity.

Kinetic Energy

You're in your kitchen, making a meal for your family, when suddenly the cupboard doors begin flying open and slamming shut again on their own. Appliances roar to life as the refrigerator bangs open and the food inside hurtles across the room. You escape into the living room, where the TV comes blasting on all by itself and wildly changes channels. While lights blink insanely on and off, you reach for the phone to call for help. At that same moment it leaps off the end table and falls to the floor, static hissing from the receiver.

A mean-spirited ghost trying to chase you out of your house? Maybe. But it's more likely that you've just witnessed a dramatic display of kinetic energy, caused not by some external force but by you or a member of your family who's either blessed or cursed, depending on how you look at it, with kinetic energy.

Kinetic energy is the unintentional, spontaneous manipulation of inanimate objects through no obvious physical means, causing its possessor to become kind of a hapless walking force field.

There are several theories about what creates kinetic energy. And, of course, there are just as many skeptics who will swear it doesn't exist at all, which I'd be happy to consider if I hadn't witnessed it with my own eyes a few thousand times. Some believe that kinetic energy can simply appear in a person from out of nowhere and then vanish just as inexplicably. Others believe, as I do, that it's a power some people are born with and others aren't, a power that ebbs and flows in irregular cycles through the course of a lifetime.

Kinetic energy is often at its strongest when the body is going through dramatic hormonal changes—during prepubescence or puberty, for example, or in pregnant or menopausal women. But it can manifest itself in young children, too, who have no idea of the chaos they might leave in their wake by simply walking through a room. My granddaughter, for example, when she was only three or four years old, could crash computer hard drives and entire phone systems and cause paper to fly out of giant Xerox machines simply by coming to visit me at my office. Her kinetic energy seems to have calmed considerably in the last few years, but I'm already bracing myself for her becoming a teenager, which is when my son Paul's kinetic energy hit its peak. In his case, just when he hit puberty, he would inadvertently cause all his shoes to zoom around his bedroom like missiles every night as he fell asleep. Today, twenty-five years later, Paul's incidents of kinetic energy are virtually nonexistent.

All of which I bring up to illustrate why I'm not convinced that kinetic energy is an inherited phenomenon. Paul and my granddaughter, who is Paul's niece, are the only two members of my family in at least three generations who were born with kinetic energy, and the many other cases I've studied support my belief that it's about as random a gift as it can possibly be. I almost wish it weren't. If it were more traceable and reliable, it might be more widely understood and not mistaken so often for hauntings, preposterous satanic possessions (emphasis on "preposterous") or, maybe most insulting of all, overactive imaginations and/or publicity stunts.

So if you or someone you know seems to make all hell break loose among inanimate objects by doing nothing more than simply being there, remember, it's no one's fault, it's not a physical or mental illness, it has nothing to do with evil, it doesn't require an exorcism, and it's not some perverse punishment from God (as if God has a perverse streak to begin with). It's only a temporary, passing spasm of innate, purely unintentional kinetic energy.

Kirlian Photography

Kirlian photography is a method of capturing on film the auras, or energy patterns, that surround living things. It was discovered by two Russian scientists, Semyon and Valentina Kirlian, in 1939, and it involves passing a high-frequency electrical current through an object while photographing the object either directly or through glass. The result is an image of the object along with colored auras around them that are capable of indicating stress, illness and other disturbances in the body of the object itself.

Kirlian photography has been a favorite target of skeptics for decades, and on some occasions the skepticism has been deserved. Photographing auras is a ripe area for frauds and scams, and there were more than enough victims of faked Kirlian photography at the height of its popularity to inspire a barrage of question marks.

At the same time, though, legitimate researchers around the world were conducting well-documented, successful experiments with the vast potential of Kirlian photography and the study of aura images in all areas of the life sciences. The brilliant UCLA neurologist and researcher Dr. Thelma Moss was a leader in exploring what Kirlian photography could do and how it could be put to practical use, and she was among many who contributed such discoveries as:

* 100 healthy lab rats were easily distinguished from 100 lab rats whose tails had been injected with cancerous tissue, simply by the visible difference in the auras of the injected tails.
* When a seed whose aura is blue begins to sprout, the seed's aura remains blue, while the sprout photographs a bright pink color; the pink aura follows the tip of the sprout as it continues to grow, and more and more of its stem becomes the same blue of the original seed.
* In a large group being screened for cancer, Kirlian photography revealed six more tumors in patients than conventional medical testing uncovered.
* There's a visible transfer of energy when a freshly picked leaf is laid beside a leaf picked hours before.
* Fertile plant seeds have conspicuously larger auras than infertile seeds.
* Spikes occur in the aura during stressful and traumatic situations.

* The aura dramatically increases in size when the subject becomes intoxicated with either drugs or alcohol.
* With practice and concentration, we can withhold or significantly project our auras.

Kirlian photography can be a valuable diagnostic tool in the hands
of experts in the medical and scientific communities.

It also continues to enjoy great popularity among scam artists who,
for a fee, will be more than happy to photograph and interpret your
aura, I'll bet. While I've never personally taken a Kirlian photograph or
examined the equipment involved, friends in the research field who
have extensive experience with it tell me it's one of the easiest forms
of photography to doctor and manipulate to create almost any result
you're hoping for. There are also some handy do-it-yourself Kirlian
photography kits you can send away for, presumably to explore your
auras in the privacy of your own home. It's your money, of course, and
you can and should do anything you want with it, but in these cases
I'm pretty sure you'd get the same value for your money if you took it
out in your backyard and set fire to it.

In the hands of trained reputable researchers whose lives are committed to finding cures and breakthroughs through the Life Force
called auras, Kirlian photography is a great tool whose potential even
now is only in its infancy.

The Left Door

The Dark Side, as you can read in that designated section, is made up of the true sociopaths among us, those without conscience or any capacity for remorse, those to whom love is strictly a means of manipulation and ego inflation and most of all, those who, no matter what rhetoric they've devised to gain your trust, have turned away from God. Let me repeat that, to make a point I don't ever want you to question: The Dark Side is those who have turned away from God. God has not turned away from them, any more than He ever could or would turn away from any of us, because we truly are His children. If someone's life is devoid of God, it's always his choice, not His choice.

There is an actual place called the Other Side, but the closest thing to an actual place called "hell" is this earth we're living on, this tough boot camp we voluntarily come to from time to time for progress along the eternal journey of our souls. That being true—and it is—it's fair to wonder what happens to the spirits on the Dark Side when their lifetime ends. The answer isn't pretty, but again, they have no one to thank but themselves.

When a person on the Dark Side dies, his spirit never experiences the tunnel and the sacred light at its end. Instead, he's propelled straight through the Other Side's Left Door, or, as my granddaughter used to call it when she was a little girl, Mean Heaven. Please don't let me create the mistaken impression that when we reach the Other Side we see two doors and have to choose between the left and the right. Only a handful of times have I heard of a near-death survivor being conscious of finding two doors at the end of the tunnel, and there was no danger of their stepping through the wrong one.

The Dark Side has already chosen the Left Door through a remorseless lifetime of physically, emotionally and/or spiritually abusing God's children, so no other door is ever visible to them when they die. And inside the Left Door is an abyss of Godless, dark, joyless, all-encompassing nothingness.

The only permanent residents of this abyss are faceless beings in hooded cloaks, who've become the artistic and literary archetype for the persona of Death, aka the Grim Reaper. These beings don't act as dark spirit guides or avenging angels. They function more as a Council, overseeing the paths of the spirits who make a brief appearance in their presence.

And the spirit's time in the void behind the Left Door is nothing if not brief. Unlike spirits on the Other Side who can choose when and whether to return to earth for another incarnation, Left Door spirits travel straight from their bodies at death, through the Godless darkness they've chosen, and right back in utero again, on a self-inflicted horseshoe-shaped journey that leaves them as dark at birth as they were at death in their previous life.

In other words, taking Ted Bundy as a perfect example of the Dark Side: The instant he died, his spirit traveled through the Left Door and entered the womb of some unsuspecting woman, who is probably still wondering along about now where she went wrong as a parent, when the truth is that the dark course of her child's life was already determined before it was born. So if there's someone in your life from the Dark Side whom you're convinced you can change for the better with enough love and patience, please remember that you're fighting a perpetual soul cycle that makes spiritual progress impossible, and that's a fight you can't win.

I can't tell you how relieved I was, and how many of my long-standing questions were answered, when I learned the truth about the Dark Side's journey through the Left Door and back into the womb. For one thing, as a psychic, I can look at most people and see a whole crowd of spirits from the Other Side, from Spirit Guides to departed loved ones to Angels. But from time to time I'll notice someone who seems to have no spirits around them at all, who seems isolated from the divine loving support that constantly surrounds most of us. I used to worry that I was developing blind spots where some people were concerned, and if that were true, I would need to do something about it. Now I know that there's a perfectly good reason why some people don't have a team from the Other Side around them: It's impossible to accumulate a team from a place you've never been. Those solitary people are dark entities who, by their own choice, take the Left Door, and pay a horrible spiritual price for it.

I've found great spiritual comfort in the truth of the journey of the Dark Side. On one hand, I know that the perfect God I believe in could never be vindictive enough to banish any of His children from His sacred presence for eternity. On the other hand, I couldn't make peace with the idea that Ted Bundy and I, who are what I'll politely call polar opposites on the subject of the sanctity of humanity, could end up in the very same embrace of the Other Side between lifetimes, as if there is no significant difference between my soul and the soul of a serial killer.

Now I know what sends Bundy and Hitler and other card-carrying members of the Dark Side through the Left Door for countless dark incarnations while most of us make it safely Home to the Other Side: The Dark Side members defiantly turn their backs on a God who never did and never will stop loving them, which is the one thing most of us find as spiritually inconceivable as the Dark Side itself.

And to prove that our Creator really does love each of His children eternally and unconditionally, not even dark entities are doomed to horseshoe from the Left Door into the womb again forever. The spirits and Angels on the Other Side are well aware of these lost spirits, and sooner or later they literally catch them in their quick transit from one dimension to another and bring them Home to be embraced by God and infused with love again by the white light of the Holy Spirit, the only force powerful enough to reunite them with the sanctity of their soul.

Lemuria

Lemuria is also known as "the lost Pacific continent." Like Atlantis, its Atlantic lost-continent counterpart, the debate about whether or not Lemuria actually existed has raged on for thousands of years. Many believe it was located between Madagascar and Malaysia in the Indian Ocean. The sacred texts of Hinduism refer to "the three continents that were," one of which was called Rutas. Rutas was destroyed by a cataclysmic series of volcanoes, according to the Hindus, a tiny fraction of it remaining as Indonesia and a handful of its survivors finding their way to India and becoming Brahmans, a highly elite caste. The brilliant prophet and healer Edgar Cayce thought that South America's western coast was once a part of Lemuria. Easter Island mythology contains stories of a place called Hiva, which was swallowed by the sea. Many other South Pacific civilizations speak of a sinking island, sometimes called Bolutu, sometimes called Hawaiki, where paradise existed, and the population was happy, amazingly sophisticated and particularly gifted at telepathic communication and other highly developed extrasensory techniques.

Lemuria, it is said, existed prior to and during the time of Atlantis and was destroyed in an apocalyptic series of volcanoes, earthquakes and tsunamis. The legend goes that a few of its residents managed to escape, their beloved land's highly advanced wisdom stored in crystals they cradled reverently on their rough-hewn rafts, and made their way to a northern shore, where they became the ancestors of the first Native Americans, whose artifacts have been found off the California coast dating back to around 25,000 B.C.

I'll say it again—there absolutely was a Lemuria, and, like Atlantis, it will rise from its grave beneath the sea again, during this century, exactly where I mentioned earlier that it's believed to be, between Madagascar and Malaysia in the Indian Ocean. Estimates of its size—approximately 5,000 miles long by 3,000 miles wide—will prove to be remarkably accurate.

There's an ancient Hopi legend that is widely believed to refer to the catastrophic sinking of Lemuria and the subsequent arrival of the first Native American ancestors on the western North American coast:

> "Down on the bottom of the seas lie all the proud cities,
> the flying patuwvotas (shields made of hide),
> and the worldly treasures corrupted with evil.
> Faced with disaster, some people hid inside the earth while others escaped
> by crossing the ocean on reed rafts,
> using the islands as stepping stones."

Leprechaun

According to Irish mythology, leprechauns (from a Gaelic word that means "pygmy," by the way) are little people who possess a treasure, usually a pot of gold, that will belong to any human who can capture the leprechaun. The downside of capturing a leprechaun, though, is that if you ever look away from him, even for an instant, he will disappear. Leprechauns are said to speak entirely in poetry and, as a trade, make shoes for elves—never a pair of shoes, mind you, but only one. They're also mischievous and, while having virtually no contact with humans, love to rearrange and/or hide small objects in people's houses while the people sleep.

In truth, where most mythology has some basis, leprechauns are among the inhabitants of the First Level of the Underworld, which you'll find discussed at length in the section entitled "the Underworld."

Levitation

Levitation is the phenomenon in which the human body is physically elevated several inches or farther into the air and suspended there for a discernible length of time without the use of any external or artificial devices.

There are those who include the lifting of objects into the definition of levitation as well. I happen to think that falls more appropriately under the heading of psychokinesis, which you'll find discussed at length in its own section.

What lies at the heart of levitation, in my opinion, are astral projection and/or astral travel (also discussed in their own sections), physically manifested through either a deliberate or spontaneous disbursement of the body's cellular energy.

Whether they're spontaneous or deliberate, levitation incidents reportedly can last from a few seconds to a couple of hours, and by all accounts, if a person is touched while being levitated, she instantly falls to the surface beneath her.

One of the most interesting facets of levitation is the diverse cross section of belief systems in which the phenomenon has been recorded. Mediums, shamans and mystics have reported levitations for thousands of years, but then, so have Hindus, Buddhists, yogis, Brahmans, Japanese ninjas, Indian fakirs, Catholic saints, Christians and followers of Islam. Just a handful of fascinating accounts:

* Saint Joseph of Cupertino, who levitated frequently, was said to have once remained elevated for almost two hours.
* Saint Teresa of Avila, whose levitations were involuntary, was witnessed to remain more than twelve inches above the ground for periods lasting up to thirty minutes.

* Several Tibetan yogis have demonstrated the ability to both walk and sleep while levitating.
* A medium named Daniel Douglas Home, in the late 1800s, was witnessed by several people to levitate out of a third-floor window of a building and then waft back into the building through a completely different window. The Catholic Church ultimately excommunicated him as a sorcerer.

I've never personally witnessed a levitation, but I've certainly talked to enough reputable colleagues who are convinced that it's a rare but very real phenomenon.

Life Force

The Life Force is that energy within us and the entirety of creation that elevates us from nothingness to alive, vital and part of the great "I Am," as the ancient Eastern religions referred to the honor of existence.

You'll find references to the term "Life Force" throughout this book, but its most complete description can be found under its synonym, Etheric Substance.

Life Themes

One of the many decisions we make on the Other Side when writing our chart for an upcoming incarnation is the specific purpose that will satisfy what we're hoping to accomplish. The purpose we choose, and weave into our chart, is called our "life theme."

We actually select two life themes to round out our game plan and make sure we get the most we can out of our brief, tough camping trip on earth—a primary theme, which is essentially who we plan to be, and a secondary theme, which is another aspect of ourselves we'll have to deal with along the way. For an easy analogy, think of it as planning a trip. The chart is the highly detailed road map of the entire journey. The primary theme defines our basic itinerary as we travel from Point A to Point B. The secondary theme is an ongoing obstacle we'll be faced with as the journey unfolds.

We all arrive on earth with both a primary and secondary life theme. Figuring out what they are, and which is which, is a valuable exercise for clarifying and simplifying our lives. Having an easy frame of reference for the basic itinerary of this life can help keep us on track, and recognizing that one recurring hazard that is continually trying to pull us off course will keep us from being blindsided and overwhelmed by it. It's the difference between seemingly random confusion and a well-informed, "I know what this is, and I'm prepared for it."

A case in point: My primary theme is "humanitarian." That's who I am, my joy, my passion, as essential to me as breathing. But my secondary theme is "loner." How's that for conflict? I admit it, there have been times when I've resented having to sacrifice the "loner" part of me and wished I could just disappear to Kenya under a nice big baobab tree for the rest of my life. The challenge of the secondary theme, though, is not to look at it as a burden but to recognize it, respect it as an aspect of myself that I chose and find ways to make peace with it.

There are forty-four life themes. As you read them, and their brief descriptions, pay close attention to your responses to them. I have no doubt that your spirit will resonate when you recognize your primary theme. You may have a more subtle response as you search for your secondary theme, but as a guideline, look for something that has pulled strongly at you in your quiet moments for as long as you can remember. If it's something that would complicate your primary theme or even make it impossible, chances are, as in my case, that is indeed your secondary theme—one of the challenges you chose to do battle with this time around.

* **Activator**—troubleshooters; gratified by accomplishing the task in front of them; have to be careful not to spread themselves too thin.

* **Aesthetic Pursuits**—driven to create some form of artistic beauty; can lead to fame and privilege, enjoyable if the secondary theme is compatible, but tragic if the secondary theme is in conflict. Judy Garland, Vincent van Gogh and Marilyn Monroe are examples of a primary "aesthetic pursuit" theme in unresolved conflict with a secondary theme.

* **Analyzer**—need to scrutinize the intricate details of how and why everything works; invaluable in scientific, electronic and forensic areas; difficult for them to relax and stand back far enough to see the bigger picture.

* **Banner Carrier**—frontline warriors against what they perceive as injustices; sometimes need to learn the effectiveness of tempering passion with tact and diplomacy.

* **Builder**—the often invisible but essential cogs that keep the wheels of accomplishment turning; not those who stand onstage to accept trophies, but those who actually built the stage; can feel unappreciated, but need to remember that the rewards for the builder theme lie not in trophies but in the accelerated advancement of the spirit.

* **Catalyst**—the movers and shakers, those who make things happen and mobilize inactivity into action; seem to particularly excel in stressful situations; feel empty and depressed without a goal to conquer.

* **Cause Fighter**—the generals who command the banner carriers—vocal, active and passionate about their efforts toward a better world, sometimes at the expense of their own and others'

safety; run the risk of vying for a bigger spotlight on themselves than on the cause they're promoting.

* **Controller**—when successful, take charge of every task at hand through wise, discreet, supportive supervising and delegating; when unsuccessful, compelled to dictate and judge every detail of the lives of those around them.

* **Emotionality**—deeply feel the highest of highs, the lowest of lows and every shade of emotion in between; need to recognize the exceptionally great importance of balance in their lives.

* **Experiencer**—insist on trying any pursuit or lifestyle that happens to catch their eye because of a need to live life as an active, varied series of participation events; biggest hurdle is potential excessive self-indulgence to the point of irresponsibility.

* **Fallibility**—usually undertaken by those who were born physically, mentally or emotionally challenged; a theme taken on only by the most extraordinary spirits; when they find this choice discouraging, need to be assured what an inspiring example they're setting for the rest of us who weren't so brave.

* **Follower**—as essential to society as leaders, since without them there would be no leaders; strong, reliable support can be a follower's greatest and most generous contribution; their toughest challenge is being discerning about whom and what to follow.

* **Harmony**—will go to any extreme to maintain peace, calm and balance in their lives and the lives of those around them; on the plus side, cooperative, and calming in chaotic situations; on the minus side, can find it difficult to adjust to life's inevitable bumps, bruises and stress.

* **Healer**—often but not necessarily drawn to the physical or mental healing professions; their theme can express itself in any

form of easing pain and improving well-being; always vulnerable to empathizing too closely with those they're trying to heal.

* **Humanitarian**—born to extend themselves to humankind one on one, addressing the world's hunger, poverty, illness, homelessness and other inequities head-on; face the twofold challenge of knowing there's an infinite amount of work to be done, but also knowing when and how to stop and rest to keep themselves from burning out.

* **Infallibility**—seemingly born with everything—looks, talent, intelligence, privilege, wit, grace, etc.; can be an unusually difficult theme, with problems rarely taken seriously, frequent resentment for their advantages and secret feelings of inadequacy from not having had to earn advantages; often drawn to such excesses as obesity, promiscuity or substance abuse and can feel emotionally inept in situations that challenge their character.

* **Intellectuality**—the ultimate thirst-for-knowledge theme; use their wealth of education to improve life on earth; at its worst, the professional student whose sole purpose is the self-directed goal of knowledge for the sake of knowledge, hoarded instead of shared.

* **Irritant**—faultfinders, never at a loss for something to complain about; helpful in teaching us tolerance and refusal to engage in negativity.

* **Justice**—lifelong pursuit of fairness and equality; at best, Abraham Lincoln and the Reverend Dr. Martin Luther King; at worst, can result in riots, anarchy and vigilantism.

* **Lawfulness**—a driven concern with safeguarding that line between legality and illegality; usually devoted public servants dedicated to social order and balance; corrupted, they abuse their power.

＊ **Leader**—often gifted at their ability to lead, but rarely innova-
tive, choosing to become leaders in already established areas;
would benefit from expressing their leadership in more socially
relevant frontiers.

＊ **Loner**—often socially active but choose lifestyles that will allow
them to be isolated; content alone and struggle to overcome
feeling drained when other people spend too much time in their
space.

＊ **Loser**—seek attention through being martyrs; if there is no
melodrama in their lives, they'll create it; can teach us to dislike
behavior without judging the people responsible for it.

＊ **Manipulator**—approach their lives like a one-sided chess game,
often with remarkable talent; can have an enormously positive
impact on society; when talent is abused, are self-absorbed at
everyone else's expense.

＊ **Passivity**—perceived as weak but, more accurately, uncommonly
sensitive; trouble coping with extremes; occasional tension can
be valuable for spurring them to action.

＊ **Patience**—indicates more eagerness to move quickly on the
spirit's journey than those who choose less difficult themes—
patience theme indicates spiritual impatience; ongoing battle
against snapping at stress; frequently fight the guilt of suppressed
stress and anger.

＊ **Pawn**—the fuse that ignites something of great magnitude, either positive or negative, to emerge; Judas, whose betrayal of
Christ was a critical element to the birth of Christianity, a classic example of a pawn; have to be vigilant in aligning themselves
with only the worthiest, most loving causes.

＊ **Peacemaker**—typically accompanied by surprising aggression;
can be overzealous in efforts to stop violence; not opposed

to achieving a bit of celebrity in their noble, highly visible cause.

* **Performance**—might pursue careers in entertainment fields, but often content being local life of the party; nourished by the spotlight, however large or small; tend to form opinions of themselves through the eyes of others; need to learn to provide their own spiritual and emotional nourishment.

* **Persecution**—convinced they've been singled out for extraordinary bad luck and negative attention; avoid happiness as potentially too disappointing; remarkable spiritual advancement in choosing and overcoming this theme.

* **Persecutor**—aggressive, self-justifying sociopaths; will abuse and kill without guilt or remorse; inadvertently inspire progress in our laws, judicial systems, forensics techniques and moral boundaries.

* **Poverty**—prevalent in third-world countries; also exists in the advantaged who feel that no matter how much they have, it's not enough; perspective on irrelevance of material possessions can provide brilliant spiritual growth.

* **Psychic**—often choose strict childhood environments in which their ability to sense things far beyond normal is met with severe disapproval; challenged to put their gift to its highest, most unselfish, most spiritual use.

* **Rejection**—usually alienation or abandonment in early childhood that continues throughout life; the challenge is to learn that when the spirit is whole and self-reliant, it can no longer be held hostage by others.

* **Rescuer**—gravitates toward victims, wanting to help and save them, even if the victims have created their own crises; typically

strongest in the presence of the weakest; can end up being victimized if they don't learn to be selective.

* **Responsibility**—find joy in active, hands-on accomplishments
and feel guilt if they leave something undone; need to remember
that people around them also benefit from responsibility and
accomplishment.

* **Spirituality**—spend a lifetime in search of their own spiritual
center; at its highest potential, creates boundless inspiration
and tolerance; at its lowest, can manifest itself in narrow-
mindedness and fanaticism.

* **Survival**—see life as a relentless, ongoing struggle; usually excel in crises but have trouble distinguishing between a true crisis
and an everyday challenge.

* **Temperance**—typically accompanied by an addiction; even if
actual addiction never manifests itself, constant sense of vulnerability to potential addiction; have to avoid the opposite extreme of becoming fanatically repelled by the object of what
they perceive to be a potential addiction.

* **Tolerance**—feels compelled to find a way to tolerate even the
intolerable; growth accomplished by recognizing that being tol-
erant is not the same thing as being weak and indiscriminate.

* **Victim**—life's sacrificial lambs; throw a spotlight on injustice
and inspire us to take action; abused children, targets of hate
crimes and the wrongly convicted among those whose victim
theme is devoted to the highest good.

* **Victimizer**—achieve control for the purpose of being surrounded by visible proof of their own power; insatiable, hypersensitive ego; on a small scale, the controlling lover or spouse,
the stalker, the pathologically overzealous parent; on a larger

scale, Jim Jones, David Koresh, Bo and Peep of the Heaven's Gate cult; any and all sacrifices of their followers an homage not to God but to the narcissistic needs of the victimizer.

* **Warrior**—fearless risk takers with the courage to step up to a physical, moral or spiritual challenge; when focused, especially with secondary humanitarian theme, can make historic contributions of global significance without our ever knowing their names or their ever needing us to.

* **Winner**—an active, pervasive compulsion to achieve; perpetual optimists; in its finest form, the winner's unfailing ability to pick themselves up from every failure and move on is inspiring; without reality checks, can squander money, security and lives with impetuous, undisciplined and uninformed decisions.

Lilith

Jewish folklore defines Lilith as the first wife of Adam, made of dust exactly as Adam was. When she refused to be submissive to him, she was banished from the Garden of Eden, and Adam was given Eve, who was created from his rib to guarantee obedience to Adam's will.

When she was cast out of the Garden of Eden, Lilith took up residence in a cave, where she set up her favorite belongings, most particularly a mirror that she proudly displayed. She entertained demons in her cave, the legend goes, and gave birth to legions of demon offspring who emerged from that cave to spread insidious evil throughout the world. It was said that whenever these devil progeny wanted to return to their mother, all they had to do was enter the nearest mirror, since by then, through Lilith's powerful vanity, all mirrors had become direct passageways to Lilith's cave.

In some translations of the Bible there is one (and only one) reference to the name "Lilith," in Isaiah 34:14: "And wild beasts shall meet with hyenas, the satyr shall cry to his fellow; and there shall repose

Lilith and find her a place of rest." This is believed by some to be the "period at the end of the sentence" that starts in the Kabbala and its description of the Holy One destroying "the wicked Rome" and reducing it to ruins "for all eternity. He will send Lilith there, and let her dwell in that ruin, for she is the ruination of the world."

Now, I'm no feminist, but it hasn't escaped my notice that the most hideous possible interpretations of the Lilith folklore began springing up right around the same time the concept of Azna, the Mother God, began fading from church documents, and religion itself became a patriarchy. Maybe it's just me, but respectful as I am toward everyone's beliefs on a large scale, provided they begin with a basic premise of the sanctity of all living things, I detect a certain lack of restraint and objectivity in a statement that reads "for she is the ruination of the world," no matter who this particular "she" is referring to.

In fact, Lilith is a great, positive, highly misunderstood power, the ruler of the First Level of the Underworld. And let me quickly add that, contrary to popular belief, the Underworld has nothing to do with evil. You'll find a full discussion of it in its own section, so I won't belabor it here, except as it applies to Lilith herself. The first of the Seven Lower Levels of Creation, as they're called, is home to wonderful, mystical beings, beings that are often conveniently dismissed as delusions— the elves, the leprechauns, the sprites, the fairies and the gnomes. Lilith, Queen of the Fairies, is the governess of that magical domain.

The entities on the first of these Lower Levels, including Lilith, are on the same frequency level as earth itself, which is why "the little people" are seen even more often than in the spirit world, if those who see them would just admit it. And believe me, until I began researching this marvelous creation called the Underworld, I didn't buy it either, and might never have bothered to look into it until I saw a fairy in Ireland with my own eyes and couldn't blink her away as imaginary, no matter how hard I tried. Their life spans average hundreds of years, and Lilith is said to be 4,500 years old. Her power allows her to travel with ease from the First Level to Earth to the Other Side if she chooses to. Neither she nor the other First Level beings ever reincarnate—they're a separate, independent phylum, with no need to advance, but they're every bit as valued a creation of God's as we are.

For practical purposes here on earth, we can use Lilith as one of our most valuable untapped resources. She is a loving, vigilant and formidable protector of our children and animals, and eager to help when they're in trouble or missing if we just call on her. Notice I didn't say pray to her—I always will strictly reserve my prayers for the Godhead, and Lilith is not a god. She is, however, a force, a brilliant champion of ours with an undeserved mythical reputation for evil, and for bearing legions of the devil's children, and for being so contrary that she was banished from the Garden of Eden, and for being the ruination of the world—which, when you stand back and take a long, objective look, hints at widespread acknowledgment that, tabloid headlines aside, there's nothing mythical about the power, the impact and the very existence of Lilith herself.

Master Teachers

Many spiritual writers use the term "Master Teachers." I'm not holding out on you by ignoring it. I simply refer to them as "the Council," with "Master Teachers" thrown in from time to time because it's familiar to me, as it might be to you. You'll find a full description of the Master Teachers, in other words, under the synonymous section, "The Council."

Medium

The word "medium" is referred to throughout this book, and since it's a term that not all of you might be familiar with or clear about: A medium is simply a person whose God-given psychic abilities are complemented by an expanded range of frequency perceptions. The result is that they're able to see, hear and experience spirits from other dimensions who operate at higher frequency levels than ours on earth.

In other words, in addition to my other psychic gifts, I'm innately able to tune in to the higher frequency of the Other Side. That allows me to communicate with the spirit world, which means I can be considered a medium.

Now, just to differentiate between some of these words in the context of how I define them, although I'm sure there are those who would exhaustively debate the semantics:

My **psychic** skills, oversimplifying the definition to a fault, involve the use of such gifts as clairvoyance (seeing things from other dimensions), clairaudience (hearing things from other dimensions), clairsentience (sensing things from other dimensions), infused knowledge (information received with no awareness of where it came from) and many other paranormal abilities you'll find throughout this book, for the purpose of giving readings on the past, present and future, as well as health concerns, relationship concerns, career concerns, etc. Since this definition is deliberately oversimplified, I'll stress that if I'm functioning strictly as a psychic, contact with the spirit world doesn't come into play. (Technically, everything comes from God, of course, not from me, and there's other interaction with Home on my part that we don't need to get into here—we're keeping it simple, remember?)

As a **medium,** still using many of those same skills I use as a psychic, I'm able to act as a go-between, or messenger, between you and the spirit world. You ask if your mother, your aunt Jane, your son, your husband is safe and happy on the Other Side, and my clairvoyance allows me to see them and describe them to you, while my clairaudience allows me to hear and pass along their answers to your questions, or initiate conversations with you that they might want to have. My function as a medium isn't that much different from those interpreters you see at the United Nations—I'm just there to make sure the questions and answers get repeated accurately, and offer enough validation, by way of a physical description or some other very personal bit of information I couldn't possibly know, that you're in touch with the person you think you're talking to.

As a **channel,** I literally absent myself from my body for a while and let my Spirit Guide Francine borrow it to speak through me, using my vocal cords and the lower frequency of this dimension, because frankly, the rapid-fire, high-pitched chirping from her dimension is still tricky for me to understand, and I've had more than sixty years of practice at it. If this provides a useful image, I empty myself and provide a clear *channel* for her to flow through, and/or transmit/communicate through. There are channels who'll let almost any and every spirit come in and blather away. I've seen them do it, and I've seen how it depletes them. I applaud their courage, but I never have and never will regret my exclusive contract with Francine.

I really do hope these distinctions help clarify those three common terms a little, instead of complicating them even more.

Merging

Merging occurs on the Other Side when we literally blend our spirit with that of another "living" entity. The word "living" belongs in quotes because while merging usually refers to an intimate event between two spirits, it's also a means by which we can become an actual emotionally involved bystander at a time, place or moment in someone else's chart. Merging means "fully experiencing," or "becoming one with" in a way that we here on earth can create only a pale replica of, no matter how often we try to toss that term around at weddings, as if we mean it.

Merging between two spirits on the Other Side has nothing to do with lust or hormones, nor is it thought of as sex. It's a blending together, physically, spiritually and emotionally, to a state of mutual bliss, without either spirit losing its own identity. During an act of merging, each spirit shares another's wisdom, passion, history, sorrow and joy, so that between those two, for that brief time, there is ultimate, all-encompassing knowing. Its intended result isn't procreation—we don't procreate on the Other Side—nor is it any kind of eventual exclusivity for the two spirits involved. Instead, merging is meant to be nothing more and nothing less than what it is—an episode of perfect harmony and joyful reciprocal acceptance between two spirits in heaven.

Mind Theory

The Mind Theory is something I developed in an effort to illustrate—literally—the difference between how our typical human minds are trained to function (and become our worst enemies if we're not careful) and how we can retrain our minds to be our finest, most elevated, most elevating tools.

When we're newborns, with no conscious memories of our past lives or the lives we've just left behind on the Other Side, our minds have the structure you'll see in Figure A, the two vertically stacked equilateral triangles that meet at their points (marked "Point X"). We know there's a conscious mind, and we've heard over and over that there's a subconscious mind. In fact, throughout this and other books you'll see me refer to the subconscious mind as that higher, deeper place where our spirit minds reside. I do that for simplification and familiarity—for the sake of most discussions, dividing the mind into just two parts, the conscious and the subconscious, helps get to the real point much more easily.

My Mind Theory, though, more appropriately divides the mind into the Conscious/Subconscious and the Superconscious, a device that originated with Carl Jung, one of my heroes in the world of psychology.

So again, we're born with the traditional human mind structure of Figure A, with the Conscious/Subconscious represented by the lower triangle and the Superconscious represented by the upper triangle. Each of them is divided into levels.

CONSCIOUS/SUBCONSCIOUS MIND

FIRST LEVEL: THE WAKING STATE

We begin basic recognition and interpretation. "This is a tree. That is another tree."

SECOND LEVEL: SENSES, DEDUCED REASON

"I have now deduced what it is: That looks like a tree; it must be a tree."

THIRD LEVEL: MEMORY and KNOWLEDGE

"Now I have stored it. In imagery, I cannot possibly store a tree if I do not know what a tree is."

FOURTH LEVEL: IDEAS, CONCLUSIONS, CREATIVITY

"I have seen a tree. I know it is a tree. I have now deduced that it is a tree. I have stored it to be a tree. And now, maybe I can draw a tree, or I can do something creative with a tree."

But here's the problem with the typical human mind we're born with: No one tells us we have access beyond that point, that yes, you

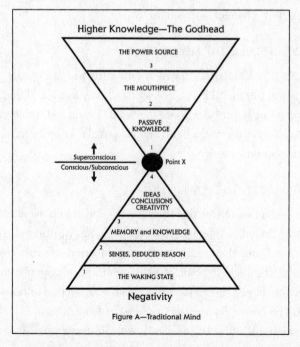

Figure A—Traditional Mind

really can get beyond that Fourth Level to the Superconscious. It's sitting right there, just beyond Point X, which sadly tends to be choked off by nothing more than our conditioning from a free, easy flow of information.

Instead, we're much more conditioned to accept passively the wide-open bottom of the Conscious/Subconscious triangle, where the negativity of life on earth flows to the point of occasional flooding and no one ever tells us it doesn't have to be that way.

SUPERCONSCIOUS MIND

FIRST LEVEL: PASSIVE KNOWLEDGE

It's in the first level of the Superconscious mind that all our knowledge is stored, all the memories and wisdom and skills our spirit minds hold safe, our own personal Akashic Records. All that knowledge, so close to our conscious minds, if it weren't for that choked-off channel between the two.

SECOND LEVEL: THE MOUTHPIECE

It's in this level that, newly armed with the knowledge you've gained in the First Level, you essentially say to God, "I don't want to keep this beautiful wisdom to myself. I want to be able to share it, say it and do it eloquently." Your passive knowledge, in other words, becomes active.

THIRD LEVEL: THE POWER SOURCE

The perfect image for this third level is waking up every morning, saying, "May the White Light of the Holy Spirit surround and protect me," and then reaching for an industrial-strength electrical cord at the highest point of your mind and plugging it into the ultimate Power Source directly above you, around you and with you. The Power Source, the Godhead, is to all of us like the Superconscious Mind is to the Conscious/Subconscious Mind—right

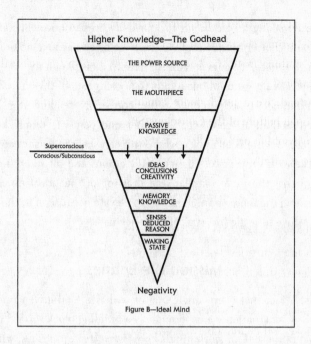

Figure B—Ideal Mind

there, that close, available every moment, just waiting for us to access it.

And the wide-open end of the Superconscious Mind allows a constant flow of the Higher Knowledge the Godhead possesses as we continue striving to expand our capacity to contain it.

Now: Using those exact same definitions of the Conscious/-Subconscious Mind, the Superconscious Mind and their respective levels, take a look at Figure B. This is a portrait of what we can train our typical human minds to look like. Same levels, different configuration, different proportions. It's the senses that are given the lowest priority, and negativity, not the Superconscious Mind, that's choked off, while the Higher Knowledge of the Godhead is now available to flow freely through the Superconscious and the Conscious/Subconscious Minds like a divine, uninterrupted funnel. No more blocking ourselves at the exact point where our most valuable resources sit waiting, no more making it so difficult for our daily lives to have constant access to our Power Source that we waste so often because no one tells us that it's there, it's ours and all we have to do is plug it in.

And how do we train our minds to accomplish all this? You've just finished ninety-nine percent of the course by reading this Mind Theory section. To complete the other one percent, simply keep a drawing of Figure B in a place where you can see it at least once every day. I know from years of clients, study groups and my church membership that the more familiar that drawing of the "ideal mind" becomes, and the more your life begins to elevate because of it, the more you'll refuse to settle for "typical" ever again.

Mission Life Entities

It's just a fact that every single one of us has a God-driven purpose, and every incarnation we experience is a building block toward fulfilling that purpose. Our spirit minds know what that purpose is, whether our conscious minds can define it or not.

It's also a fact that there is no one purpose that's more important than any other. Ditchdiggers and teachers and paramedics and charity volunteers are every bit as essential as kings and presidents. Armies of generals without foot soldiers would never win a battle. Never doubt that, especially in God's eyes, every purpose toward His greater good is indispensable and of equal value.

All of which is to introduce the Mission Life Entity. Those who sign up for the designated purpose of "Mission Life Entity" are among the most advanced spirits in our midst. *Not among the most important*, just among the most advanced, so don't even think about feeling diminished if you don't happen to be one.

Mission Life Entities have said to God, "Wherever on this earth you need me, I'll willingly go." They'll sacrifice their comfort and yearnings for Home in the name of the mission they've signed on for—not to convert or preach any specific religion or dogma, but compassionately to rescue, reconnect, affirm, ignite and celebrate the spirit of the divine in every child of God they encounter, whatever their belief system.

Mission Life Entities are kind, never superior, and they never try to gain control over those around them, let alone intimidate or frighten with threats of hell and eternal damnation. They don't claim an exclusive closeness to God, or to have more effective access to Him. They don't isolate or estrange anyone from loved ones or from the world in general, and they never lose sight of the fact that it is God, and only God, who is the Real Answer.

Mission Life Entities can be found in any and all walks of life. Their purpose is visible through their quiet generosity, their ready empathy, and most of all, their gift for elevating the spiritual well-being of humanity without making shrill, annoying, judgmental pests of themselves.

Mission Life Entities work the hard way up through the spirit ranks, writing exceptionally difficult life charts for their exceptionally numerous incarnations, so that finally there's no level of life on earth they can't relate to. The path to achieving the purpose of Mission Life Entity is filled with hardship, turmoil and disappointment, in exchange for profound satisfaction and a journey of the soul only a rare few choose to take.

Morphic Resonance

Morphic resonance occurs when the spirit mind is confronted with a place, or a person, so profoundly familiar from a past life that it experiences almost total recall. Deeply affected by that recall, the spirit mind infuses the conscious mind with that same factual and emotional information, to the point where the whole body—mentally, physically and spiritually—*resonates* with a familiarity that only the spirit mind can genuinely claim. It's a relative of cell memory and déjà vu. In fact, my Spirit Guide Francine describes it as déjà vu multiplied by about a trillion.

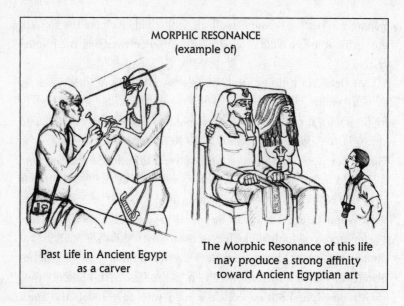

MORPHIC RESONANCE
(example of)

Past Life in Ancient Egypt
as a carver

The Morphic Resonance of this life
may produce a strong affinity
toward Ancient Egyptian art

A case in point was a client named Bill, who'd just returned from London, a city he'd yearned to visit all his life without ever having read a thing about it or knowing why he felt drawn to it. On his first day there, during a guided tour of the city, he suddenly realized that he knew exactly where the tour bus was, where it was headed and what they were looking at, several seconds before the guide announced it over the loudspeaker. His mind kept up a silent running monologue that both fascinated and frightened him: "Right around this corner is St. Paul's Cathedral. . . . We're in Chelsea now. . . . We're coming up on Scotland Yard on our left. . . . We'll be at Harrods in a minute. . . ."

He was shaken by his precise knowledge of a strange city, but it paled in comparison to his trip to the countryside a few days later. He was alone in a rented car, going wherever his whim took him, he thought, when it slowly became apparent to him that he was on very familiar roads, on a very deliberate mission. Three hours from London, on the outskirts of a village he knew would be there, he found himself sitting in front of a perfectly ordinary white stone house on an acre of land, tears in his eyes, inexplicably feeling as if he'd lost his best friend, as over and over again the same strange thought repeated itself: "My pub is gone. My pub is gone. My pub is gone."

Bill hadn't talked to anyone about the details of his trip after he returned home for fear they'd think he was either delusional or just plain crazy. He also hadn't been able to shake the depression that had taken root in front of that white stone house, and it only intensified when he went back to his busy, successful life in Cape Cod. I'll always believe he sensed what had happened—he flew 3,000 miles to spend an hour in my office, after all, and I'm not exactly secretive about who I am and what I do.

Thanks to regressive hypnotherapy, Bill was able to explore not one but two happy lifetimes in England. In one of them he was a doctor in London, a general practitioner who made house calls and knew the city better than he knew his own name. In the other, he married his childhood sweetheart in a small village in the northern countryside and joyfully supported her and their two children by way of a simple, friendly pub on the outskirts of town that he built with his own hands from the ground up.

It takes a concept as potent as morphic resonance to encompass Bill's detailed familiarity with those places he knew nothing about in this life and, far more than that, his overwhelming sense of belonging there, of being home, that he couldn't even define, let alone understand or shake off after he left.

One of the most wonderful aspects of morphic resonance is that I don't know anyone who's experienced it, including me, who saw it coming. It's as if in the blink of an eye your life goes from "just another day" to "will never be the same." If and when it happens to you, shine a spotlight on that moment when a seemingly impossible familiarity rang as the truth in your spirit and you'll understand exactly what morphic resonance is. And never forget to thank God for still more proof of the infinite survival of your soul.

Mystical Travelers

Mission Life Entities are rare advanced spirits who've essentially said to God, "Wherever on this earth you need me, I'll willingly go." Mystical Travelers can most easily be described as Mission Life Entities with a broader range. What they have said to God about their soul's journey is, "Wherever in this universe you need me, I'll willingly go."

In other words, Mystical Travelers devote themselves to the same eternal purpose that Mission Life Entities do: strengthening the divine spiritual connection between us and God as a thriving, active force. But while Mission Life Entities keep their sights focused on earth, Mystical Travelers volunteer to incarnate and continue that purpose on any inhabited planet in any galaxy that God needs them. Most Mystical Travelers have experienced many lifetimes on earth and are ready to graduate to more expansive horizons. It's as if their learning on earth earned them their Ph.D.s, and they're yearning to go elsewhere for their postgraduate work.

Mystical Travelers have all the transcendent qualities of Mission Life Entities—the peaceful acceptance of sacrifice and discomfort, the uncommon empathy, the generosity, the kindness, the unwillingness to sit idle if someone needs help. The only two I've met in my sixty-nine years had the added bonus of seeming to have taken and excelled in every theological course ever conducted, coming away with none of the rhetoric and all of the joy of actively loving and being loved by God. Both of these Mystical Travelers made me feel like a beginner, and neither of them lived long enough to reach adulthood. They came, they gave us a glimpse of our spirits' greatest potential and then they quickly left for their next assignment on the other side of the universe.

To a five-year-old boy in Kenya named Jared, and to a thirteen-year-old boy named Mattie Stepanek: The privilege was all mine.

Near-Death Experiences

I wouldn't know where to begin to count the number of books, studies, debates, societies, TV specials, research projects, theological forums, etc., etc., etc. that have been devoted to the subject of near-death experiences. The overwhelming focus: Are near-death experiences real?

And I have to say, there's one fact about near-death experiences among all that noise that's irrefutable: I've never met or heard of anyone who's actually had one, including me, who doesn't know it was real. So while the scientific, theological and philosophical skepticism rages on, some respect, please, for those of us with involuntary firsthand expertise.

I've told parts of my near-death experience in other segments of this book, but here's the whole thing:

I was forty-two years old. I'd had major surgery, and there were catastrophic postoperative complications, to the point where my family and close friends were keeping a twenty-four-hour vigil around my hospital bed. There were four or five of them there when my body temperature suddenly dropped like a rock, my heart stopped and by every physiological definition in any medical dictionary you can name, I was dead.

I've talked a lot about fellow near-death survivors who were mesmerized by the realization that they'd left their bodies and could hover above themselves, eavesdropping on what everyone in the room was saying and doing now that they were "gone." (You might want to bear that in mind when and if you find yourself at someone's deathbed—just because they're dead doesn't mean they're not listening to every word you say.) I, on the other hand, was apparently in sprinter's position to get out of there and couldn't have been less interested in hovering.

When you read "the Tunnel" section, you'll find that it doesn't descend toward us from up in the sky somewhere. It actually rises from the etheric substance of our own bodies, at maybe a twenty- or thirty-degree angle, and instead of leading up, it leads across, to Home on the Other Side that isn't far away beyond the clouds, where happy little bluebirds fly, but is really right here, only three feet above our ground level, in another dimension with a much higher vibrational frequency than ours.

As I moved through the tunnel, I remember thinking that even on the best, happiest, healthiest day of the lifetime I was leaving behind, I'd never felt as alive as I felt now that I was dead and free of that inconvenient albatross of a body that had conked out and was of no further use to me. I was thriving, I was free, I was exhilarated, and I knew without giving it any conscious thought that everyone and everything I had ever worried about was perfect, exactly as it was meant to be. I didn't consciously wonder about eternity at some specific moment in the tunnel, but I became filled with the peaceful, certain truth of it, which included the knowledge that my loved ones on earth would be with me again in what would seem like no time at all. I had no sense of leaving a life behind me. Instead there was a thrilling sense of returning to a life that brought me endless joy.

The legendary white light appeared ahead of me. Its brilliance is sacred, and its penetrating, welcoming purity somehow contains all the wisdom that ever was and ever will be.

A figure stepped into the large opening at the end of the tunnel. At first it was just a silhouette against the brilliant light. As I got closer I could make out the features of my cherished Grandma Ada, who'd gone Home when I was eighteen and whom I'd missed every minute of every day since then. I joyfully cried out her name without making a sound, and she smiled back with indescribable love. I could see a meadow beyond her through the opening at the end of the tunnel, grassy and filled with flowers with earthly colors enriched and magnified by a thousand.

And then, two things happened at exactly the same moment:

I reached out my hand to Grandma Ada, and she reached out her hand to me. But her fingers were pointing upward, with her palm toward me, in a gesture meaning "stop." I kept reaching for her, either not understanding or refusing to, and I was a breath away from touching her. . . .

During which I clearly heard the distant voice of one of the friends who'd been standing at my hospital bed when I left. It was a plea so urgent she almost shrieked, "Sylvia, don't go, you're so needed!"

At the sound of those words, you would have thought a giant rubber band had been stretched to its limit around my waist. One instant I was about to take my beloved grandmother's hand and step through the glorious threshold to the Other Side. The next instant I was snapped away from her and Home, and slammed back into that weak, painful, leaden body in that cold, sterile hospital room, staring into weeping, agonized faces that surrounded my bed. I tried my best to be philosophical, to be thankful I was back because it was clearly for a worthy purpose, but the truth is, I was angry, frustrated and depressed about it for weeks afterward.

In the long run, though, in the many years since, I've cherished the opportunity to hear countless near-death experiences of clients, friends and colleagues from every faith and every continent on this planet, not as a curious researcher and regressive hypnotist but as someone who's been there too. And without exception, we all share a gift no skeptic could ever diminish, no matter how snide and superior they might try to be.

It was put perfectly by the late poet, pacifist and international treasure Mattie Stepanek, whose passing in 2004, at the age of thirteen, left the world poorer for his absence but infinitely richer for his having been here at all. I had the great pleasure of appearing on *Larry King Live* with Mattie. At one point Larry King asked Mattie, who'd had a near-death experience of his own, if he was afraid of death. Mattie Stepanek, then eleven, with the peaceful smile of an angel, answered for each and every one of us who's ever come back from even an instant in the presence of that light:

"I'm afraid of dying," he said. "But I'm not afraid of death."

Night Terrors

You'll find a thorough discussion of night terrors, and what to do about them, in "the Boogeyman" section. In brief, for now, night terrors are those events beyond nightmares that jolt children awake in a state of utter panic, and they're caused by a child's memories or astral trips to past-life traumas while the child sleeps.

Noir

There are dualities to be found throughout creation—male/female, yin/yang, land/water, day/night and, of course, light/dark.

So just as there is a cosmic Other Side that is Home to the most advanced spirits of the universe, and just as those divine, advanced spirits are sent for new God-centered incarnations from a sacred site on the cosmic Other Side called Nouveau, there is also Nouveau's exact opposite, called Noir. It functions identically to the Left Door of our Other Side: Dark entities from inhabited planets in every galaxy pass directly through the godless void of Noir when they die and are immediately horseshoed back in utero to the same planet or any other inhabited planet they choose. The dark spirits who pass through Noir exist for the same reason our Left Door beings exist: not because God has turned away from them, but because they have turned away from

God. And they have the same mission that the Dark Side has on earth: to destroy God's light in as many spirits as possible, because darkness cannot survive where there is light.

Completing these particular dualities of light/dark and Nouveau/Noir, you'll find a description under "Nouveau" for how to find the ancient image of "the Great Man" using the constellations as its outline. Where the heart of "the Great Man" would be in that beautiful image is where the sacred Nouveau lies. How appropriate that in that same image, you'll find Noir exactly opposite the location of the heart.

Nouveau

There is a cosmic Other Side that is the embracing Home to the spirits of the universe just as our Other Side is Home to the spirits of earth. And the most cherished site on the cosmic Other Side is Nouveau, where Mystic Travelers and other highly advanced spirits from Other Sides in every galaxy return to be trained for their next incarnation on another inhabited planet in the universe.

Yes, that means there are people among us who've lived previous incarnations on other planets. Most of them are going about their divine spiritual assignments quietly and anonymously. A few have gained unsolicited fame as great humanitarians. If we on earth weren't so silly about the whole concept of aliens and likely either to imprison them or permanently banish them, they could teach us infinitely more than our hysteria allows.

To help you visualize the actual location of the sacred Nouveau, picture the ancient image of "the Great Man" in the night sky. His head is the constellation Aries, His feet are the constellation Pisces, and the rest of His body is outlined by the other ten constellations that make up the Zodiac.

Now, with that starry portrait of "the Great Man" in mind, find where His heart would be, and you've found Nouveau.

Numerology

Numerology is another tool for divination in which the birth date and the full birth name of a person are used to unlock the secrets of that person's past, present and future.

Numerology employs 11 numbers—1 through 9, 11 and 22. Letters of the alphabet are each assigned a number from 1 through 9, and any number that exceeds 9 or the two master numbers of 11 and 22 are found by simply adding their digits until the sum becomes one of the numerological numbers. (The number 1255, for example, would be reduced to $1 + 2 + 5 + 5$, or 13, which would again be reduced to $1 + 3$, resulting in the numerologically applicable number 4.)

Each number, in turn, has its own list of meanings and attributes:

0—empty but whole, like an oyster hiding a pearl; potentially very creative but can also be very scattered and disorganized

1—powerful, original, a leader, good at innovating, but can also be stubborn and resentful of authority

2—sympathetic, helpful, appreciates routine, an excellent confidant, but can be insecure and unambitious

3—most comfortable as the center of attention, usually more sensitive than initially perceived to be, but can be vain and superficial

4—practical, steady, honest, a great money manager, but can be overly cautious and quick to lose their temper

5—resourceful, an optimist, funny, makes friends easily, loves anything new, but can be opportunistic and irresponsible

6—the ultimate diplomat and peacemaker, loves beautiful things, but can be a chronic worrier

7—introspective, philosophical, a mystical outlook on life, but can be isolated and secretive

8—ambitious, materialistic, focused on power and success more than family and relationships, can be self-centered and thoughtless

9—humanitarian, generous, compassionate, an idealist, but can be egocentric and overly sensitive

10—powerful, dominating, inspiring, but can be rigid and unreceptive to others' ideas

11—the "2" vibration, amplified, i.e., all those qualities multiplied

12—the "3" vibration, amplified, i.e., all those qualities multiplied

22—the "4" vibration, amplified, i.e., all those qualities multiplied

Using those attributes for each number, numerology then applies them to the specifics of your information.

Very basically, the number your birth date reduces to is an indication of your life path, the qualities at your core that need to be put to their best use in order for you to to make the most of your time here.

The number your full given name reduces to tells you what your destiny is in this life, your true purpose for being here.

The number the vowels in your full given name reduce to is the key to the deepest desires and priorities of your soul, the wisest part of your essence that must be acknowledged in order for you to be fulfilled.

The number the consonants in your full given name reduce to illuminates how the outside world perceives you, your personality, the first impression you make on others and how others might try to influence you.

I've met some gifted numerologists. And every single one of them was wise enough and gifted enough to use numerology not as a literal series of results etched in stone because the numbers say so, but as a complement to their own psychic skills.

Omens

Omens are signs we look for, or sometimes inflict on ourselves, to predict the future. A shooting star we've wished on to ensure the wish, a groundhog and its shadow to clue us in about the next six weeks of weather, a broken mirror supposedly dooming us to seven years of bad luck (or guaranteeing it, if we believe it)—all omens, and all so ingrained in us that our responses to them seem like second nature.

An earnest search for answers, reassurance and hints of our destiny in what we know is an orderly universe is as old as humankind. In fact, the Greeks and Romans so highly valued the ability to interpret omens accurately that they made it an esteemed profession and/or bestowed those they considered to have that particular gift with the title of "priest." Ancient Romans even developed it into two particular specialties:

The white buffalo is a strong
Native American omen

augurs, who predicted the future based on the flights and flight patterns of birds, and *haruspex*, who made their predictions based on signs they found in the entrails of sacrificed animals. "Augury" is still a part of our language, used as a synonym for "omen," while, not surprisingly, the popularity of "haruspex" never has caught on.

Most omens have been adapted from ancient times to the present, spread and plagiarized from one culture to another and generally adopted as either fact or "that's silly, but I'll play along with it just in case" by subgroups within cultures to the point where it's impossible to tell exactly where and when they originated. That doesn't make them any less fun or any less fascinating, though, so here are a handful that are still believed somewhere, by someone, to this very day:

* It's unlucky to meet a cat, a dog or a woman when first going out in the morning.
* You'll have a bad day if you give away water before breakfast.
* Killing a robin dooms you to a lifetime of bad luck.
* If an owl flies around a house three times, a member of that household will die soon.
* Finding the back tooth of a horse by chance guarantees money.
* It's guaranteed bad luck to throw your hat on a bed.
* It's very unlucky to carry red and white flowers onto an airplane.
* An itchy elbow means you'll soon be changing bed partners.
* To bring a fisherman good luck, throw a hot coal into the water in the wake of his boat.
* Seeing a cloud shaped like an oblong box means you'll soon be running across a dead body.
* It's bad luck to mention fire at a banquet. If it should happen inadvertently, the only antidote is to pour water on the table.
* There's irreversible doom ahead if a snake falls off the roof into your yard.
* If you turn out a light while people in your house are still eating supper, there will be one less person at the table within the year.

* All sorts of bad luck will follow if you kill a cricket, not the least of which is that other crickets will destroy your clothing as an act of revenge.
* A sneezing cat means rain is on the way.
* It's bad luck to find a spider in the morning but good luck to find a spider in the evening.
* When you spill salt, you must avert otherwise inevitable bad luck by gathering the salt into your left hand and flinging it over your right shoulder into a fire.
* It will always bring good luck to have Christmas breakfast by candlelight.

Option Lines

There is no one on earth whose life is perfect. I don't care how many advantages they seem to have or how tempted we might be to envy them. You know this from your own experience—no matter how beautifully things seem to be going or how on top of your game you feel at any given time, there's one recurring area of your life you just can't master, despite your best efforts.

That one recurring area isn't random, it's not an accident and it's not just one of those things. It's deliberate, and you picked it as part of the chart you wrote on the Other Side to map out the lifetime you're living now. That one recurring area you can't seem to master is called an Option Line, and count on it, we've all got one. If we appropriately think of incarnations on earth as tough trips away from Home at boarding school, our Option Lines are those courses we know we have to take, and we know we have to pass one way or another; but we also know it will take every ounce of effort we've got because it's not going to come easily.

There are seven Option Lines to choose from. You'll probably have no trouble recognizing yours:

* Health
* Spirituality
* Love
* Social Life
* Finance
* Career
* Family

Notice that this list could also be called "Seven Essential Elements of a Well-Balanced Life." So when one of them is in constant turmoil, you can try to conquer it, you can try to avoid it, you can try lying to yourself by saying everything's fine or it doesn't matter. But in the end, because it really is essential and because it's the Option Line you chose, it never stops affecting you.

I've never made it a secret that my Option Line is Family. That's not to imply that there haven't been bumps along the way in the other six areas on the list, but I seem to have the tools to keep up the ongoing repairs they require. When it comes to family issues, I honestly feel as if the harder I try to solve them, the more I look like Lucy Ricardo in the candy factory, earnest but completely inept. You'd think I'd never read a book on charts and Option Lines, let alone written one, or almost thirty of them.

I chose Family as my Option Line. I then chose a wonderful father, an abusive mother, two sons, one of whom has a father he would happily trade for almost anyone else, and three husbands who almost make me wish I had a drinking or drug problem so that at least I'd have a lame excuse for marrying them instead of none at all. And around those various scenarios I was hoping to build a white picket fence and have bluebirds swooping down to trim the piecrust cooling on my windowsill?

All of which is to say, when we write our charts, we choose our Option Line before we start filling in the details of our upcoming lifetime. So it makes all the sense in the world that we design our Option Line and our chart to be compatible with each other. That doesn't necessarily make the ongoing struggle with the specifics of our Option Line easier. Take it from me. What being aware of it can do, though, is keep us from feeling ambushed every time yet another obstacle comes up in that same seemingly impossible area of life.

Most of all, whichever Option Line you've identified as yours, keep reminding yourself that it's not something that's been inflicted on you, it's not some burden God has cursed you with; it's a choice you made before you came here. There's some challenge in it, some valuable growth for your spirit, that you may never conquer or understand this time around, but I promise it will make all the sense in the world the minute you're Home again.

Orientation

Orientation is an essential part of our transition from life on earth to our busy, joyful lives on the Other Side. It takes place in one of the countless satellite rooms in the Hall of Wisdom, immediately after we've studied our most recent incarnation through the Scanning Machine. During Orientation we're debriefed on the lifetime we've just lived and reviewed, with the help of our Spirit Guide, a team of trained Orientators and any other spirits whose input can give us perspective.

For example, maybe there's someone you deeply hurt during your life, and watching your own cruelty through the Scanning Machine has left you devastated. The Orientators and your Spirit Guide, with your chart for that lifetime in front of them, can help you see if your actions might have resulted in some long-range unimagined progress in your soul's journey, or in the journey of the person you hurt. You can even summon that person to join the discussion if they're on the Other Side as well, or summon their Spirit Guide if they're not, to get a complete overview of the impact and inevitable ripple effect of your behavior—none of which we can begin to fathom in our rushed, short-sighted lives on earth, let's face it.

One way or another, this first phase of Orientation is devoted to a deep, honest understanding of the most troublesome parts of your life. It lends infinite value to the life you've just lived, and you leave eager to make amends, to forgive yourself and move on with greater love and compassion, or to start preparing for another incarnation to take care of business you've decided is unfinished.

Another function of Orientation is to ease the transition to the Other Side for those spirits who were unprepared for the trip and are too confused or annoyed to be at peace when they first arrive. Not everyone is exhilarated about going Home, and the Orientators are impeccably trained to help. After the unprepared spirits experience the Scanning Machine and the debriefing afterward, they're given the kindest, most insightful counseling by their Orientators to quiet their turmoil and resentment. They're then given as much time as they need to do activities that brought them comfort on earth—fishing, reading, hiking, golf, computer games (and let's face it, there are those who wouldn't consider it heaven if there weren't computer games), whatever will allow them to decompress at their own pace and renew their spirit's awareness that our *real* lives are those we live on the Other Side.

The Other Side

The Other Side is where our spirits come from when we enter the womb, and it's where our spirits go when we die. It's a very real place, more beautiful than our earthly minds can imagine, but our spirit minds remember it and are Homesick for it from the moment we leave until the moment we get back.

Rather than being "far, far away" or "beyond the moon and the stars" or any of those other lovely but vague descriptions, the Other

Side is right here among us, another dimension superimposed on ours, just three feet above our version of ground level. Its vibrational frequency is simply much higher than ours, which is why we don't perceive it. Its topography is a perfect mirror image of ours, with one exception—because there's no erosion or pollution on the Other Side, its landscape is an image of the earth from thousands of years ago, when bodies of water were pure blue and mountains and coastlines were perfectly intact. On the Other Side, Atlantis and Lemuria, the earth's lost continents, thrive. So do the world's great architectural and artistic masterpieces, even if they're now crumbling or have long since been destroyed on our struggling planet.

We on earth are constrained by the laws of time, space and physics. The residents of the Other Side happily function without those laws and instead enjoy such universal laws as infinity and eternity. Our lifetimes here are the blink of an eye in the context of the Other Side. As for living without physical laws, the approximately six billion spirits at Home have no word for "crowded" in their vocabulary—hundreds of them could easily fit into an SUV if they weren't so adept at astral travel that they have no use for cars.

All spirits on the Other Side are thirty years old, no matter what age they were when they died. They can assume their earthly appearance when they come to visit us, to make sure we recognize them; but going about their business on the Other Side, they can also choose their own physical attributes, from height to weight to hair color, and change any or all of those attributes whenever they like.

The spirits on the Other Side are constantly active, studying, working, researching, enjoying parties and concerts and dancing and sporting events, even working on cures for earthly diseases to transmit to our doctors and scientists telepathically so they can "discover" them.

Telepathy is actually the most popular form of communication in the spirit world, but all languages are fluently spoken and understood.

The universal language on the Other Side is the eloquent Aramaic, originally from ancient Syria, a dialect of which was spoken by Christ and His disciples.

Every spirit on the Other Side has access to all knowledge, including everything from the life charts of everyone who was ever incarnated to the sacred Akashic Records, which are the written depiction of God's memory.

To complete the perfection of the Other Side, there is no negativity there, no aggression, no ego or jealousy or pride, and no judgment. God didn't create those emotions. We did. And yet, incredibly, it's those exact human-made emotions that inspire our seemingly inane choice to leave our Home on the Other Side from time to time and slog through another round of what we hilariously call "life."

There are those who believe we reincarnate because each incarnation brings us closer to God. I couldn't disagree more. God created us. We're part of Him, just as He is part of us. It's impossible to get any closer than that. We take brief trips away from the glory of the Other Side for the growth and education of our souls. We do that at our own insistence, because it's our journey and our joy. God, on the other hand, appreciates every breath we take, particularly in His name, but He adores us exactly the way we are.

Ouija Board

Ouija boards were created and became popular in the late 1800s. As most of you probably know, they consist of a board with the letters of the alphabet, numbers, the words "yes," "no" and "good-bye" and usually some mystical-looking symbols. A planchette, or felt-footed triangular piece of plastic with a pointer, moves around the board when hands are placed lightly upon it, theoretically spelling out words and messages from the spirit world.

There's been an endless amount of debate about whether or not the movement of the planchette is attributable to the spirit world or simply to the person or persons whose hands are resting on it.

I don't think it's an either/or debate. I'm sure there are plenty of cases in which both have happened and will always happen as long as Ouija boards are around.

Here's my position on Ouija boards in general: I would consider it a personal favor if you would take yours, if you happen to own one, and throw it straight into the Dumpster where it belongs. The reason is very simple. On those occasions when the board is being used by an opportunistic spirit to convey messages, there is absolutely no control over the identity and intentions of that spirit. If it's a dark entity, for example, or a manipulative and terribly confused ghost, sitting and listening to it or, even worse, following orders from it is a preposterous, potentially harmful way to spend your time and energy.

The image to use next time you take out your Ouija board, even if it's just for the fun of it, is to picture your doorbell ringing and your throwing open the door without taking the slightest precaution to find out who's there, a friendly neighbor with a pot of coffee or a band of armed robbers. If you see nothing wrong with doing that, then by all means, enjoy your Ouija board. If the thought horrifies you, *throw your Ouija board away*.

Oversoul

The oversoul is simply that essence that is part of us, but beyond us. It's not a physical element of the body; but the "we" that our bodies are a component of could literally not exist without it. It is the divine spark that genetically links us to God.

Eastern religions, particularly Hinduism, refer to this divine spark as "atman," which simply means "the self." Whether we call it the oversoul or atman, it doesn't concern itself with ego or earthly status or anything to do with our self relative to the rest of humankind. It's an essence, intangible but real, that is self-relative to God, identical in every one of us on earth. Just as our parents' DNA is an undeniable presence in us even though we can't experience it with any of our five senses, our Creator's DNA is every bit as much of a presence, emanating from within us and around us, a sacred, inherited Life Force we don't need to search for or earn. It's already there. It already *is*.

Your oversoul is your hallowed birthright. In those dark nights when you feel separate from it, don't pray to your Father to help you find it, because it's never been lost. Simply pray to Him to help you remember what it's like to experience it, and then thank Him when, before long, at some moment when your mind is still enough to notice, you feel that spark again in the depth of your spirit.

P

Palmistry

Palmistry is the interpretation of a person's past, present and future through the study of the lines, mounts, skin patterns and other natural markings of the hands. Your dominant hand—the hand you write with—is thought to reveal your life's path, while the other hand is thought to indicate your ultimate destiny.

The mounts, or raised mountains of flesh like those at the base of the fingers and the thumb, are each named after a celestial body—the Sun, the Moon, Jupiter, Saturn, Mercury, Upper Mars, Lower Mars, and Venus. Each mount signifies a specific list of attributes, with the size of the mount indicating how much or how little of that attribute the person possesses. The Sun, for example, which is the mount below the ring finger, indicates creative talent; Venus, the mount at the base of the thumb, indicates love relationships; the Moon, the lowest mount on the hand beneath the little finger, indicates imagination; and so on.

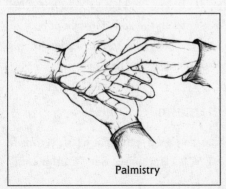

Palmistry

Each finger also has its own designated name and list of indicated attributes, with the fingers' lengths and shapes hinting at the quantity and quality of those attributes the person possesses. The index finger, or Jupiter finger, represents qualities associated with leadership. The second, or Saturn, finger holds keys to the person's destiny. The ring finger, called the Apollo finger, represents health and metaphysical consciousness. The little finger, aka the Mercury finger, deals in general with communication. The thumb is Venus and hints at mental and emotional flexibility. Each of the three divisions of every finger has its own meaning, and even the spaces between the fingers are given significance.

The lines on the hand are also meaningful. The Life Line is that line that surrounds the Venus mount at the base of the thumb, ending at the wrist. There's significance not just in its length but also in the other lines it's connected to. If it doesn't intersect with the Head Line, for example, which runs horizontally across the palm, the person is probably an independent thinker. The Fate Line runs from the Saturn finger down to the wrist and indicates careers and goals. The Heart Line is the top horizontal line across the palm and suggests the balance between the mind and the emotions, the importance of love relationships in the person's life, the active or passive role one takes in a relationship, etc.

My feeling about palmistry is the same as my feeling about the use of other physical tools for the purpose of readings: If it's helpful to the reader and used in conjunction with other God-given psychic skills, great. But if it's taken too literally, without the added insight of psychic input, it has no more value (except financially, to the reader) than a cleverly disguised scripted reading on a psychic hotline.

Phantasm

Simply another word for a visible (to some) spirit that hasn't yet made it to the Other Side. That's all it is, I promise. See "Earthbound," "Ghost" and/or "Poltergeist."

Phenomenon

Since *Phenomenon* is the title of this book, it certainly deserves a brief section of its own.

According to the dictionary, the word "phenomenon" (plural: phenomena) means "an observable event, particularly one that's remarkable or in some way extraordinary." Philosopher Immanuel Kant thought of phenomena as our compilation of the world as we experience it, as opposed to the world as it would exist without the benefit of our experience of it. Consistent with that approach is a quote from Niels Bohr that goes, "No phenomenon is a phenomenon until it is an observed phenomenon."

This book, for the most part, deals with an actual category of phenomena called "anomalous phenomena." Those are defined as phenomena "for which there are no suitable explanations in the context of a specific body of scientific knowledge." A euphemism for "yeah, right" at first glance, although God bless a whole lot of open-minded researchers in all fields of study who are beginning to think maybe a lot of the topics in this book aren't so anomalous after all.

There are basically three kinds of anomalous phenomena:

1) Mental—including clairvoyance, infused knowledge, telepathy, etc.
2) Physical—including psychokinesis, apportation, doppelgängers, etc.
3) Astral—including astral projection and travel, near-death experiences, etc.

All are observable events just scratching the surface of what's covered in this book, and all probably inspiring, consciously or unconsciously, a quote from J. B. S. Haldane that accurately observes:

> "The universe is not only queerer than we imagine;
> it is queerer than we *can* imagine."

Phrenology

Phrenology is (or, probably more accurately, *was*) a form of divination in which various shapes, bumps, indentations and other characteristics of the head were interpreted for the purpose of discovering a person's intellectual and emotional skills, or lack of them.

It was invented/devised by a German physician named Franz Joseph Gall in the late 1700s. Gall believed that since the brain is the organ in which the mind is contained, and the mind contains a whole array of distinct abilities, then each of those abilities must have its own distinct "organ" within the brain. The size of each "organ" indicates the strength of the abilities within it, and the shape of the brain is the result of the varying sizes of these distinct "organs" as they develop. As the skull forms around the brain, it reflects these various-sized "organs" and becomes a tangible indicator of abilities, tendencies and weaknesses when interpreted by a trained, qualified phrenologist.

Let's say, for example, that at the bottom right of your skull, behind your right ear, you had a slight indentation. That location happens to correspond to an "organ" phrenology refers to as Amativeness, which means "amorousness," in the sexual sense. A phrenologist, noticing your indentation in that area, would be likely to interpret it as an indication of indifference toward sex, or at the very least a lack of affection. A pronounced protrusion in that same area might lead to the conclusion that you're promiscuous. Obviously there's more than a little subjectivity involved in judging the size of an indentation or bump, and what's slight or what's pronounced, but those judgments were part of what separated the experts from the amateurs in the science of phrenology.

The popularity of phrenology spread like wildfire throughout Europe and Great Britain and on to America around the 1830s, proclaimed "the only true science of the mind" at a time when so little was known about the mind and the brain that there was a certain "it's better than nothing" enthusiasm toward what phrenology might have to offer.

The Fowlers—two brothers, a sister and her husband—were probably the most influential and financially successful American experts on phrenology. They'd begun a lucrative reading practice in New York in the 1830s. By the 1880s they'd developed their angle on this particular science into an industry of lecture circuits, societies, a publishing company and the manufacture of their own interpretation of the phrenologically divided skull, with its thirty-five or forty (the number seemed to vary) separate "organs" intricately mapped and labeled.

Phrenology techniques were a matter of preference and fee size. Some phrenologists exclusively used the palms of their hands to examine their clients' crania. Others insisted that accuracy could be achieved only with the fingertips. Still others put on flashy displays of using both the palms and the fingertips, depending on which part of the head they were reading. For added flair, precision and profit, a measuring device, especially the very scientific-looking caliper, might be brandished.

While there are still a few practitioners of phrenology, its popularity had pretty much come and gone by the time the twentieth century rolled around. Part of the reason for that was its unreliability, despite avid phrenologists' attempts to explain away inaccuracies. If someone was known to be a miserable, humorless human being, but a phrenology reading revealed that they had a very pronounced Mirth organ, the typical explanation would be that the brain's other organs were somehow interfering with the Mirth organ—*never* that there might be some flaw in the basic theory of phrenology, or a misinterpretation by the phrenologist.

Another more significant reason phrenology lost the majority of its steam, though, was the simple, inevitable fact of biological and scientific progress, which led to the simple, inevitable fact that our skulls are not perfect, bone-sculpted replicas of the surface of our brains. A bump or indentation on the head isn't necessarily reflected in the brain, and vice versa, and that reality in itself flew in the face of many basic theories on which phrenology was based.

To be fair, phrenology did turn out to be right about the fact that specific parts of the brain are dedicated to specific mental and physical functions. So to you phrenology fans out there, please don't go away claiming I didn't find a single good thing to say about it.

Points of Entry

One of many touching things I've discovered about the spirit mind in my decades of doing regressive hypnosis is its eagerness to release its pain. It will go wherever it needs to go, with me or without me, no matter how long it takes, to expose any embedded thorns that have been causing discomfort for too long. And once those thorns are revealed, where the sunlight and air of the conscious mind can reach them, the healing is almost instantaneous.

I'll call the client "Mr. A." He was from New Orleans, and he'd flown all this way for help with what he described as a "sheer terror" of being alone. He'd structured his life in such a way that it rarely happened, but when it did, when he was by himself for more than just a brief time, he'd be overwhelmed by a feeling of having done something horribly wrong, that was beyond his ability to atone for it.

I don't lead my clients during regressive hypnosis. They lead me, with only the most occasional objective questions from me. So within minutes of his arrival in my office, Mr. A. was in Egypt, living a happy, successful life as a member of the Royal Guard and a father of ten children. As sometimes happens with clients recalling their fondest incarnations, he went into exhaustive detail, and it took a while to get to the fact that he died in that life from a sudden heart attack well into his sixties.

He'd been so long-winded about his incarnation in Egypt I couldn't imagine what I was in for when he got from that heart attack to the Other Side. He'd told me the names of all ten of his Egyptian children. I prayed I wasn't about to hear the names of every loved one who was there to welcome him Home.

He mentioned the tunnel, and the light, and then he paused. I took a deep breath and asked, "Where are you now?"

His voice grew very quiet. "In a green field. Beautiful. With mountains all around. And animals."

Far be it from me to tell him the meadow on the Other Side is the first thing everyone sees—that was for him to figure out at his own pace. Instead I simply asked, "How do you feel?" prepared for the usual variations on ecstatic, euphoric, joyful, peaceful. What I wasn't prepared for was what he actually said.

"Desolate."

I quickly regrouped as best I could, but he definitely threw me. "Where are you?"

"Peru," he said.

So much for a long-winded tour of Home. He'd already leapt to another life. "What are you doing in Peru?"

At which he began sobbing. I kept repeating, "Go to the observant position. What you're feeling isn't happening now. It's in another life. We'll get rid of it so it can't hurt you again. Observe it. Just watch it and tell me what you see."

My Spirit Guide Francine never interferes with my readings or hypnosis sessions, but she stopped by just long enough to cue what came out of my mouth next. I didn't know what it meant, but if it would help calm him down I didn't care. Quoting her, I said, "Go to your point of entry."

It was as if I'd hit a fast-forward button. He became focused and objective, and the words almost spilled out of him.

"My wife and son were killed. It was my fault. My mistress killed them, to punish me for refusing to leave them. I was responsible for the death of my family as far as I was concerned, and I'd forfeited my right to another moment of happiness. So I disappeared to the mountains where no one knew me and tended sheep in exchange for a place to sleep, and I died of exposure there. I never did ask God to forgive me. I couldn't imagine why He'd even want to hear the sound of my voice."

No wonder the poor man associated solitude with punishment, and what an awful burden for him to carry without knowing where it came from. As you can read in the "Cell Memory" section, it's because of unresolved wounds from past lives, connected to our bodies through cell memory, that we react to those wounds as if they've just now been inflicted.

Hands down, though, the eye-opener of the day for me was this point-of-entry business. Francine told me later that the point of entry is simply the moment at which the event or events happened that created the painful cell memory to begin with. I couldn't believe it. A way for clients struggling with a specific issue to jump to its cause, without spending half our session or more wading through past lives that aren't relevant to the problem at hand, sounded too good to be true.

I had just one hesitation, and I shared it with Francine. "What are the odds of my clients even knowing what 'point of entry' means when they hear it? I didn't."

She simply replied, "You didn't need to. It's for them."

That was almost twenty years ago. And I will swear to this: Without exception, every regressive hypnosis client since, when I've asked them to tell me their point of entry, has known exactly what I was talking about and skipped to the relevant lifetime and the relevant event in the blink of an eye. Out of curiosity I tried asking a few "awake" clients to tell me about their point of entry, and without exception they all said, "What's that?"

Just more of that insider spirit vocabulary, I guess, that will all come rushing back to us as soon as we get back Home.

Poltergeists

"Poltergeist" is a German word that literally translates to "noisy spirit." Poltergeists, in other words, are the mischievous and intrusive residents of the ghost world. All poltergeists are ghosts, but not all ghosts are poltergeists, which simply means that not all ghosts are as intent on being disruptive as poltergeists invariably are.

As you'll read in the section on ghosts, it's almost surprising that all ghosts *aren't* poltergeists, considering how confused and disoriented they invariably are. And the reason for that is, because ghosts haven't experienced the tunnel and the light that provides their transition to the Other Side, they have no idea they're dead. As far as they're concerned, nothing particularly noteworthy happened, and yet one day, for no apparent reason, everyone around them, family, friends and strangers alike, literally began treating them as if they no longer existed. If that's not enough to confuse and disorient someone, I don't know what is.

Some ghosts take this confusion passively, getting their bearings as they go along and almost hoping not to be noticed so they won't be disrupted any more than they already have been. Others are eager to be noticed, wanting to make friends, wanting help, wanting to just be acknowledged, which might manifest itself as playfulness but not intentional aggression. A small minority, though—the poltergeists of the group—are so disturbed, resentful or territorial of a space they still fervently believe is theirs that they'll be as noisy, ornery and obnoxious as they feel they need to be to drive intruders away or just scare them for the sheer sport of it.

A letter from a client described a poltergeist experience far better than I ever could.

"I was stuck for a night at Miami International Airport, waiting for a connecting flight to South America. It was deserted, around two thirty or three o'clock in the morning, and all the seats around me were empty. I was so immersed in the book I was reading that at first I didn't notice the man who suddenly appeared and sat down next to me. When I did notice him I was immediately annoyed and uncomfortable, wondering why he'd insisted on sitting beside me when there were hundreds of vacant seats in plain sight. Then he asked me a question. I don't remember what it was, but I do remember that it was personal, and I stood up to walk away and said, very sharply, as I pointedly turned my back to him, 'Leave me alone.'

"His reply was, 'You know, I am the devil,' and he let out a loud laugh that gave me a chill right up my spine. After I'd walked about twenty steps from him I glanced over my shoulder to make sure he wasn't following me, and he was gone. I looked everywhere, but he was gone. Vanished. That gave me even more of a chill—even running at superhuman speed, there was no place for him to hide or disappear to in those empty, echoing, endless hallways." —John

As it happens, that particular poltergeist was the ghost of a man who, in the late 1950s, had been convicted of a horrific child murder and was being transported by federal agents to Rikers Island when he and one of the agents were killed in a traffic collision less than a mile from the Miami Airport. If the murderer was simply a ghost, trapped at that airport, maybe too ashamed or too thoroughly evil and cowardly to take his chances on what eternity might mean for him, he had an endless expanse to hide in, staying out of the way, or at most just walking by to see if my client happened to notice him.

It virtually defines a poltergeist that, instead, he saw my client sitting alone and vulnerable in the middle of the night and, for nothing but the sheer, mean sport of it, couldn't resist terrorizing him. As I said before, all poltergeists are ghosts, but all ghosts are most decidedly *not* poltergeists.

Possession

Possession, in its paranormal definition, is when a spirit invades and completely overtakes a body without consent and to the total submission of the spirit who's already inhabiting that body. In its most commonly reported/publicized form, the invading spirit is satanic or some other per-sonification of evil and has to be driven from the body through an often violent series of exorcisms by an ordained member of the clergy.

Now, to get something straight right up front that I'm absolutely passionate about: I believe possession is a physical, psychic and spiri-tual *impossibility*, and I encourage you never to waste one minute of your time being afraid it might happen to you or someone you love. It's inarguable that exorcisms have been used over countless millennia as an excuse for horrible abuse, as a substitute for desperately needed psychiatric and medical help, as punishment or just an effective threat for disobedient members of various religious faiths, and as a lucrative scam of the lowest order aimed at the most earnestly God-fearing by those whose only interest in God is in using His name to gain unde-served trust. I promise you from the bottom of my heart, no spirit can enter your body without your full awareness and permission. That's called "channeling," and you can read about that in its own section.

That having been said, there are times when what I believe has to take a backseat to what a client believes if I'm going to give them the help they come to me for. An example from early in my career was a woman who was referred to me by a clinical psychologist friend who was getting nowhere with her. She was terrified of snakes, he told me. That could have been dealt with if it hadn't been for an added compli-cation: She was completely convinced that there was a huge snake wrapped around her waist. I would love to tell you that I devised a wise, cunning game plan while I waited for her to arrive, but the truth is, I was a nervous wreck without a clue how I was going to handle this until she stepped through the door. Then, on pure impulse, I leapt to my feet and yelled, "Oh, my God, you've got a snake around your waist!" With which I sprang to her side, grabbed the imaginary snake, wrestled it all over my office and beat its imaginary head to death against the wall. She left an hour later snakeless, calm and relieved.

The same approach of working as best I can within my client's reality applies even when their reality includes a subject I feel as strongly about as I feel about possession. A few months ago a beautiful, soft-spoken, deeply upset Jamaican gentleman came to see me. He was almost too frightened and ashamed to tell me what the problem was: His right hand, he finally confessed, had been possessed by the devil for many months. The anxiety of this terrible secret was beginning to affect everything in his life, from his generally level-minded, quiet demeanor to his ability to concentrate to his orderly schedule, to the extent that he was afraid of losing his job and his family.

I did test the waters on my chances of convincing him that something else was going on. But his religious and cultural beliefs in exorcism and the devil were generations old, absolute and nonnegotiable, and the last thing this proud, intelligent man needed was for me to disrespect his truth.

And so, thanking God one more time for my years of study of world religions and my upbringing in Catholic schools, I took his right hand in both my hands and performed an exorcism that would have made the pope himself proud: "Most glorious Prince of Heaven, Saint Michael the Archangel, defend us against the rulers of this world of darkness, against the spirits of wickedness. God of Peace, crush Satan beneath our feet, bind him and cast him into the bottomless pit . . ." I was amazed at how much I'd retained from catechism classes, but I knew I was on exactly the right track when I said, "From the snares of the devil," and this dear man, his voice trembling with emotion, replied from his memories of the very same Catholic texts, "Deliver us, O Lord."

In less than half an hour his body suddenly slumped, not as if he'd gone unconscious but as if for the first time in far too long all the tension had left him and he was allowing himself to be totally relaxed. I was silent for several minutes, not wanting to interrupt his peacefulness. When he finally looked up at me there were tears in his eyes, but he was smiling from ear to ear.

"The devil is gone," he said. "He escaped like a coward through my left hand."

He'd come believing he was possessed; therefore he was. He left believing the devil had been banished from his right hand; therefore it had. All the rhetoric and dogma in the world can't beat that result.

As for what was really going on, it was actually far more fascinating than a possession if he'd been open to hearing it. The right brain controls the emotions, and the left brain controls the intellect. In his case, a new love relationship was making him behave in ways that made him feel foolish and illogical (a show of hands, please, of everyone who knows what that's like) and preoccupying his mind to the point where he couldn't focus as easily on his work and other responsibilities (another show of hands, please). Because of his religious and cultural upbringing, the unfamiliar discomfort of his emotions overriding his intellect was most easily explained as "the devil has possessed my right hand," and later, with satisfaction, "he escaped through my left hand." He walked out of my office actually feeling as if his intellect were in charge again, as he's accustomed to. Which will last only until she starts playing games with him, and she will, but that's another story for some other book. In the meantime, I can't resist closing by wondering out loud if, considering what this woman has in mind for this uniquely naive man, he might be better off if there *were* such a thing as possession.

Psychic Attacks

See if these words, or some version of them, sound familiar: "I'm kidding myself thinking I'm accomplishing anything in my life. No matter how hard I try, I'm not making any difference in this world at all. Nothing I've ever done really amounts to anything, and it never will. What's the point of even getting out of bed in the morning when the truth is, no one cares whether I do or not?"

If so, chances are you've experienced a psychic attack. Rather than assaulting the body, psychic attacks target our minds, our self-confidence, our hope, our sense of power and even our faith in God's unconditional love for us. They diminish us, they separate us from our joy and humor and enthusiasm, and they drain us of enough energy even to try to pull ourselves out of it. Rarely if ever do we see a psychic attack coming, and rarely if ever can we trace what brought it on, which makes us feel even more helpless and out of control. Without recognizing what caused it, we can't begin to imagine what we can do to stop it.

To understand psychic attacks, you need to read the definition of the Dark Side, that group of spirits and humans among us who embrace and perpetuate negativity, chaos and evil. The goal of the Dark Side is simple: to extinguish light, which, let's face it, is the only way darkness can exist. And in the eyes of the Dark Side, we white entities, a reference having nothing to do with race but simply meaning those of us who love God and are repelled by negativity, are the lights to be extinguished. They know better than to try to convert us to their side, since that can't be done. So instead, they try to destroy us—not physically, necessarily, but by making us so emotionally impotent that we lose the power, the self-confidence, the optimism and the focus to beat them. In other words, the dark entities of the Dark Side attack us *psychically*, thus the term "psychic attack."

Many years ago I went through what I knew only to call a "spiritual desert" at the time, an almost paralyzing period of doubt in myself, my worthiness and the meaningful use of my faith in God. Nothing in particular had brought it on, and I'd gone to great lengths to keep it to myself. But I was facing a speaking commitment at my church, Novus Spiritus, and since the large congregation knew me very well, I knew I couldn't fool them for long into thinking I was my usual strong, confident, spiritually passionate self. I thought of canceling rather than exposing myself as the failure I felt like. But finally I decided I owed them the same honesty I'd promised them from the day I founded my church. So I stepped up to the lectern, took a deep breath, looked out at the eager faces of those people I loved and knew I was about to disappoint, and confessed every weak, hollow, empty moment of self-doubt I'd been going through.

But instead of looking disappointed, every person in that congregation sat there nodding and even smiling a little with recognition. As we
talked afterward I learned that not only had they all experienced those
same feelings; they'd heard those same words playing in their heads
that had been plaguing me: "I'm kidding myself thinking I'm accomplishing anything in my life. . . ."

Starting first thing the next morning, and feeling better already, I
started taking an informal poll among my clients throughout the world
during readings. I was shocked to hear that every one of them, at some
time or other, had been victimized by the same kind of psychic attack,
and that during it, no matter what country or culture or circumstance
they were living in, those same words of futility kept nagging them
too, like a tape recording permanently set to replay.

The more people I talked to about psychic attacks, the more I realized that we all have a copy of the very same tape of self-doubt cued
up to start droning at our first sign of vulnerability. I fully believe it's
the Dark Side, those negative forces around us, simply catching us off
guard and using our inevitable moments of weakness to try to diminish us. I'm also sure it's no coincidence that psychic attacks are especially common among people who are about to begin a spiritual
journey of some kind. After all, few things are more threatening to
dark entities than the growth of spirituality and the unstoppable ex-
pansion of the brilliant light and love of God.

I would never claim to be able to rid you of psychic attacks forever,
any more than I would claim that I'm not still occasionally plagued
with them myself. But I can promise it will lessen their frequency if
we take avoiding negativity as seriously as we take our efforts to avoid
the common cold—believe me, in the long run, colds don't do a fraction of the harm that negativity does.

I've also found a way to help remind myself during a psychic attack
that those ugly, discouraging insults in my mind aren't the truth at all;
they're just a tape, planted by the Dark Side to try to bring me down. I
simply reach up to that spot between and slightly above my eyes

where my third eye would be and give a little push with my forefinger, as if I'm ejecting that insidious tape from my head. While I do that I say, "I refuse this tape and all other tricks of the Dark Side, and I release its negativity from my mind to be resolved forever into the white light of the Holy Spirit."

As I say so often, I understand completely if you don't believe me. But it's harmless and takes only a couple of seconds, so try it anyway. Next time a psychic attack hits you, won't you be pleasantly surprised if I'm right?

Psychic Energy Vortex

"Psychic Energy Vortex" is a synonym for "Imprint," which you'll find discussed at length in its own section.

Psychic Forensics

Since at least as far back as the Jack the Ripper murders in 1888, and probably much farther back than that, skeptics have been debating the value of psychics in the area of criminal investigation. And while the debate rages on today, a lot of us psychics have been busily working away with law enforcement, declining pay and publicity, ready to help in any way we can. Finally, thanks to TV shows like *Psychic Detectives* and *Medium*, the investigative potential of psychics is being acknowledged and, I hope, more universally validated, so that all of law enforcement will take advantage of our special skills as some of law enforcement has been quietly doing all along.

I'm sure other investigative psychics—Dorothy Allison, Noreen Renier, Phil Jordan, Nancy Weber and too many more to name—understand as I do why there's been hesitation for the agencies who call on us to "come out of the closet" and say, "You bet I've used psychics, and I'd do it again in a heartbeat." There are phonies in our profession who waste valuable time with nothing but guesswork. There are publicity hounds. There are crisis groupies, and there are those who see every tragedy as an opportunity to enhance their bank accounts. And of course there are plenty of law enforcement officers who would come as close to consulting even the most reputable psychic as they would to solving cases with Ouija boards and Magic 8 Balls.

But as criminal investigators around the world, including Scotland Yard, the FBI and other indisputable experts already know, those of us with proven skills, proven integrity and a track record for avoiding exploitation and ambulance chasing can make significant contributions as evidence is gathered and leads are pursued. Psychics don't solve crimes. Law enforcement solves crimes. We simply bring another set of tools to what's usually a long, exhaustive, difficult process of identifying criminals and putting them behind bars. We're no different from the criminal profilers, the geographic profilers, the forensic anthropologists, sculptors and other experts who were viewed with initial skepticism until they proved their worth, as any participant in an investigation should be expected to do.

The word "forensics" is a reference to the use of science, technology and other specialized techniques in investigating and confirming the validity of evidence. Psychic forensics is simply the application of our brand of specialized techniques. And while most if not all of us have a variety of skills at our disposal, we tend to have a few that are more highly developed than others. Some psychics, for example, find that their major contributions to an investigation come in the form of visions (clairvoyance) and mental signals from the criminal or the victim (telepathy). Others are brilliant at holding photos or articles of clothing and receiving valuable information from the energy contained in them (psychometry), or hearing distant words and phrases that can give clues to the location or identity of a missing child or an elusive felon (clairaudience).

One of my most useful strengths when it comes to helping law enforcement is my ability to channel, or act as a tube through which the spirit world can communicate. And let's face it, especially when it comes to murder, who's a more reliable eyewitness to the crime than the victim himself?

Years ago a friend and colleague, psychology professor Dr. Bill Yabroff, always a delightfully open-minded skeptic about the paranormal, asked if I would let him test me—or more precisely, my Spirit Guide Francine, who's able to speak through me with my permission while I step aside by means of a deep trance. I trusted Bill to be fair, objective and completely honest, no matter what the results turned out to be, so I not only agreed; I was frankly pretty curious about the results myself and welcomed the opportunity.

At my insistence, Bill didn't tell me, until I arrived in his office the night of the test, what he had in store for Francine. He had a list of names, he told me, randomly selected from hundreds in his university's psychology department files. There were twenty names on the list, all former clients, all deceased. Bill's intention was to read the list to Francine—just the names, nothing more. If Francine were really speaking to him from the Other Side as she/I claimed, she should have access to the deceased clients and be able to identify their exact cause of death. If she were a fraud, it would take about two seconds to figure out that she/I was guessing, in which case she'd fail the test and make an idiot of herself/me.

Accurately and in detail, Francine identified the cause of nineteen of the twenty deceased clients. I have no memory or awareness of what goes on when Francine's "in" and I'm "out," so I didn't know the specifics until Bill played the tape for me later that night after the test was completed. But when I say "in detail," I mean *in detail*. She didn't just say, "Died from a gunshot," for example, or even, "Died from a gunshot to the head." She said things like, "Died from a self-inflicted gunshot wound to the right temple, with an exit wound below the left ear."

The twentieth cause of death, the one Francine missed, was a drug overdose. She said there were three different drugs involved. The initial autopsy report said two. Bill called the client's family the next day and discovered that they'd requested a second autopsy, which revealed that it was actually three drugs, not two, that their loved one used to kill himself.

And by the way, just to clarify that this wasn't a mind-reading exercise for Francine, Bill had taken the added precaution of not looking up the twenty causes of death himself prior to the test, so that information wasn't available in his mind for Francine to read. Not even on his best day could Bill telepathically slip answers to Francine when he himself didn't have a clue what they were.

Many years ago I tried to set up a panel of reputable, responsible, discreet psychics to convene on a regular basis, pro bono, to tackle a variety of challenges from cold cases to missing children to all sorts of health and humanitarian crises. Without going into detail, I'll simply say it didn't work. I would love to try it again. Maybe the problems that prevented it last time around could be avoided this time. Separately we're each making a difference. Together we could move mountains.

Psychokinesis

Psychokinesis, also called telekinesis, is the ability to move or manipulate objects without applying any physical or other scientifically explainable force. It's a word with Greek origins: *psyche,* which roughly translates to "mind," and *kinein,* which means "to move." Unlike kinetic energy, which you'll find in its own section and which is completely random and involuntary, psychokinesis is deliberate, focused and specific on the part of its possessor.

Probably the most renowned and unfairly criticized demonstrations of psychokinesis in American culture were the repeated televised appearances during the 1970s of Uri Geller, an Israeli psychic who was able to bend spoons and other metal objects through the power of his mind, without ever touching them. The appearances were live, mesmerizing and, I promise you, completely authentic. But because Geller was unable to duplicate the same phenomena during strictly controlled lab experiments, many skeptics and critics were delighted to leap on the bandwagon of calling him a fraud who'd simply tricked TV audiences by substituting the metal objects involved through sleight of hand.

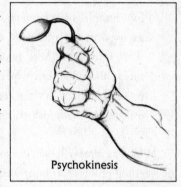

Psychokinesis

But fair is fair as far as I'm concerned—if Uri Geller's credibility was compromised by his inability to prove his psychokinetic gift in a laboratory environment, the skeptics' and critics' credibility should be called into question too, for their inability to ever prove that Uri Geller was performing any kind of fraudulent sleight-of-hand tricks.

This is not to say there haven't been literally millions of faked cases of psychokinesis. But exhaustive studies have been done, starting most notably with Dr. J. B. Rhine of Duke University in 1934 and proceeding through such other reputable researchers as physicist Helmut Schmidt; engineers and psychologists at Princeton; experts at the Chinese Academy of Sciences; physicist John Hasted at the University of London; biochemists throughout the world; and far too many more to list here. The results seem to add up to the following:

* The validity of the existence of psychokinesis can't be dismissed or disproved.
* Harnessing and productively guiding the power of psychokinesis has enormous biological and humanitarian potential. Antibodies,

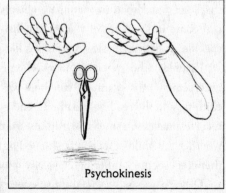

Psychokinesis

for example, have been shown to grow more rapidly in test tubes exposed to the proximity of psychokinetically energized hands than antibodies those hands never had access to. And various molds and fungi have experienced more retarded growth under a psychokinetic influence than those same molds and fungi not exposed to those influences.

Which is simply to say, no one's more in favor of skepticism, and demanding proof, than I am. But once there's a strong indication that a phenomenon exists of potentially limitless benefit to this planet and all its residents, isn't it time for the normal and the paranormal to start working together and show that as a united force there's virtually nothing on God's earth we can't accomplish?

Psychometry

As you'll read in the section on imprints, the energy that emanates from all things living on earth is powerful enough to impact and be absorbed by all nonliving things around them. On a huge, dramatic scale, an energy vortex called an imprint is formed. On a small, mundane scale, every inanimate object around us has absorbed and still contains the sum total of all living energy with which it's come in contact.

Psychometry is the ability to sense and interpret the living energy that's been absorbed by inanimate objects. Perceptions of that energy can come in the form of visions, smells, sounds, emotions and even specific empathic physical sensations like pain, heat and cold.

Psychics who specialize in psychometry when working with law enforcement, for example, can hold an article of a missing child's clothing and, by reading the child's energy contained in that clothing, receive images or smells or sounds from where the child is, sense whether the child is feeling frightened or is with someone who makes them feel secure, and/or perceive any injuries the child might have.

Other psychics and mediums, some of them very successful, find it helpful during readings to hold a possession of their client's, or of a deceased loved one the client might be hoping to contact. I don't happen to be one of those psychics, but whatever works, as long as it's legitimate and helps the client, is fine with me.

For the most part, I use psychometry the way you do—I pick up an object while shopping, let's say, and react to whatever feeling it gives me. I might see a purse that's exactly what I've been looking for, but when I pick it up and hold it there's something about it that makes me put it back and keep looking. That's psychometry. Or I'll be house-hunting or apartment-hunting and walk into a place that's gorgeous and ideal in every way, with the one exception that for some reason I can't wait to get out of there. That's psychometry. And if you really want to give your psychometric skills a good workout, spend a few hours in an antiques store, where every object is filled with decades or centuries of energy from its previous owners, their families and friends and houseguests, the happy or sad or angry or ice-cold emotional dynamics of the households themselves, and even the store's buyer and previous shoppers who've inspected it.

The vast majority of you don't need me to tell you to follow your instincts and surround yourself only with things to which you have a positive psychometric response. But every once in a while a client will walk in with a doll or a crystal bowl or a piece of artwork and say, "This has been in my house for thirty years and I've always felt as if there might be something evil about it. Should I get rid of it?" Uh . . . hello . . . ? I wouldn't let something stay in my house for thirty minutes if I felt there might be something evil about it. I don't care if I love the way it looks, I don't care how much it cost, I don't care if it's a potential museum piece, I don't care if my high-strung aunt Betty gave it to me and she'll pitch a fit if it's not on display every time she comes over, it will not be in my house.

It's important to clarify that it's the absorbed energy in objects that creates our psychometric response to them. The objects themselves aren't haunted, possessed or evil. Spirits and ghosts can manipulate inanimate objects, and they can contribute to the energy held inside them, but they can't occupy them. "Inanimate" means "not alive," and "not alive" means they're uninhabitable for anything living, from earth or from the spirit world.

So when I say I won't have anything around me that gives me a bad feeling, please don't let me mislead you into thinking I'm psychometrically detecting anything more than its energy history. And sometimes that's quite enough. Not always, but often, when I pause to focus, I do get the full imagery and impact of where an object has been. I was at a business dinner recently in the home of a woman who has an unfortunate tendency to devote far more attention to her material worth than she does to her spiritual worth. Spotlighted in her living room so that none of us could miss it was her newest acquisition, a hideous ancient twelve-inch-tall stone Portuguese gargoyle she was eager to tell us cost tens of thousands of dollars. From a distance, I found it only ugly and repellent. But when the opportunity presented itself, I quietly slipped my hand around it for maybe two seconds. It took no longer than that to know that this repulsive statuette was once part of the décor in a pagan arena where children and animals were sacrificed, and it had retained every vicious, godless moment of it too. I wasn't asked, so I kept my mouth shut. But if I had tens of thousands of dollars to spare, I'd spend it to keep that thing away from me before I'd bring it home, throw a spotlight on it and subject myself and my loved ones to that constant, horrifying little presence.

Whether you're highly skilled at psychometry or just capable, it's a very common, wonderfully useful tool that I hope you'll pay attention to. Understanding what you're feeling (energy imprints) and what you're not feeling (hauntings or possessions) in the inanimate world around you can help you discard even more of the negativity in your life, and after all, that is what we're here for.

Quadrants

As you'll read in the discussion of the Other Side, that dimension just three feet above us is a duplicate of the earth, essentially our planet's Oversoul, as Earth once existed in its geological perfection. Our seven continents exist there, along with Atlantis and Lemuria, earth's two "lost" continents.

The continents on the Other Side are each divided into four quadrants. This has nothing to do with politics and governments, since there are no laws at Home and no need for them. Instead, the quadrants are simply areas of each continent that are devoted to specific purposes corresponding to the Seven Levels of Advancement (see under its own listing), which are our chosen vocations in our lives in paradise.

One quadrant on a continent is devoted to Orientation, for example, one to all the sciences, one to the creative arts and one to research. There's complete movement among the quadrants, with no area off-limits to anyone. A sentry is posted at the entrance to each quadrant, but only to take note of the whereabouts of everyone who works there in case someone comes by to visit them or ask them to consult on a project in some other quadrant.

And for the ultimate in convenience, if you drop by to say hello to a friend in, let's say, the third quadrant of Atlantis, and the sentry tells you they've gone off to meditate in the Gardens of the Hall of Justice, you don't have a long journey ahead of you to catch up with them, no matter where they are. On the Other Side, where we're free of our bodies, and our minds are brilliant and finely tuned, we elevate our astral travel on earth to an art form—wherever we want to go, we simply think or project ourselves there, and we're there.

The quadrants, then, are divisions of the continents at Home devoted to the infinite choices available to us there, just another example of perfect order within the perfection God created for us to share with Him on the Other Side.

Quickening

"Quickening" simply means "to come to life." Or, in the bigger, more accurate picture, "to have the spirit enter and activate the earthly body." The Bible (Romans 8:11) states, for example, "If the Spirit of him who raised Jesus from the dead dwells in you, he who raised Christ Jesus from the dead will quicken your mortal bodies also through his Spirit which dwells in you."

It's an obscure word, and not one that's likely to come up often in conversation. I bring it up only to address a question I'm asked time and time and time again: When exactly during pregnancy does the spirit enter the fetus?

If you've ever seen me dodge the question, it's only because I can smell someone trying to pull me into a debate on abortion, and that happens to be one of those rare subjects, like politics, I simply won't debate.

Of course, the actual answer to the question about when the spirit enters the fetus sounds like dodging, so I don't often bother to sidestep it. Here's the answer: It varies. Helpful, huh? But it's the truth. The spirit enters the fetus when it and God decide it's ready. Which makes no sense at all if you believe our spirits kind of drop into this life from out of nowhere and nothingness. But if you believe our spirits are eternal, then you believe they always were and always will be, which means they already exist and enter the womb from wherever they've been.

Where they've been, of course, is the Other Side, preparing to undertake another incarnation, and it's a long process once they've made the decision that it's something they need to do. They spend time with their Spirit Guide and Orientation team, defining and refining the goals that are compelling them to leave Home for a while. Based on those goals, they then compose an intricately detailed life chart to ensure that one way or another those goals will be accomplished. After further refining their chart with the Council, and being blessed with the Angels the Council is sending along to watch over them, they gather with their friends and loved ones in a magnificent building called the Towers to say farewell. They're then taken to a site of their choosing on the Other Side, where they're granted two hallowed audiences—one with their Messiah, followed by a brief, awesome glimpse of the materialized presence of Azna, the Mother God, to receive their prayers and promise them a safe trip Home again. From there they return to the Towers, to one of the departure rooms, where they're covered with warm blankets, gently eased into the peace of a twilight sleep and begin the process of descent into the womb they've charted for their lifetime on earth.

There's no such thing as time on the Other Side, so it's impossible to calculate how long that entire process takes from beginning to end. But it's not something they rush, nor would we want them to, since leaving Home for this often overwhelming challenge called life is the bravest, most difficult series of decisions our spirits ever undertake.

Maybe now you'll understand that I'm honestly neither dodging nor sidestepping when I say: The spirit enters the fetus when the spirit and God decide it's ready.

And that moment when the spirit enters is the real quickening.

R

Rapport

I was eighteen years old when I suffered the first great loss in my life and understood the bottomless, numbing pain of grief. Grandma Ada died—my best friend, my inspiration, my most loyal supporter and my brilliantly psychic teacher since the day I was born. Thanks to her, I knew a whole lot about the spirit world and the Other Side and why she wasn't sad when she left this life. I wasn't grieving for her. I was grieving for me, for the unimaginable emptiness of being here without her. Yes. Even then I could clearly see and communicate with spirits. But everyone else who can see and hear them too will back me up on this—it's not the same. It's hard to hold someone you love when you're living in two different dimensions.

Two days after Grandma Ada died I was alone in my bedroom, sitting at my vanity, going through the motions of brushing my hair, when the feeling came over me that I was not alone. I checked the mirror. I turned and looked behind me. I was mistaken. No one was there. I focused on my hair again and could have sworn I felt a warm breath on the back of my neck.

Not even seconds later, two things happened almost simultaneously: There was a sudden deafening crack, as if a bolt of lightning had struck inside my bedroom just a few feet away from me, and I distinctly heard Grandma Ada's strong voice call out, "Sylvia!"

I leapt up and urgently scanned the room. Everything looked perfectly normal. But there was an intense stillness in the air, like that thick, uneasy silence after an electrical storm, and my heart was pounding.

I raced out of the room and literally ran into my father, who was rushing up the stairs almost as fast as I was flying down them. He stopped me, put his hands on my shoulders and studied me.

"Sylvia, what on earth happened? You're white as a sheet. And what was that horrible cracking noise? It sounded like the roof fell in."

Still trembling, I told him about the last minute or two of my life. He'd spent eighteen years living with a very psychic daughter and an even more psychic mother-in-law named Ada, so not much surprised him anymore.

"She told you she was going to send you a sign within three days that she made it Home safely," he reminded me as he held me. "I guess she kept her promise. But that loud crack scared the hell out of me. What was it?"

I had no clue. But you can bet I was going to move heaven and earth (pardon the expression) to find out if I had to, because I knew it was a sound, and a moment, I would never forget.

That deafening crack, I learned, is a phenomenon called a "rapport," and it's the spirit world's version of a sonic boom. Occasionally, when a spirit pierces that invisible veil between the high-frequency dimension of the Other Side and our much-lower-frequency dimension here on earth, it creates the same shock waves in the atmosphere that any other object creates when it moves faster than the speed of sound. Those shock waves cause sudden buildups and releases of atmospheric pressure, and it's in the release of that intense pressure that sonic booms and rapports are created.

The more I've researched rapports over several decades, the more aware I've become that it's not all that uncommon for them to accompany spirit visits from Home.

In my sixty-nine years of personal and professional experiences all over the world, I've probably been on the receiving end of tens of thousands of spirit visits. And yet I've been in the presence of only one rapport.

Which doesn't make me doubt for a moment that rapports happen more often than I can attest to. It just makes me cherish even more that sad, hollow morning when I was eighteen and my Grandma Ada found a way I couldn't possibly miss to keep her promise and let me know she'd made it Home safely.

The Rapture

To many Christians, the rapture is synonymous with the Second Coming of Christ. By all accounts its inspiration is 1 Thessalonians 4:16–17:

> "For the Lord himself will descend from heaven with a cry of command, with the archangel's call, and with the sound of the trumpet of God. And the dead in Christ will rise first; then we who are alive, who are left, shall be caught up together with them in the clouds to meet the Lord in the air; and so we shall always be with the Lord."

As for those who've been left behind because they lived lives too wicked to be saved, *"The Son of man will send his angels, and they will gather out of his kingdom all causes of sin and all evildoers and throw them into the furnace of fire"* (Matthew 13:41–42).

There seems to be an ongoing debate among those who believe in the impending rapture about whether it will occur before an era on earth when Christians will be persecuted, during that era of persecution or at the end of that era of persecution.

Every time I read or hear something about that particular debate I think, "That's your issue with the rapture? The timing?"

Here's my issue: I'll never understand the depiction of a God who is all-knowing, all-loving and all-forgiving, unless you displease Him, in which case He'll have you thrown into the flames of hell for all eternity. What kind of mean, vindictive, compassionless God is that? What kind of parent is that? Can you imagine raising your children like that? "I love you very much, and I always will. Now, behave, or I'll throw you into the furnace."

To the core of my soul I believe in God, a God who really is all-knowing, all-loving, all-forgiving and incapable of cruelty and vengeance, let alone the irreversible vengeance of eternal damnation. I believe the pitiless God of the rapture is an interpretation through the eyes of some church founders who, being human and having their own agendas, decided that the best way to keep their membership in line would be to turn God into a bully.

Please, by all means, believe what truly makes sense to you and what truly resonates in your spirit as the truth. Don't take my word, or the church's word or anyone else's word for anything until you've gathered enough information to make a genuinely educated decision about what *your* word is.

The perfect, loving, compassionate God I worship makes sense to me. I couldn't devote my life to Him if He didn't. I wish no less than that for you, and I'm simply urging you to insist on it rather than be bullied into being afraid of something you secretly can't make heads or tails of.

Regressive Hypnosis

I've been a certified master hypnotist since the 1970s. I know how beneficial hypnosis can be. It's a fact.

I believe we've all had past lives, on earth and on the Other Side. Or, more accurately, I know we've all had past lives. I've known that all my life, and long before. It's a fact.

Somehow, bright as I am, it had never occurred to me to take those

two facts and blend them together. It took a weight-reduction hypnosis client suddenly leaping to a previous incarnation without my having a clue what he was doing to make the lightbulb go on over my
head—duh! If our spirit minds reside in the subconscious, and hypnosis provides access to the subconscious, then of course hypnosis could
provide access to the past-life memories held in our spirit minds.

I started studying and researching like a madwoman to devise an
effective bridge for my clients to use to make their own smooth transition to an earlier lifetime without my guiding them. It was exciting,
stimulating work, but in the back of my mind I kept feeling something
was missing. Giving clients the opportunity to prove to themselves
that they've been here before, and that they've survived death over and
over again, would be great. But on a practical, day-to-day basis, what
use would it be to Client Smith to discover that in 1682 he was a ship-
builder in Norway with a wife and two children? If hypnotically re-
gressing people to their past lives would not make a real difference
in the lives they're living now, if it would be nothing more than an

Hypnosis

interesting exercise with a punch line of "so what?" I wasn't sure I wanted to waste my clients' time or mine.

After a lot of soul-searching I finally turned to my Spirit Guide Francine and essentially asked, "If there's a useful point to going ahead with this, what is it?"

"Healing." That's all she said. It was enough. I wasn't even sure how healing could be found in past-life regression, but if it were hiding in there and I could uncover it—now, *that* would be a useful point. The key word was "if." Francine never lies, but I don't take her word, or anyone's word, for anything. I'm never convinced until I've checked something out for myself, and healing through past lives was no exception.

Throughout my career I've had the luxury of close relationships with members of the medical and psychiatric communities. Several of these friends had been doing their own exploring on the subject of reincarnation, and we'd scheduled a two-day seminar about the truth or fiction of past lives. What a perfect opportunity to try this healing regression premise on a volunteer from the audience—no setup, no rehearsal, just me and a total stranger winging it in front of several hundred witnesses.

One colleague in particular tried to talk me out of it, never a likely success once I've made up my mind.

"What if it doesn't work?" was his argument.

"Then it won't work. But we'll never know if we don't try, will we?" I'd rather fall on my face any day than waste time wondering.

The auditorium was packed. I had more volunteers for this experiment than I could count, and I perversely chose the most obviously reluctant of them, a conservative-looking man in his thirties who turned out to be Neil, a mortgage broker from Texas. I briefly explained the hypnosis process, and then, before we started, I asked him if there were any physical or emotional problems he'd like us to get to the bottom of. He thought of two: a chronic pain in his right foot that his podiatrist couldn't seem to diagnose, and a fear of being a disappointment to the people he loved, no matter how hard he tried or how successful he was.

He was bright and honest, my favorite kind of subject. I relaxed him into a hypnotic state and slowly guided him back through this life, his death in a previous life and then into the heart of that life itself. He took a breath and suddenly seemed to shrink into himself. His voice became thin and barely audible. His right foot twisted and turned under and in. I asked him to tell me about himself.

His name was Calvin, he told me. He was twelve years old and lived on a farm in Virginia.

"What's today's date?" I asked.

"June 10, 1821."

"What's wrong with your right foot, Calvin?" I asked.

It had been clubbed since birth, which made him a burden to his parents, who'd counted on a healthy son to work the fields. He'd stopped going to school because everyone made fun of him, so he spent his time taking care of the farm animals, who loved him and didn't seem to think there was anything wrong with him or his foot. By the time I brought him back to the present, there wasn't a dry eye in the house.

Then, before I woke him, I found myself adding, "And whatever pain or fear or negativity you might have carried over from a past life, release it and let it be resolved in the white light of the Holy Spirit."

His posture straightened, his foot returned to normal and he offered a preoccupied "thank you" as he left the stage. He called my office several weeks later to report that the pain in his foot was completely gone, and that ever since his hypnosis he'd noticed a huge improvement in his self-confidence.

I've been asked a thousand times by clients and colleagues, "How do we know these supposed 'past lives' aren't just fantasies the mind dreams up to relieve pain?" It's a fair question, which I found myself asking too. So parenthetically, my staff and I started verifying the existence and details of as many past lives as possible as described by my clients. As this was long before computers, I've got storage units filled from floor to ceiling with proof that these "fantasies" come with some very obscure, very authentic-looking birth and death certificates.

In the long run, though, the answer I keep coming back to, and that keeps me going, when it comes to the authenticity of regressive hypnosis is, "Who cares, as long as it helps?" I'm not about to insist you believe in it. If I don't take anyone's word about what's true and what's not without needing to see for myself, how can I ask you to take my word for it? This is simply an explanation of what regressive hypnosis is, where my belief in its ability to heal came from, and why thousands of clients whose lives have been freed from long-buried burdens believe in it too.

Reincarnation

Reincarnation is nothing more and nothing less than the belief that the human spirit, because it's eternal as a promise from God, survives the death of the body and returns to recurring lifetimes in a variety of chosen circumstances and bodies—i.e., incarnates again and again—for the purpose of the growth and learning of the soul.

For much more on the subject of reincarnation, see the sections on "the Chart" and "Regressive Hypnosis."

Remote Viewing

Remote viewing is a skill that allows us to perceive and describe details about a specific item or location that we're separated from by time, distance or a physical barrier. Unlike telepathy, there's no living sender passing along information for us to translate into precise images. And unlike astral travel, we can accomplish this particular skill without having to leave our body. With practice at remote viewing, we can, for example, walk down a street in a strange city halfway around the world and accurately describe the shopwindow displays, each of the parked cars and the weather at a particular moment; tune in to a loved one's hospital room to see if they're in bed or out of bed, who's visiting them, what if any doctor or nurse is checking on them right then and what kind of flowers in what color vase someone sent since you were last there; or even view the guests, the china pattern and the seating arrangement at Teddy Roosevelt's inaugural ball.

Like any other mental skill, remote viewing means nothing if it's not accurate, which makes it a breeze to test. If I claim to be remote viewing a friend's hospital room and describe two visitors and a blue vase of white roses, and then call my friend and discover that there were no visitors and the flowers are yellow tulips in a green vase, my remote viewing was nothing but noise. But if I go into breathtaking detail about the gold-rimmed Waterford china, the seating arrangement of Mr. and Mrs. Rockefeller directly across from Mr. and Mrs. Morgan, with Mrs. Morgan in a dark blue silk gown that had a beaded bow at the waist, and historical archives confirm that information, I've accomplished successful remote viewing. That's one of the reasons researchers, including me, are so drawn to this particular skill: It's either accurate or it doesn't count. There's no gray area, no such thing as "close enough."

Which, by the way, makes a governmental experiment on remote viewing even more interesting. In the 1970s the CIA and various branches of the military began studying its potential usefulness, particularly in the areas of intelligence and defense. In 1995 they disbanded the program and published an official report dismissing remote viewing as having no value to the United States government. With the results of every remote-viewing experience being so clearly and immediately accurate or meaningless, what in the world took twenty-five years? Why continue exploring something as clear-cut as remote viewing for twenty-five years or even twenty-five days unless you're getting too many positive results to dismiss it? I don't know why the official conclusion on remote viewing was "valueless," but I can't help but wonder if maybe the government, in the end, just couldn't bring itself to endorse something even vaguely perceived as paranormal.

Remote viewing is a wonderful skill to explore, as simple as can be to practice and, most of all, surprisingly useful—not for the debatable accomplishment of being able to call a friend and tell him how many dirty dishes he has in his sink at that moment, but for sharpening aspects of your own mind. Remote viewing depends on the conscious and subconscious minds working together and communicating as a team. The subconscious mind does the actual viewing, but in order to do it effectively, the conscious mind has to stay out of the way so that the subconscious mind can receive a clear signal from the object or location it's focusing on. And while the subconscious mind is doing its work, the conscious mind needs to be able to express what the subconscious mind is receiving, either verbally or through writing or sketching, and express it accurately without interfering or trying to edit the information.

Practicing remote viewing is no more complicated than this: During some quiet moment when your conscious mind can take a nice safe break (when you'd typically be daydreaming instead, in other words), relax yourself with a few deep calming breaths and then select a target location you want to explore. Don't choose a place that you have no way of validating later, since validation is your only way of grading yourself. Start with someplace familiar, like the living room in a friend's house. Start with a wide shot and then begin asking yourself specific questions, ignoring your conscious mind's assumptions and letting your subconscious mind's first impressions provide the answers instead. Are the draperies in the room closed or open? Is the TV on or off? Is the room completely tidy or is there clutter? Is there anything on the furniture or on the floor that usually isn't there—a coffee cup, a newspaper, a magazine? What if anything do you smell in that room? What do you hear? If the TV or radio is on, or if someone is on the phone in that room, try to make out a word or two that you can check out later. Keep asking questions until you're satisfied that you've created a detailed snapshot of that room at that moment, and then call your friend and see how well you did.

It really is no more complicated an exercise than that, and it takes no longer than you want it to. Don't get discouraged if your accuracy is less than dazzling at first. Just one or two hits are a great starting point to work from, and remote viewing really is a skill that improves with practice.

A researcher named Ingo Swann, one of the leading experts on remote viewing during the 1960s and 1970s, wrote that developing this skill can "expand the parameters of our perceptions." That's exactly right. And those expanded parameters when our conscious and subconscious minds are clearly communicating with each other are bound to include everything from remembering our dreams more reliably to consciously accessing our spirit minds' knowledge of our past lives, our chart for the lives we're living now and the glorious lives on the Other Side we'll resume when we go Home again.

Saints

I mean no disrespect to our many, many centuries of saints when I say that sainthood is an earthly title, and of no particular status on the Other Side. That's not to imply that those who've been beatified, or declared saints, aren't advanced spirits, or that they don't deserve our most profound esteem. I'm just convinced that God doesn't have a more honored place set aside in paradise for those who made the cut than He has for the rest of us who are just plugging along every day doing His work as best we know how.

Elevating a person to sainthood is a complicated process, as you probably know. Just for starters, it requires committees, nominations and votes. And I'm sorry to say that, even at the most elevated and well-meaning levels, I have yet to experience a committee in which egos and personal agendas magically disappear until the work is done, or where God could get a word in edgewise, let alone have His wisdom factor into the equation. And no one is even worthy of consideration for possible sainthood unless they've performed three miracles. Who evaluates the submitted acts to judge whether or not they're miracles? More committees. Which means more egos and more personal agendas. There's something about the idea of God sitting breathlessly on the edge of His seat waiting for the outcome of a committee vote on miracles or saints that seems unlikely to me.

And of the billions of people on earth, I know, and so do you, that there are probably hundreds of thousands who are quietly, selflessly, courageously and reverently performing miracles every day, in corners of the world too remote for word to work its way to the appropriate attention of the appropriate committee members. They'll never be nominated for sainthood. They'll never be heard of outside their own small circles. But that doesn't make them any less worthy of the honor. God knows that, whether we on earth think it matters or not.

So in case you're wondering, we walk shoulder to shoulder with the saints on the Other Side. And, in the perfect, loving wisdom of Home, they're equally proud to walk shoulder to shoulder with us.

The Scanning Machine

There's usually some truth in every cliché. So it's probably not surprising that shortly after we return to the Other Side after we die, our whole lives really *do* flash before our eyes, thanks to an amazing device called the Scanning Machine.

As soon as we've arrived back Home and joyfully worked our way through the beloved animals and people waiting at the Other Side's entrance to greet us, we're escorted by our Spirit Guide through the vast doors of the Hall of Wisdom to the stillness of a sacred room deep inside its gleaming white walls.

In the center of the room, surrounded by marble benches, sits the Scanning Machine, a huge convex dome of blue glass. And inside that glass dome, we watch each and every moment of the life we've just lived unfold before our eyes. Rather than appearing like a movie, our life plays out in the form of a three-dimensional hologram, so that no matter where we move around the Scanning Machine, we can see every detail, good or bad, right or wrong, with perfect clarity.

You might wonder as I once did if reviewing our entire lives doesn't take a lifetime to accomplish. I admit it, I know intellectually that time is an earthly concept, and that on the Other Side there is no such thing as time; I just still occasionally have trouble grasping that fact. At Home, though, past, present and future have no meaning—everything is now. Bearing that in mind as best you can, or as best I can if that's more accurate, we review our lives for as long as it takes, even "rewinding" as much "footage" as we want, as often as we want.

Obviously our encounter with the Scanning Machine is more than just an entertaining way for us to make the transition from earth to the Other Side. It's an essential step in the eternal journey of our spirits. As we trudge along through our lives on earth, we have no significant memories of the charts we wrote for those lives to help us accomplish the specific goals we came here for. But the moment we return Home and arrive at the Scanning Machine, we have total recall of our charts. So it's not just a matter of watching our last incarnation unfold in three-dimensional detail for the sheer nostalgia of it; it's a matter of seeing how that incarnation stacked up against the detailed plans we laid out for it ahead of time. And make no mistake about it: It's the toughest judge of all who ultimately evaluates our success and failure—not our Spirit Guide, not God, but *us*. Us as our spirit selves, mind you, from the perspective of the Other Side, where not only is there no negativity but there's also no defensiveness and no ego-driven self-justification to prevent us from facing the truth of our actions and being accountable for them.

According to my Spirit Guide Francine and clients who've described their experiences at the Scanning Machine during regressive hypnosis, the vast majority of us leave it feeling sad and preoccupied with a sense of having let ourselves down. Oddly, the big mistakes we made don't bother us nearly as much as the times when we could have helped but didn't, when we needlessly inflicted pain for no other reason than to flex our muscles, when we were too busy to be kind—as if it saves time to be cruel, when we knew the truth but lied anyway because it was easier at that particular moment.

Those are the highlights, or lowlights, of a carelessly lived but closely reviewed life that can crush us, it seems. Which undoubtedly explains why it's on the sobering occasion of leaving the Scanning Machine that many of us first begin considering the possibility of returning to earth to try again.

During our lives on the Other Side, the Scanning Machine is one of our most valuable research tools. In the same way we study our just-completed incarnation when we first return Home, we can also study every other incarnation we've spent on earth, and, for that matter, every incarnation of anyone and everyone who interests us, by essentially playing any chart we choose through the hologram projector of the Scanning Machine. We can be an eyewitness to any event in our spirit's history or the history of humankind, or if we prefer we can even merge with that event, becoming a part of it, feeling all the emotions its actual participants felt, without altering its dynamics or its outcome in any way. So yes, your whole life can flash before your eyes, as can all the lives you've lived, as can all the lives ever lived by anyone on earth, thanks to the brilliant, sacred, incalculable wealth inside the Scanning Machine's pale blue glass dome in the heart of the Hall of Wisdom.

Scrying

Scrying is an ancient approach to fortune-telling that employs the use of an object for the fortune-teller to focus on or stare into until a vision appears. The clichéd clairvoyant in a turban and robes gazing into a crystal ball is the stereotypical portrait of scrying in action, but stones, mirrors, coins, even ink have replaced crystal balls as scrying vehicles in various cultures around the world.

Without a doubt, no natural substance is more popular than water when it comes to scrying. Long before crystal balls were conceived of, fortune-tellers were drawn to water for answers. And it's no surprise, all things factual and dubious considered. Water is essential to life. It's a powerful source of energy, irresistible to the spirit world as a conductor for their trips from the dimension of the Other Side to the much slower, gravity-ridden dimension of earth. Its movement and its potential for both sparkling clarity and secretive murkiness make it an embarrassment of riches for anyone searching for images, visions, reflections and floating omens. Water cleanses, even purifies, baptizes and washes away sins. It's rumored that evil spirits can't cross it, and that a small glass of water beside a fortune-teller, in addition to being a scrying object, can trap negative energy inside it.

I have to say, I've never used props, but I'm not one to knock anything that works for the true benefit of the client. Just please don't ever let anyone convince you that there really are answers to be found in crystal balls or stones or water or anything other than a truly God-centered spirit.

Séance

Circa 1845, in a town called Hydesville, New York, three young psychically gifted sisters named Fox began holding sessions in which they communicated with the spirit world, receiving the spirits' responses to questions in a complex code of rapping patterns. These sessions, called "spirit circles," became popular among believers, the skeptical but grieving and the simply curious. Other psychics, clairvoyants, clairaudients and mediums began arranging spirit circles of their own, with their own forms of communicating spirit messages to the assembled group, from channeling to automatic writing to telepathy and psychometry.

The name "spirit circle" gave way to the word "séance," from the French word that simply means "sitting." More than a century and a half later, séances—some of them legitimate and helpful, some of them insipid and cruelly phony—are still enormously popular in some form or other throughout the world. Early séances were typically held around a circular table in dark-curtained rooms in the dimmest possible light. Sometimes that was for the logical purpose of creating the most conducive atmosphere for spirit visitations. On other occasions it was to help disguise highly dramatic special effects as trumpets and other objects swooping around the room (by a wire that was virtually invisible against the dark curtain) or the séance table tipping or levitating (by a lever that would be hard to see in such dim light). Becoming a superstar medium in what became a highly competitive séance circuit took extraordinary measures, apparently, especially for those whose only ability to communicate with the deceased would have to wait until they were deceased themselves.

Today's séance typically includes no more than eight people, counting the medium conducting it. The tradition of sitting in a circle continues, although the table is optional. (If a table is used, the participants sit with both hands lying flat, palms down, on the table, with their fingers lightly touching those of the participants on either side of them.) The location, either indoors or outdoors, should be dimly lit, for no other reason than to provide a relaxing, less distracted atmosphere, and there should be plenty of candles, since the spirit world is attracted to candlelight. Ideally, there should be a specific, agreed-upon purpose for the séance—to contact one participant's deceased loved one, for example, or to get in touch with the Spirit Guide of a missing person for help in locating that person. Seven people battering the medium with a barrage of "I want to talk to my mother," "Ask Aunt Mary where she put the insurance papers," "Please get my dad to come so I can finally say good-bye to him," etc., etc., is going to accomplish exactly zero.

Once the purpose has been agreed upon and the group has taken their positions in the circle, there should *always* be a prayer, since nothing can or will happen that God shouldn't guide and be thanked for, and a request for protection from the white light of the Holy Spirit, to protect the séance from any wandering negative ghosts who might try to take advantage of the opportunity. A meditation should follow, to cleanse, relax and focus the minds and energies involved.

And then, once the séance begins, the medium—an experienced medium with a reliable and traceable reputation—is in charge and should never be interrupted in the two hours maximum the session should last.

As hard as it can be to understand, there is no guaranteed result to a séance. You'll read far more about the reasons why in the section on spirits. But simply put, specific residents of the spirit world are not always at our beck and call, any more than our friends and family here on earth sit at home by the phone twenty-four hours a day in case we might want to get in touch with them. It might take several sessions to accomplish the desired goal, or to unearth and accomplish a more valuable one. (Aunt Mary, for example, never does communicate, but her husband Uncle Bob comes through, with information that makes the location of those insurance papers seem too trivial to be bothered with.)

With a truly legitimate medium and an appropriately supportive group of participants, séances can be wonderful experiences, still more affirmation that we're surrounded by a world of spirits who have a million things to say to us if we'll just open our minds and ears and listen, starting with, "You see? There's no such thing as death."

The Seven Levels of Advancement

There's nothing haphazard in God's universe, which means there's nothing haphazard about the advancement of our spirits on the Other Side as we continue to learn. We don't go through this rough school on earth over and over again to stay in kindergarten, after all, and we all need and appreciate markers of our progress.

There are seven designated levels of advancement on the Other Side. They're simply available categories of growth, based on our experience. We can spend as long or as short a time as we want on any one level, based on our own interests, aptitudes and comfort levels. No level is considered inferior or superior to any other, and they're separated by nothing more than the specialties each of them involves—our choice, thanks to the free will God gave us as part of our birthright.

Here are basic descriptions of the Seven Levels of Advancement we can choose from and aspire to at Home:

LEVEL ONE: Our return to the Other Side, including the reunion with our Spirit Guide and loved ones and our review at the Scanning Machine of the lifetime we've just lived.

LEVEL TWO: Our Orientation process, in which we're given whatever help we might need for our decompression from earth to Home. It might just be a debriefing session with our Orientators and Spirit Guide about what we accomplished and what we might have left unfinished on earth. It might be cocooning, or a period of extra care and tranquillity for those who've arrived on the Other Side upset, unsettled and in emotional turmoil. Or it might be intensive care and twilight sleep in the Towers, for those on whom serious mental damage has been inflicted—torture and brainwashing victims, for example—who need a long period of expert rehabilitation before they can reunite with their own inherent joyful spirits again and resume their busy, peaceful lives of bliss at Home.

LEVEL THREE: The physical and science skills. This level embraces every vocation that is literally hands-on, ranging from agriculture and animal husbandry to botany and hydroponics to chemistry and physics to carpentry and stonemasonry to forestry and geology.

LEVEL FOUR: The creative arts, all of which thrive on the Other Side, including writing, sculpture, dance of every kind, music of every style, painting and performing.

LEVEL FIVE: Every area of medical, scientific, psychiatric, environmental and sociological research. This area is particularly tuned in to us on earth, so that the results of their research can be passed along through infused knowledge to our own experts and "discovered" as our health, environmental and humanitarian crises here continue to escalate.

LEVEL SIX: The teachers, Orientators, lecturers and seminar leaders who help, guide and instruct those in Levels One through Five. It's no coincidence that some of our most uncommonly gifted and charismatic "teachers" here on earth, by whatever occupation we technically classify them, from Joseph Campbell to Dr. Martin Luther King to Winston Churchill, are highly sought-after teachers and lecturers on the Other Side.

LEVEL SEVEN: The level to which only a handful of rare souls aspire. On Level Seven, the spirit forfeits its identity and the sum total of its energy and accumulated wisdom and experience. Instead of proceeding in the universe as its own separate being, it's willingly absorbed into the great uncreated mass, an infinite, mysterious, unfathomable force field from which all the love and power of God emanates.

Now, just to clarify, we don't work our way back through each of the levels every time we leave the Other Side for another incarnation and return again. Obviously we go through the first two levels on every arrival back Home. But once we're acclimated again, we simply resume our work on the level we were on when we left. We also have the luxury of constant mobility from one level to another, with the exception of Level Seven, needless to say. For example, I happen to be an Orientator on the Other Side, a Level Six responsibility. But that doesn't keep me away from the Level Three animal husbandry centers that own a big piece of my heart, or from joining the archaeological researchers on Level Five at every opportunity. That mobility doesn't work in reverse—if you've only reached Level Three, you can't leap to Level Five and skip Level Four, since each new level is achieved through learning. There's no exclusivity involved; it's simply the same logic that keeps us from going from the first week of our freshman year in college to the second semester of our senior year without taking any of the required courses in between.

I'll be the first to admit that my knowledge of Level Seven is limited to a couple of basic facts. I know that once a spirit has given itself to God's infinite force field, it never incarnates again or reclaims its own identity. I also know, though, that even though it's been absorbed into the most awesome and unfathomable of all entities, that spirit never ceases to exist. The best analogy I've been given is that it's like pouring a cup of water into the Pacific Ocean. While that cup of water can never again be separated from the massive body of water that's consumed it, the cup of water technically still exists.

If you're wondering if you'd ever have the courage, or the trust, or the selflessness, or the ultimate commitment to aspire to the seventh level, let me step right up and assure you that I'm with you. In sixty-nine years on this earth, traveling the globe, meeting hundreds of thousands of people, I can honestly say I've met only one seventh-level entity, one spirit who is already cherishing his awareness that he'll be heading Home from here to offer his whole identity to God's uncreated mass. He's a theology professor, and his persona is so ethereal and translucent that even from across a room you can feel the presence of a rare, extraordinarily powerful soul.

The rest of us can still take heart and hold our heads high, knowing that whichever level we're on and whichever we aspire to, we're not disappointing ourselves and we're certainly not disappointing God. As long as we dedicate our gifts to Him, He needs us all.

Shamanism

Shamanism is a fascinating practice of holistic healing techniques that start at the spirit level and "work their way out." While the specifics vary from one culture to another, shamanistic practitioners thrive in countries throughout the world and in almost every religion, from Christianity to Buddhism to Judaism to Hinduism to Bahaism. One of its most effective distinctions in comparison to Western medicine is that shamans look at each condition and each healing as unique, while Western medicine prefers one cure that works for as many of the masses as possible.

Shamans believe that everything in nature is alive, from rocks, rivers, plants, trees and the earth itself. As a result, everything in nature possesses information. Shamans work with that information, and with the spirits of humans and animals around them, to diagnose, to treat and to heal the soul and whatever illness is creating a shadow around it.

A shamanistic healing begins with the shaman shifting his state of consciousness so that he can examine his patient's spirit through an elevated awareness. That shift of consciousness is accomplished through astral travel, which the shaman calls the "soul flight," during which he retrieves whatever natural information he needs and also searches for any essential life elements his patient might have inadvertently lost or picked up along the way.

For that to make sense, it's important to understand a few basics of the shamanistic approach to health problems:

* Illness results from a loss of power, and healing requires restoring that power. This is usually accomplished through a "power animal retrieval." In shamanism, a "power animal" is a spirit protector whose strength is available to us whenever we need it, very much like totems, which you'll see defined in their own section. In a power animal retrieval, the shaman astrally travels to the patient's power animal and gathers however much restorative strength the patient needs.

* Either all or parts of the soul will leave the body when the need arises to protect itself from a serious physical trauma. From time to time parts of the soul get trapped outside the body, uncertain

about how to return. Shamans respond to this soul loss, which is often considered the cause of schizophrenia and other mental illnesses, by performing a soul retrieval, literally bringing back those lost fragments and making the spirit whole again.

* Your own negativity, or negativity someone might feel toward you, is very real and physically invasive, becoming imbedded in the body and resulting in ulcers, chronic headaches, indigestion and disabling back and joint pain. Shamans locate and remove the imbedded foreign energy in a technique called "shamanic extraction."

Because of their profound reverence for and connection to all aspects of nature, shamans are also called upon to heal infertile land and polluted bodies of water and diseased crops, and to perform rituals that will create shifts in weather patterns to restore stability to the environment itself. We owe shamanism a debt of gratitude for countless discoveries in the world of natural healing resources, and for its quiet, largely unreported efforts to make up for our ongoing abuse of this sad, struggling planet.

Shamballa

"The way appears but fleetingly,
The vision lasts not long.
But lifetimes lived in time
Are as ashes to this flame.
O dreamed-of Shamballa,
I come to thy Pure Land."
"Shamballa," by Hermes

One of the world's most gorgeous legends is that of the sacred hidden land of Shamballa. Since the time of Buddha, if not before, Shamballa has been a beautiful myth to some, a symbol of the highest spirituality the soul could hope to achieve. To others, it's an actual place, elusive, shrouded in clouds among the highest, most impassable peaks of the Himalayas, worth a lifetime of searching on foot or by air if only for a glimpse of it. Even those who claim to believe it's nothing but a snowy, glistening mirage can't disguise a longing hint of "but what if . . . ?" in their eyes when the subject of Shamballa comes up.

Countless stories surround it, some warning of the ferocious but equally elusive Yetis who guard its entrance, others speaking of the fleeting sparkle of a vast jeweled dome peeking through a momentary break in the veils of mist over the site where Shamballa is rumored to exist. A typical story is one of an explorer who was wandering by himself at the base of the mountains one day, when he was lured toward them by the quiet echo of Tibetan monks, reverently chanting somewhere nearby. He followed the sound and found himself at a small doorway in a sheer, massive cliff. Stepping hesitantly through the doorway, he stood gaping at the impossible world inside—a warm, green, endless valley, filled with magnificent spired temples and little towns that looked like clusters of diamonds in the emerald meadows and fields of crops that surrounded them. The townspeople noticed him immediately and rushed to welcome him, inviting him to stay and rest and make himself at home. But the explorer was so overwhelmed with awe that he insisted on going to retrieve his friends, who were camped nearby, wanting to share this impossible beauty with them and knowing they'd never believe his story if they didn't see it for themselves. The residents warned him that if he left, he'd never find his way back, but he assured them that he was a world-class explorer, more experienced than they could imagine, and he couldn't possibly lose his way on such a short trip to his camp and back. As he stepped out the doorway through which he'd entered, he took the added precaution of hanging his down vest on one of the door's iron hinges to mark the site. Less than a half hour later he returned with his friends to find his down vest hanging on a jagged rock in a sheer, unbroken wall of granite.

Buddhist writings insist that Shamballa can be reached only by way of a hard journey across deserts and mountains, and even then only those who are called and who are spiritually enlightened enough will find their way. All others, even if they follow the footprints of the enlightened, will find nothing but blizzards, ice-covered barren mountains and probably death from exposure to the elements. Tibetans who believe Shamballa physically exists think it's probably in Tibet. Others who've studied for decades swear with equal passion that it's in Mongolia, the Arctic or Siberia.

A whole other school of thought is that Shamballa, every bit as splendid as our most exquisite fantasies of it, actually exists in the earth's etheric substance, or its aura, holding all our wisdom intact and safe from harm.

And yet no less than the magnificent Dalai Lama has said of Shamballa:

"Although those with special affiliation may actually be able to go there through their karmic connection, nevertheless it is not a physical place that we can actually find. We can only say that it is a pure land, a pure land in the human realm. And unless one has the merit and the actual karmic association, one cannot actually arrive there."

And in the end, the legend continues, a time will come when all spiritual integrity in the world that surrounds Shamballa will be lost to the wars of humankind.

Then, and not until then, a great king will emerge from this hidden land where the highest wisdom has been guarded since the beginning of time. And with this wisdom the king will defeat all evil, and we'll see the beginning of a golden age.

Silver Cord

The silver cord is a very real, glistening, impossibly delicate strand attached to each of us just below the breastbone and leading to the higher dimension of the Other Side. Like the umbilical cord that nourishes our bodies during our brief confinement in the womb, the silver cord nourishes our spirits with the immediate love and Life Force of God during our brief, self-imposed confinement here on earth, away from Home. It's our unbreakable connection to that Place we came from, that Place we'll go again, where our joy waits. The silver cord is God's way of making sure that He and we, no matter how far apart we might seem in this infinite universe, are always touching.

If you spend much time studying world religions and beliefs, you'll discover as I have that the concept of the silver cord is fairly common. Even the Bible refers to it, in Ecclesiastes 12:6–7: "Before the silver cord is snapped . . . and the spirit returns to God who gave it." Several clients have told me about seeing their silver cord during near-death experiences. So I really have no excuse, beyond my relentless skepticism, for the fact that until I was fifty years old, I privately thought of the silver cord as nothing more than kind of a spiritual version of Cinderella's glass slipper, just a sparkling, pretty, well-intentioned product of humankind's hopeful imagination.

And then I saw my own. So much for skepticism.

It was nighttime, after an especially long day at work. I was meditating, lying on the floor of my living room. Candles were lit, and a log was burning in the fireplace. Suddenly I realized that, thanks to the depth of my meditation, I'd left my body and was astrally hovering near the ceiling watching myself, impressed with how peaceful I looked. Astral travel during deep meditation isn't all that noteworthy for some people, I know, but it's rare for me, probably because I don't care for the sensation it gives me of not being in control. At the same instant it hit me that I was out, wafting around the room instead of inside that body on the floor, I caught the briefest, most breathtaking glimpse of something fine and glittering near me in midair. It was silver as starlight, delicate as a strand of an Angel's hair, and I saw it just long enough to understand that it started in my solar plexus and trailed off to disappear several feet away into the higher dimension that was its Source.

It was my own silver cord, beautiful and sacred and absolutely real. To this day I have no idea why I was given the privilege of seeing it only once and have never seen it again. That's not a complaint. Once was a blessing, and I'm grateful.

It's no surprise that that experience piqued my curiosity considerably, and I started reading. Some of the most fascinating books on the subject of the silver cord can be found in the works of Sylvan Muldoon, a gifted researcher and expert on the subject of astral travel from the 1920s through the 1940s. From his personal observations of his own silver cord during countless astral trips, he discovered that the thickness of the cord varies, depending on the spirit's proximity to its body. If the spirit is astrally traveling within ten or fifteen feet of the body, the silver cord has the approximate diameter of a silver dollar, with a sparkling aura that makes its exact size hard to distinguish. But when the spirit is on a very distant trip, a globe or a light-year or a dimension away from its body, the seemingly delicate cord easily stretches, never in any danger of fraying or snapping in two, and becomes no thicker than a silk thread.

In response to a request on my Web site, clients and colleagues e-mailed from around the world to share their own eyewitness descriptions of the silver cord, which they saw in situations ranging from sleep to meditation to surgery to comas. More than ninety percent of the descriptions came from people who had no idea there was any such thing as a silver cord, so they were even more shocked to see theirs than I was to see mine. They used such phrases as "a luminous length of string," "a long, slender lighted coil," "a tiny glowing ribbon," "a smoky-looking ray of sunlight" and "a cloudy laser beam." For the record, these e-mail contributors included members of six different religions, a retired law enforcement officer, a Catholic priest, a member of the Methodist clergy, two medical doctors, a heart surgeon and a Wall Street executive. And a few perceived the silver cord as being attached to the front or the back of their head, or to their abdomen.

But one of my favorite anecdotes about the silver cord appeared in Sylvan Muldoon's work *The Phenomena of Astral Projection*. It was referred to as "the Hout Case No. 2" and was a doctor's account of what he witnessed while performing surgeries on three separate patients:

> ". . . In each case I was able to see, at least part of the time, the astral cord that united these spirit bodies with their physical counterparts. This was represented to me as a silvery shaft of light which wound around through the room in much the same way as a curl of smoke will drift indifferently in still atmosphere. When the magnetic force would draw the spirit close to the physical body, this cord was more apparent, as though more concentrated. At other times this force was indistinguishable to me. . . ."

I've never doubted that our spirits receive constant, essential love and support from the Other Side during our rough camping trips here on earth. But when I least expected it, and would frankly have almost bet against it, that glistening silver cord appeared, and I was given a glimpse of divine proof that God, in His perfect wisdom, has devised a way literally to nourish us every moment we're away from Home. More and more research and more and more clients and colleagues since that night have continued to confirm and share their awe at that subtle, glittering miracle, and to remind me of a question I hope none of us ever stop asking:

How many other signs of God's hands on earth will we see if we just slow down and open our eyes?

Sorcery

Sorcery is an ancient form of magic intended to produce a desired effect on some upcoming event or person, or to reverse a negative effect someone was believed to have fallen victim to.

The basis of sorcery can be boiled down to sympathetic magic, which is virtually identical to imitative magic, found in its own section in this book. Sympathetic magic works on the principle that "like produces like," even at a distance. The most clichéd example of sympathetic magic is the voodoo doll, a representation of a specific person on which abuse is inflicted, the sympathetic magic theory being that, since like produces like, what happens to the doll will happen in some form to the designated person. And before we devote too much time to the primitive, barbaric nature of sticking pins in voodoo dolls, let's bear in mind that hanging someone in effigy is exactly the same kind of sorcery and sympathetic magic, so it's not as if we civilized nations have never heard of such a thing.

Sorcery and sympathetic magic have some fascinating interpretations throughout the world, both ancient and current, practiced not just by sorcerers and sorceresses (respectively, the male and female experts on the art of sorcery) but by the most common and most earnest among the population as well, who clearly agree that like produces like and aren't about to take any chances.

* In some cultures, young sons of whale hunters were forbidden to play the children's string game "Cat's Cradle" to avoid the probability of their hands becoming equally entangled in their harpoon lines when they grew up and followed their fathers' profession.

* Certain ancient cultures refused to allow pregnant women to tie or twist ropes during the last two months of their pregnancy, for fear they were conjuring the sympathetic magic of their baby

being strangled by its umbilical cord, or being born with its intestines twisted.

* When the man of the house was away on hunts, it was common in many African cultures for a small bowl of rice and roots to be set aside at every meal, so that the distant hunter would never be weak from hunger, and the women would not sew in his absence for fear she would prick her finger and cause him to injure himself on something sharp during his hunt.

* Sumatran rice is planted by the women with the longest, most flowing hair, so that the rice will grow with long stalks.

* Many cultures, from ancient times until today, will not allow barren women to participate in planting crops for fear the barrenness will rub off.

* The ancient Chinese village of Tsuen-cheu-fu was consistently pillaged by the nearby village of Yung-chun until the residents of Tsuen-cheu-fu figured out the reason: Their village was shaped like a fish, while Yung-chun was shaped like a fishing net. The residents of Tsuen-cheu-fu promptly built pagodas in the center of their village to stop the net before it could successfully trap them again.

* On certain South Pacific islands, November, with its relentless rains, is called "the Month of Tears." Anyone born in November is doomed to a life of sorrow unless they boil a pot of water, remove the lid and let the condensed drops of water from the lid fall at the feet of the infant's father, replacing the tears that would have fallen from the eyes of the newborn in its lifetime.

* Wives and daughters of men in Laos who were off trapping elephants were forbidden to put oil of any kind on their skin, which was guaranteed to sympathetically lubricate the skin of the elephant and allow it to escape from the traps.

In some form or another, every one of these and thousands upon thousands of others have been adopted, adapted, performed with a flourish and capitalized on by sorcerers and sorceresses, called by many names, in every culture of the world since time began. And as with every other form of spell, curse, incantation, omen, magic, etc., that claims a power of its own, I can only say about sorcery, used with the best of intentions or the worst, that your belief in it is the only power it can ever have, and your belief in God is all the protection from it you'll ever need.

Soul Mate

It is not your purpose or your divine destiny on this earth to find and spend the rest of this lifetime with your soul mate. In fact, the odds against it are astronomical.

Please don't let it discourage you that the overhyped, over-romanticized search for your soul mate is a futile expectation. Let it ease your mind. It's wrenching to hear clients take on a whole added level of sorrow during a divorce by believing they've been rejected by their soul mate, as if a genuine soul mate would be capable of rejection. Or clients, even ones with successful marriages, telling me that their life's greatest failure was in never having found their soul mate. Or clients in abusive relationships who stay because the constant emotional intensity feels to them like the passion only a soul mate could inspire. The term "soul mate" gets mistaken for everything from infatuation to lust to an excuse for stalking, obsession and domestic violence.

Once you understand what a true soul mate is, you'll stop putting so much unnecessary pressure on yourself.

We're each created with spirits that have both male and female aspects, and we live lifetimes as both genders. I've never met anyone with more than four or five incarnations who's always been male or always been female every time they came here.

At the same moment we're created, an identical twin spirit is created with us. That identical twin spirit's male and female aspects are essentially mirror images of our own. And that identical twin spirit is our soul mate. Our soul mate is not the other half of us, any more than we're the other half of our soul mate. I am not half a person. Neither are you. There are people who complement me, who have some qualities I didn't happen to choose this time around, and vice versa. But trust me, and I say this on your behalf as well as my own, with those people or without them, I always have been and always will be a whole, one-hundred-percent complete person. Why would you or I spend one minute, let alone a lifetime, looking for another half that doesn't exist and that we one-hundred-percent complete people would find useless?

During our lives on the Other Side we share a closer bond with our soul mates than with any other spirits, as identical twins would. But we're certainly not joined at the hip. We pursue separate friendships, separate interests, separate work and studies and, above all, our own separate identities. With our soul mates we enjoy a rare, singular connection—free, unconditional love, liberated and liberating, with that innate unspoken spirit intimacy only identical twins truly understand.

Like all spirits on the Other Side, both we and our soul mates can choose when, if and how many times we want to incarnate for another trip to earth. We make these decisions separately, for our own very specific reasons, and don't forget, in the context of eternity, we leave Home and come back again in the blink of an eye.

So all things considered, what are the chances of our soul mates even being here on earth at the same time we are? And why would either of us bother to coordinate our travel plans, since we're together as often as we want on the Other Side? Not to mention the odds against the two of us incarnating in the same general age range, enough geographical proximity for us to run into each other somewhere along the way, and the gender of preference for the two of us to become a couple, which seems to be the top priority of the whole soul mate myth?

So please stop setting yourself up to fail by looking for someone who's undoubtedly not even here at the moment. Please stop clinging to a bad relationship in a misguided devotion to a "soul mate" who's making you miserable—a contradiction in terms if ever there was one. Please don't devalue a potentially lovely relationship because it doesn't give you that soul-mate feeling. Please don't believe that there's only one person among the population of six billion or so on this earth that you're destined to be with. And please don't go through life resentful or discouraged because your soul mate never showed up, or cheated on you, or treated you terribly, or left you.

I feel very safe in saying that your soul mate—your identical twin spirit—is probably doing exactly what mine is right now: having a blissfully joyful time on the Other Side planning a "Welcome Home" party.

Spirit Guide

Every one of us has a Spirit Guide, someone we literally trusted with our soul on the Other Side, who agreed to be our constant, vigilant companion and helpmate when we made the choice to experience another lifetime on earth.

All Spirit Guides have experienced at least one incarnation, so they're able to empathize with the problems, mistakes, temptations, fears and frailties inevitable in the human world. In fact, most of us either have been or will be someone else's Spirit Guide during our soul's eternal journey. But remember, your relationship with your Guide was formed between your spirit and theirs on the Other Side before you were born, which makes it impossible for them to be someone you've known in this lifetime.

The Spirit Guide's job is to encourage, advise and support us toward the goals we've set for ourselves in this incarnation. And they have several tools at hand to help them with that astonishing challenge. Not only do they study us closely and objectively on the Other Side once they've agreed to take on this responsibility, but they've also

memorized every detail of our charts, while we lose conscious awareness of those charts the minute we're born. They have added perspective on our charts thanks to their direct access to the charts of those
around us, and to the sacred Akashic Records that are the written
body of God's knowledge. And like all residents of the spirit world,
Spirit Guides are able to bi-locate, or be in more than one place at the
same time, so that they can respond instantly when we yell for help
without interrupting their invariably busy lives on the Other Side.

No matter how tempted they might be from time to time, Spirit
Guides will never interfere with the choices and decisions we make,
or deprive us of our free will. At best, they'll offer possible alternatives
and warnings. But the deal we make with them from the beginning is
that we're going through this lifetime on earth to learn and grow, and
we can't accomplish that if our Spirit Guides are constantly shielding
us from the lessons we need to learn.

They communicate with us in a variety of ways, if we'll just open
up and listen. You'd think that would be easy for me, because I have
the advantage of literally being able to hear my Spirit Guide Francine,
and even channel her so that she can talk through me, but incredibly,
there are still times when I don't pay attention to her, and I always
regret it. But Spirit Guides don't need audible voices to send helpful messages. They can do it by telepathy or infused knowledge, directly into our spirit minds. What you've always shrugged off as just
instinct, or your conscience, or "something told me," is more than
likely your Spirit Guide waving flags. When you suddenly drive a different route than usual for no apparent reason and find out later you
avoided an accident; change travel arrangements at the last minute
and, as a result, are spared a disaster; act on an impulse to call a
friend, only to discover they needed your help at that moment; go to
sleep concerned about a problem and wake up knowing the solution,
rest assured that you're receiving your Spirit Guide's signals loud and
clear.

As for talking to your Spirit Guide, you can and should ask for help, advice and reassurance as often as you feel the need. But again, remember that they can't and won't intervene with our charts, and they won't participate in sparing us lessons that could be in our best interest in the long run. I also once learned a fascinating finer point of Spirit Guide communicating from Francine, by the way, when my son Paul was having a serious health crisis. I was praying with every fiber of my being for Paul's dangerously high fever to break, and I was incredulous that Francine was so slow to come to my side when she had to have heard me begging God for help. It turns out that the privacy of our conversations with God is so sacred that not even our Spirit Guides can hear them. God is part of us. We are part of Him. No one can trespass or eavesdrop, when we're already one with Him to begin with.

Don't neglect talking to your Spirit Guide just because you might not know who they are. Remember, they've been human at least once before. They're well aware that our memories of them and our lives on the Other Side are virtually nonexistent at best, so they don't expect us to remember them. If it helps your comfort level in talking to them, make up a name and call them that. Your Spirit Guide will respond to any name you choose, whether you're consciously aware of their presence or not, just for the joy of your acknowledging and embracing them.

The more you allow communicating with your Spirit Guide to become a routine, normal part of your life, the clearer the communication between the two of you will become, and the more effective they can be in their sacred promise to help you along this rough path you had the courage to choose.

Our Spirit Guides are the last to say good-bye to us when we leave Home to come to earth, our wisest and most constant advocates while we're here and the first to help us make sense of it all when we're back on the Other Side again. They're nothing more than that, but not one bit less either, and not a day should go by when we don't stop for a moment, think of them and say, "Thank you."

Spirits

First, just to clarify something, we're all spirits. Some of us are currently inhabiting a body, while others of us aren't at the moment. For this discussion I'll focus on those spirits who've already moved on from their bodies, and I'll be using third-person pronouns like "they" and "them." But please don't let that make "them" feel all that separate and all that different from "us." They *were* us, not that long ago, and not too long from now, we'll be them. The less we think of them as aliens, spooks and scary bump-in-the-night intruders we're not even sure we believe in, the more receptive we'll be when the spirit of a deceased loved one we've been yearning to see actually shows up.

Spirits are beings who have traveled through the tunnel and made it safely to that dimension called the Other Side. As you'll read in the definition of the Other Side, it's a very real place three feet above our own ground level. You've heard countless descriptions of spirits looking as if they're floating a few feet above the ground, and in a way that's exactly what they're doing—they're moving along on the Other Side's ground level, three feet higher than ours.

The Other Side is paradise, a place of perfect bliss, where the atmosphere itself is charged with God's immediate presence and eternal, unconditional love. The spirit world, living in that state of bliss and reunited with their memories of all their past lives both on earth and at Home, are incapable of unhappiness, anger, resentment, pettiness, worry, fear, negativity and every other emotion we've created and become addicted to in our world. Any emotional and physical burdens a spirit carried throughout their lifetimes here are resolved in the white light of the Holy Spirit when they return to the Other Side. So if you ever encounter a being who seems sad or mean or negative in any way, or who shows any signs of wounds, illness or disease, I promise you're dealing with an earthbound ghost, not a spirit. And if you ever find yourself wondering if a deceased loved one at Home is angry with you, or if they've forgiven you, or if they're as unhappy as they seemed during their lives, you can ease your mind, completely and forever. In the sacred perfection of Home, they're incapable of feeling anything but peace, joy and love.

The spirit world of the Other Side is unobstructed by earthly limitations, which gives spirits any number of advantages over us (and gives us a lot to look forward to when we're out of these inconvenient bodies again).

* The ability to easily communicate with each other and with us, through the use of telepathy—the immediate transference of information from one entity to another without the use of any of the five physical senses. One of the most common observations you'll hear from people who've had visitations from spirits is that the spirit talked to them without using words or making a sound.

* The ability to bi-locate, i.e., literally be in two places at once. Deceased loved ones often simultaneously visit two family members who live hundreds of miles away from each other, for example, with both visits being absolutely real.

* The ability to manipulate animate and inanimate objects to get our attention. While they'll never actually possess an animal here on earth, they can certainly cause them to respond to their telepathic commands, so that suddenly a conspicuous number of birds or butterflies or squirrels or you-name-it will be present even more than the chronically unaware can ignore. They'll move photographs or keepsakes, they'll leave coins in the most unlikely places, they'll rock their favorite rocking chair, they'll play a music box, they'll superimpose their image on a painting or snapshot—there are no limits when it comes to a spirit who's trying to say, "I'm here!"

* The dramatic ability to affect electrical devices. Because spirits have to cross from the Other Side's dimension back into ours in

order to visit us, they often attach their energy to such convenient conductors as electricity and water in order to help ease their transition. They're especially active between one and five in the morning, when the night air is at its dampest and the dew is at its heaviest. And with electricity and water being so helpful to them, it's not just a myth that the spirit world loves a good thunderstorm. It's a breeze for spirits to create bizarre behavior in TVs, appliances, telephones and other electrical devices. But again, because they're spirits, they're not motivated by meanness or a desire to frighten you. They simply want you to know that they're with you and, of far more importance, that all this talk of eternity and surviving death turned out to be absolutely true.

Spiritualism

Spiritualism is one of the world's most misunderstood concepts. It's controversial, it's often scoffed at, it's actively shunned by some religions, all without a clue of what the basic principles are—not one of which contradicts the beliefs of any major religion on earth, by the way.

Spiritualism simply means a belief that the universe and all its inhabitants were created by a sacred, supreme God.

God endowed these inhabitants with spirits, which are divine and eternal, and which by definition survive the death of the physical body. And those spirits who've survived death can and do communicate with those of us who are still occupying our very temporary bodies.

That's basically what spiritualism means. Nothing less. And not so controversial at all when you sort out all the misconceptions and get down to that simple, God-centered description.

Stigmata

Stigmata are manifestations of wounds on the body that correspond to Christ's wounds during the crucifixion, on his hands, his feet, the

Stigmata

side of his chest and his fore-head. When actual marks or blood appear, the phenome-non is called "visible stigmata." "Invisible stigmata" occur when no marks, wounds or blood can be seen, but severe pain sud-denly hits those same specific areas.

Stigmatics, as those are called to whom stigmata mani-fest themselves, seem to notice weakness and depression shortly before the marks and/or pain appear, and in most cases healing seems to take place within a few hours.

The first stigmatic is thought to have been St. Francis of Assisi, in 1224. In response to a prayer that during his lifetime he might feel Je-sus's suffering and love throughout his body and soul, Jesus appeared to him from the night sky in a blaze of dazzling stars and pierced his hands, feet and chest with streams of blood and fire.

Many of the most renowned and well-documented stigmatics in history have lived their lives devoutly but in poor health. St. Catherine of Siena suffered from chronic pain and an inability to eat. Padre Pio, the first Catholic priest to receive the stigmata, suffered lifelong fevers, lung problems and an inability to eat. Louise Lateau began suf-fering from severe neuralgia in her late teens, as well as an inability to eat. Therese Neumann suffered from occasional blindness, convul-sions, paralysis and deafness and took her inability to eat to a rare extreme—by several eyewitness accounts, she thrived on nothing but a minimal amount of water and a small, thin rice wafer, consecrated as a communion wafer, each day.

It goes without saying that there have been cases of deliberately falsified stigmata. However, it's interesting that in the thousands of

years that the phenomenon has been documented, stigmata have never been proved or disproved successfully beyond any shadow of a doubt.

Succubus

The succubus was a European mythological female demon known for entering men's bedrooms at night and having intercourse with them while they slept. Her male counterpart was the incubus, the equally mythological demon rapist of sleeping women. Like so many evil, insidious, devil-inspired beings of medieval lore, succubi and incubi were in league with each other. Succubi were not just forcing themselves on hapless, unsuspecting, sleeping men for the fun of it, for example. They were also collecting human semen to pass along to their sterile incubi brethren, so that the incubi could impregnate their female victims if and when the time was right.

It's no real surprise that there seemed to be far fewer complaints of succubus attacks than of incubus attacks. In fact, the most common victims of succubi just happened to be priests, monks and any other members of the religious clergy whose positions demanded vows of celibacy. What more convenient way to explain away the, shall we say, evidence of a forbidden erotic dream than to blame a pesky, uncontrollable, wanton succubus—and the word "succubus" is from the Latin for "harlot," by the way, so what was a defenseless celibate monk to do when faced with, of all things, a harlot demon sent from the devil himself?

Not that anyone really complained, mind you, when certain inns throughout Europe decorated their entrances with ornate carvings of succubi as their subtle way of advertising that a brothel could also be found behind those doors.

But of course there was no such thing as a succubus, any more than there was such a thing as incubi. Six times out of ten, the succubus excuse allowed a lot of men of the cloth to avoid a lot of embarrassment.

The other four times, the succubus was for frightened men what the incubus was for frightened women—the only explanation they could think of for an experience that terrified them while they slept, an experience called astral catalepsy that, in reality, is ultimately harmless and involves no other spirits than those of the sleepers themselves. And when you read the full discussion of astral catalepsy in its own section, you'll understand how and why it's so easily and frequently confused with some kind of dark, lewd assault even today.

Synchronicity

First, please read or review the definition of "coincidence," which in brief is a fleeting, conscious glimpse at a moment in our life chart that's about to happen, and a sign that we're in perfect synch with our chart.

Synchronicity is a close relative of coincidence. The word "synchronicity" was popularized by the brilliant Swiss psychologist Carl Jung, who was in his office with a patient one day discussing Egypt when a beetle known as an Egyptian scarab walked across his desk. Jung found the word "coincidence" too ordinary to describe an Egyptian beetle, thousands of miles from where it belonged, appearing at the exact moment he was talking about Egypt. It was a clear sign to Jung that this universe God created is not random and chaotic, but ordered, perfect and patterned—in a word, synchronized, from which Jung coined "synchronicity."

Synchronicity, then, is an especially meaningful coincidence. Like Jung's Egyptian scarab, it always involves some kind of unmistakable physical sign, not only to call your attention to the magical harmony of the universe but also to give you tangible proof that you are *exactly* where you charted yourself to be, *exactly* when, *exactly* with whom—God, who cowrote your chart with you, is giving you a visible thumbs-up, a nod to say, "Yes, I am with you, and I am watching, and at this moment you are in perfect synch with your blueprint. Good work."

True synchronicity is not likely to happen as often in our lives as coincidences are. But watching for it, and recognizing it when it occurs, means catching a chance for a private smile between you and God.

Synergism

The dictionary defines "synergism" as "the simultaneous action of separate agencies which, together, have greater total effect than the sum of their individual effects." How they managed to make something so thrilling sound so dull is beyond me. But if you replace a few words here and there, you at least make it seem like a phenomenon that might be worth looking into. Try this: Synergism, or synergy, is the simultaneous action of separate people who, together, have a greater total effect than the sum of their individual power.

Let's say one hundred of us have gathered in a room for some common purpose. Each of us has a belief in that purpose of "ten" on the proverbial scale of one to ten. Simple math would indicate that the total belief in that room is ten times one hundred people, or 1,000. But thanks to the force of synergy, and the power of all that combined belief, the total instead is actually 100,000 or 1,000,000. Synergy feeds and grows upon and nourishes itself, with results that literally change the world.

Jesus and twelve disciples—a total of thirteen people—gave birth to Christianity with the help of the infinite force of synergy. Prayer chains, which have been known to create miracles beyond the scope of any single participant, are brilliant examples of synergism. It was through synergism that I started my own church, Novus Spiritus, which continues to grow beyond my wildest expectations because our common purpose—the highest good in God's name for as many of His children as we can reach—is far more important than any one of us, including me.

Of course, synergisms don't have to have a religious purpose to achieve worthwhile, equally awesome power. Synergisms devoted to the highest good have any number of forms of expression—from John Walsh and his nationwide synergy called *America's Most Wanted*; to some of our extraordinary disaster and disease charities, and organizations devoted to the protection of crime victims, children and animals, and the wrongly convicted; to such inspiring groups as Alcoholics and Narcotics Anonymous, the Make-A-Wish Foundation and Project Angel Food. Each is far greater than the sum of its parts, and each has an impact beyond our ability to calculate it. Each, then, is a synergism, to which we could all lend our own individual support and experience the indescribable satisfaction of watching that support be multiplied.

T

Talismans

A talisman is a token, charm or small object of some kind that's worn, carried or kept by its owner as a superstition. It differs from an amulet in that the purpose of an amulet is to ward off evil, while the purpose of a talisman is to attract and help ensure a specific goal—good luck, protection, self-confidence, mental and emotional clarity, strength through a crisis, thriving health, etc.

The hope that an object of some kind can be blessed, supercharged or infused with the energy necessary to achieve a designated purpose is ancient, global and nondenominational. Every culture and belief system has seemed to embrace some form of good luck charm since the beginning of time. So even if our logical minds dismiss talismans as silly superstitions, and we're confident in our certainty that active faith in God is the only good luck charm we need, our attraction to talismans is almost a genetic legacy from thousands of generations of ancestors.

Dreamcatcher:
A Native American
talisman

The Greeks, Egyptians and Babylonians included a wide variety of sacred talismans in their rituals for everything from luring favorable weather to curing illnesses. Ancient Africans carried body parts of notoriously swift and agile animals to give themselves added speed. Alchemists searched for the rare Philosopher's Stone as their most treasured talisman, believing it would empower them to turn simple base metals into gold and silver. (See "Alchemy.") The Irish had/have their four-leaf clovers, which I'm sure even we non-Irish have looked for from time to time, and there are those who make the argument that rosaries and crucifix pendants are really nothing more or less than age-old Christian talismans. The gorgeous (and true, by the way) legend of King Arthur would not be complete without his talisman, Excalibur, the famous sword he withdrew from the stone that endowed him with special powers. Christian and non-Christian travelers alike have been known to carry St. Christopher medals for added protection on their journeys, and many a medal of St. Michael, considered among other things to be the patron saint of law enforcement officers, has been hidden inside the uniform of many a police officer, no matter how cynical and nonreligious that officer might claim to be. And, of course, since not all talismans were embraced for the most noble intentions, there was also a revolting favorite among thieves called the Hand of Glory, the severed right hand of a hanged felon, which would supposedly bring especially good luck to every robbery attempt.

The choice of a talisman, if you choose to embrace one, can be as simple or as complicated as you care to make it, bearing in mind that no object by itself possesses any special power—your belief is the only power any talisman will ever have. If it's simplicity you're after, a token from a departed loved one, or a piece of clothing you happened to be wearing when something wonderful happened will do the trick. If you're looking for something a little more intricate, go for connections between your goal for the talisman and color symbolism: green crystals or emeralds if your focus is health-related, for example, since green is the color of healing, or purple stones to enhance a hope for increased spirituality. Or, if you really want to make a research project out of it, you could combine the above with some ancient beliefs found in the world of nature. The sun has long been believed to be the ruler of our self-assuredness, for example. So let's say an event is coming up in which we're going to need every ounce of self-assuredness we can muster. A talisman with a symbol of the sun would be a logical choice, or a talisman made of gold, since gold is thought to be earth's metallic equivalent of the sun. See what I mean? There are enough variations on the symbolic potential of talismans that you could spend weeks searching for exactly the right one to fit your needs.

Or, you could remember what I said earlier, which is as uncomplicated and truthful as anything you'll ever hear or read no matter how much research you do, how far you travel or how long you live: Faith in God, and living that faith every day with all the kindness, compassion and peace it implies, is the most powerful talisman on this earth and the only one you'll ever need.

Tarot

Tarot is a means of fortune-telling through the use of a deck of pictorial, often beautifully artistic cards, each of them with a specific name, image and significance. It's most commonly thought to have its roots in the hieroglyphics of ancient Egypt, and it's gone through many incarnations in its thousands and thousands of years of popularity. But the most currently recognizable and often-used tarot deck was designed by an Englishman named A. E. Waite. It features a seventy-eight-card deck divided into the Major Arcana and the Minor Arcana.

The Minor Arcana of the tarot deck is the basis of today's standard deck of playing cards. It's made up of four suits—cups, swords, wands and pentacles. Each suit contains fourteen cards—ace through ten, followed by a page, a knight, a queen and a king.

The Major Arcana is made up of twenty-two unnumbered cards,

Tarot Cards

also called "trumps." Each bears its own intricate symbolism and its own *general* interpretation:

THE FOOL—the constant aspiration toward our limitless potential

THE MAGICIAN—manifesting our ideas and goals into realities

THE HIGH PRIESTESS—the balancing force between the conscious mind and the subconscious mind

THE EMPRESS—the creativity and imagination found in the subconscious mind

THE EMPEROR—orderliness, a systematic approach to the way things are brought from the mind into the material world

THE HIEROPHANT—our inner self, intuition

THE LOVERS—represents relationships, partners, the blending of two things that are sometimes opposite but compatible

THE CHARIOT—the soul, and our ability to verbalize it

STRENGTH—control over material forces

THE HERMIT—elevated wisdom, holding a lantern to light the way for others to follow

WHEEL OF FORTUNE—true understanding of your inner self

JUSTICE—righting past wrongs

THE HANGED MAN—a hint that everything isn't as it appears to be

DEATH—transformation and rebirth

TEMPERANCE—perfect balance between positive and negative, male and female, conscious and subconscious

THE DEVIL—foolish misinterpretation of facts and circumstances in our lives

THE TOWER—sudden jolts of true insight and understanding

THE STAR—gathering universal knowledge and sharing it with those around us

THE MOON—evolution of the soul

THE SUN—the fixed, unbiased, all-embracing nurturer

JUDGMENT—spiritual understanding

THE WORLD—the continuing and unending cycle of life

Telekinesis

A synonym for "Psychokinesis," which you'll find discussed in its own section.

Telepathy

Telepathy is the direct, instantaneous passing of information, knowledge or feelings from one person or entity to another without using the senses of sight, hearing, touch, taste or smell. Silent transference takes place from a sender to a receiver, sometimes over great distances, and it can happen deliberately or without either the sender or the receiver being aware of it.

Because telepathic information is often meant to have an impact on the receiver and/or to be acted upon, the conscious mind is usually let in on it sooner or later. The information is received in a variety of forms: words or phrases that pop into the mind for no apparent reason, quick flashes of half-complete images, unusually clear dreams, or a sudden preoccupation with a person we might not have seen or thought about in a very long time.

Residents of the spirit world are particularly adept at telepathy. Ask anyone who's had an encounter with a deceased loved one, or most especially an Angel, and they'll describe having had entire conversations in which neither of them spoke a single word. And if you have the joy of being close to an animal, you don't need me to tell you how much those divine spirits telepathically send if you'll simply take the time to slow down, tune in and receive. Telepathy is their most common form of communication with each other, after all, and they happen to be brilliant at it.

Telepathy isn't limited to communication from one person to another, or from one spirit to another. It can be transmitted from any energy source (a city, for example, or a country, or any body of consciousness) to any other energy source or sources (a person or any number of people, whether they know each other or not).

Any number of "experts" and skeptics insist that telepathy never actually has been proven. I'm not quite sure what that means, but it inspires me to include a telepathy story I've told before and can't resist telling again. It's documented, it's fairly famous and it's wonderful.

A man named Victor Samson was a news editor for the *Boston Globe*. One night he did a little too much unwinding after work at a nearby bar and, eager to get to the closest bed as quickly as possible, he decided to go back to the *Globe* and sleep there.

Passed out on his office sofa, Mr. Samson had a horrifying dream about a devastating volcanic eruption on an island called Pele in his dream. Thousands of helpless residents of the villages that surrounded the mountain were killed in the fiery rivers of molten lava.

Deeply shaken by his dream, Mr. Samson grabbed the nearest piece of paper, which happened to be a reporter's work sheet, and wrote down every detail he could remember. Then, still shaken and more than a little hungover, he decided to head on home for a few more hours of sleep before he was due back at work again.

Early the next morning, the *Globe*'s publisher happened by Mr. Samson's office, noticed the work sheet on his desk, read the heartbreaking story of those thousands of people, trapped on a tiny island, decimated by a violent volcanic eruption. Unaware that the story was nothing but Mr. Samson's dream, the publisher breathlessly printed it and then sent it out on wire services throughout the country.

Not until Mr. Samson arrived at the office later that day did the publisher discover that the *Boston Globe* had printed, and then distributed to all of America, nothing more than an alcohol-induced dream.

And not until weeks later did a fleet of ships arrive in Boston Harbor with the news that on the Indonesian island of Krakatau, an island the natives called Pele, a volcanic explosion had killed almost 40,000 people, within the same hour Mr. Samson had his dream.

It was August in the year 1883, you see, and news traveled slowly back then.

But again, remember, telepathy has never actually been proven.

Please.

There are those who believe that some of us are senders and some of us are receivers when it comes to telepathy. An oversimplified yardstick is that if you find yourself thinking of someone and they call shortly afterward, you're probably a sender, while if you tend to know who's calling before you pick up a ringing phone, you're probably a receiver. I don't happen to think any of us need to be categorized or limited to being one or the other. We can just celebrate that, proven or not, telepathy is just another one of those gifts we brought from Home for those times when it might come in handy.

Third Eye

If you were to point to a spot on your forehead that's centered between your eyes and slightly above them, you'd be pointing to the place where your Third Eye exists. It's also called the Spiritual Third Eye or the path to the Seat of the Soul, which simply means the throne from which the spirit rules the link between the physical body it's temporarily inhabiting and the dimension of Home and its God-given eternity.

Belief in the Third Eye is ancient and has its basis in physiology. Its location corresponds to the pea-sized pineal gland that's located in the exact center of the brain. All the way back to Descartes, and the ancient Greeks and Romans in general, the pineal gland has been thought to be our connection to the spirit world, the Other Side, our higher knowledge, our ethereal energy and our innate ability to perceive higher frequencies than our earthly senses allow, which paves the way to communication with realms beyond this one. You've heard stories of people who found themselves with psychic gifts after head injuries, lightning strikes and other physical traumas and illnesses. To name a tiny handful:

Third Eye

* Renowned Dutch psychic Peter Hurkos was perfectly normal (whatever that is) until, at the age of thirty, he fell from a ladder. The brain injury he suffered left him in a coma for three days. When he regained consciousness, he immediately realized that he'd awakened with the ability to know the unknown, and he devoted his life to his psychic gifts on behalf of everyone from law enforcement to U.S. presidents until his death in 1988.

* Edgar Cayce, unparalleled healer and "the Sleeping Prophet," was, by all accounts, a glaringly average Kentucky farm boy whose education ended with grammar school. An illness in his early twenties caused him to lose his voice, and after a year of one unsuccessful medical treatment after another, he subjected himself to hypnotism purely as a last resort. He suggested to the local hypnotist that he put himself to sleep, an ability he'd had since childhood, and both the hypnotist and a friend of Cayce's witnessed what happened when he sank into a deep trance: Edgar Cayce, who barely made it through grammar school and notoriously hated to read, described with the precision of a skilled physician the exact cause of his throat condition and the physiological suggestions the hypnotist should give him while he was still "under" to cure him. The hypnotist did as he was told, Cayce followed his own instructions as repeated to him by the hypnotist and he awoke from that one session with his full voice restored for the first time in a year. He spent the rest of his life modestly and almost reluctantly performing astonishing healings for clients around the world, always while under hypnosis and never with a single page of medical, biological or anatomical study to his name.

* Best-selling author Dannion Brinkley, in his book *Saved By the Light*, tells about, among other things, his first well-publicized near-death experience. It was 1975. He was talking on the phone during a thunderstorm when a bolt of lightning hit the line and literally electrocuted him—his body was clinically dead for twenty-eight minutes. He watched himself being lifted into the back of the ambulance. He heard a technician pronounce him "gone." He experienced the tunnel and a "Being of Light," which surrounded him with "feelings of love [that] intensified until they became almost too pleasurable to withstand." On his return to his body, he found himself able, for the

first time in his life, to predict the future, particularly world events.

All this and countless more cases, less famous but no less remarkable, simply because, as a result of the trauma, the pineal gland has been stimulated and has begun functioning at its peak capacity. Or, symbolically speaking, the Third Eye has opened and is wide awake.

The Third Eye corresponds to the Brow Chakra, which you'll find discussed at length in the "Chakra" section.

Tools of Protection

We make our brief trips here from the perfect paradise of the Other Side for the spirit growth that overcoming negativity and darkness can provide. By definition, we chart new challenges for ourselves with every new incarnation, and they're invariably quite enough for us to deal with. What we don't need is to be further weighed down with the added negativity and darkness that's guaranteed to come at us from out of nowhere as we go about our business trying to take care of what we're here to accomplish.

There are two ways we can combat that added negativity: We can spend our lives under the bed, where nothing at all can get at us, and waste this lifetime completely, or we can make good use of every moment we're here and let our Tools of Protection handle the darkness.

Tools of Protection are suits of armor we create within ourselves to surround us like a divine force field wherever we go. Use any or all of them that appeal to you—in fact, the more the better. And using them means nothing more than firmly fixing the images in our conscious mind and our spirit mind. Take an hour meditating on the images around you, or take two minutes during your shower. It doesn't matter. Any amount of time, day or night, is fine, as long as you get into the habit of using your Tools of Protection and reach a point where you'd feel naked leaving home without them.

If you don't believe they'll work, try it for a week or two to prove me wrong. They're free of charge, and they certainly won't do you any harm. They also won't make your life free of negativity and darkness from this moment on. Tools of Protection can't and shouldn't circumvent your chart. But when it comes to the uncharted interference around you that undermines your confidence, blurs your focus and tries to pull you off track, a combination of God and your Tools of Protection will take care of it for you from now on.

* **The Circle of Mirrors**—Picture yourself inside a perfect circle of mirrors, taller than you, facing away from you. White entities are drawn toward mirrors, while dark entities are repelled by them and will go out of their way to avoid you.

* **The Bubble of White Light**—While you should always surround yourself with the white light of the Holy Spirit, here's a variation on the image that makes me smile: I'm sure you remember in *The Wizard of Oz*, that Glinda, the Good Witch of the North, traveled inside a beautiful, transparent bubble. Move through your day that same way, inside a bubble made of the sacred, transparent white light of the Holy Spirit.

* **The Golden Sword**—Picture a gleaming golden sword, its hilt ornate and sparkling with jewels. Hold the sword up in front of your body, so that the hilt forms a cross over your Brow Chakra, and the blade extends like a slender, impenetrable declaration of divine strength down the length of your body, deflecting the inherent cowardice of the Dark Side.

* **Gold and Silver Nets**—The image is a fisherman's net, of finespun gold and silver gossamer, strong but light as air, its fibers braided and glistening with the white light of the Holy Spirit. Drape it over yourself to cover and protect yourself from head to toe in divine white light. As you move through your day, drape a

matching gold and silver net over any dark entities you encounter, to contain and neutralize their negativity.

* **The Dome of Light**—Picture a magnificent dome, its curved walls and ceiling made of the radiant white light of the Holy Spirit, covering you and those you love. The Dome of Light is especially effective as a car cover.

* **Worry Beads**—Borrowed and blended from the Catholics, the Greeks and the Tibetans, with thanks. Either buy or make yourself a four- to five-inch-diameter circle of beads. It's essential that the beads be made of a natural material, preferably wood—nothing artificial. Every night before you sleep, go one bead at a time around the little circle, assigning one thing you're worried about to each separate bead. When each bead has its own designated worry, place the circle of beads in a small container of sand on your nightstand, to let the sand absorb the worries from the beads and neutralize the worries.

May you and the other white entities of this world find each other and, armed with God's love and your Tools of Protection, walk together safe and confident through the negativity of the Dark Side as you follow the lighted path you've chosen to lead you Home.

Totems

To understand this definition of a totem, you should first read or review the word "chart," which, put *very* simply, is the highly detailed "preautobiography" we write for ourselves on the Other Side before we come to earth for another incarnation. We never take these trips away from Home for trivial reasons, and we're well aware ahead of time that we're setting ourselves up for enormous challenges—let's face it, if we didn't feel we had important knowledge and growth to gain from those challenges, we'd stay right where we are, in busy, blissful joy, surrounded by perfection. So precisely because we know it's going to be a difficult trip, we recruit a team of protectors from the Other Side to be with us every step of the way while we're gone. We choose a Spirit Guide. We choose a certain number of Angels. And we choose a totem.

Our totem is any member of the animal kingdom we choose to be our most loyal, constant companion away from Home, whichever glorious spirit beast we prefer tirelessly standing guard over us, its pure, perfect, devoted heart utterly committed to our well-being. Animals are revered on the Other Side, understood for exactly what they are: among God's most divine creations, incarnating one time purely for our benefit but never having to incarnate again because

Totem

they already possess the sacred wisdom we keep coming back to search for. We would never consider venturing to earth without our totem, and along with every pet we've ever owned in every life-time we've lived on earth, our totem is among the first to greet us when we complete our trip through the tunnel and arrive safely back Home.

Totems reveal themselves in any number of ways here on earth. The most obvious is if there's a particular animal you find yourself inexplicably drawn to and/or fascinated by, whether or not you've ever actually owned one or, for that matter, seen one in person. I have a friend who's mesmerized by rhinoceroses and another one who collects any miniature representation of a pig he can get his hands on, and neither of them has ever been closer than Animal Planet to the real objects of their enchantment. Another manifestation that many of my clients have mentioned is a distant and completely incongruous animal sound during the night—a trumpeting elephant in the woods around a Canadian cabin for example, or the indescribable shriek of a peacock during a red-eye cross-country flight. One client I'll always smile about never saw his own totem, a panther, but was constantly getting complaints from his landlord about the huge black cat that was so flagrantly visible in the front window of his no-pet apartment.

As for those of you who have trouble believing you have a totem because you think you don't like animals, let me assure you that if you're here from the Other Side, you arrived with a chart, and if you arrived with a chart, you have a totem. To dislike animals, and deny their sanctity in God's eyes, is to turn your back on one of the great sources of loyalty and protection you brought with you from Home. It's worth exploring and overcoming if you can, because you're need-lessly depriving yourself, and isn't life on earth tough enough without finding ways to make it even tougher?

The Towers

Among the buildings at the entrance to the Other Side, rising majesti-
cally behind the white marble triumvirate of the Hall of Wisdom, the
Hall of Records and the Hall of Justice, sit two identical monoliths
called the Towers. Hushed waterfalls glisten down their massive fa-
cades of blue glass, misting the forest of jasmine whose scent leads
the way to their etched golden doors.

The locals of Home revere the Towers as sites of unparalleled se-
renity for study, meditation and reunions with astral travelers from
earth. The natural atmospheric light on the Other Side is an eternal,
achingly beautiful pastel of pinks, violets and greens. Filtered through
the Towers' blue glass walls, that light becomes so exceptionally potent with God's love that these two beautiful buildings are largely devoted to the most challenging healing the spirits at Home ever face.

There are spirits whose circumstances at death were too extreme
for the more traditional procedures of Orientation or Cocooning to
help and heal them. Through no fault of their own, these spirits arrive
on the Other Side desperately disoriented or deranged, and they can't
experience the peace of Home until they've been deprogrammed back
to their rightful sanity and identity. POWs who died in captivity after
being brainwashed and tortured; many Holocaust victims; some of the
most severe casualties of Alzheimer's and other diseases that deeply
affect the mind; Joan of Arc, interestingly—all who were robbed of
their ability to understand who and where they were when they died
are taken immediately from the Other Side's entrance to the sacred
embrace of the Towers. They're escorted there by their Spirit Guide
and usually a close loved one as well, both of whom stay with them
throughout their recovery.

The deprogramming process within the Towers is really just a
highly sophisticated version of the deprogramming process on earth.
The most brilliant minds in the field, as well as the finest psychiatrists
and physicians the world has ever known, attend each spirit with

techniques we have yet to be infused with here on earth, while loved ones and Angels gather to lend their divine support. The spirit's earthly birthplace or childhood home or some other site of happy familiarity is re-created, therapists telepathically relate stories from the spirit's past lives on earth and at Home, loved ones travel from every corner of the Other Side to lend shared stories of their own, and all the while the ailing spirit lies still, basking in that amazing, healing pastel light pouring in through blue glass walls.

The treatment continues for as long as it's needed. It ends only when the spirits have regained total recall of their own identity, the lifetime they've just completed, all the lives that preceded that one and the sacred significance of being Home again. Only then can the eternal journey of their soul continue intact, and only then do they emerge from the Towers and resume their busy lives on the Other Side.

Obviously, we all pray for ecstatic trips Home for ourselves and our loved ones. Unfortunately, that doesn't always happen. But I believe it's essential to focus on what does always happen: All spirits who make it to the Other Side, no matter what their circumstances when they died on earth, are immediately embraced and brilliantly cared for until they're fully restored, thriving and filled with the safe, blissful ecstasy of being Home again in their Father's arms.

Trance

A trance is a condition in which there is an actual, dramatic, measurable drop in the body's vital signs, an equally measurable decrease in mental activity and a complete, temporary halt to all voluntary movement. In a way, a trance simulates death, although there's never any actual danger of dying.

If you've ever seen my Spirit Guide Francine speak, you've seen me in a trance—by "going out of my body," as I tend to call it, or "stepping aside" for a while, I can allow her to borrow my physical being to make it easier to communicate on this dimension. And because my mental activity has been tested while Francine is "in" and proven to be nonexistent, I never have the slightest awareness of anything that goes on during the time when she's taken over.

Tulpa

Tulpa are beings that originate in the mind and then, through intense belief and visualization, become actual physical realities. It's not a case of a person or group of people strongly imagining a being, or projecting it as some kind of shared hallucination. It's a case of one mind, or several minds, creating a very real, physical, living being that eventually takes on a life of its own, gathering strength as more and more people believe in its existence and usually becoming harder to get rid of than it was to create in the first place.

It's impossible to write about the tulpa phenomenon without talking about a woman named Alexandra David-Neel. She was a fearless adventurer, writer, lecturer, researcher and scholar, born in Paris in 1868, who traveled throughout Asia, usually on foot, to study and experience everything from Eastern mysticism to mind-over-matter techniques to the teachings of Buddha to Tibetan spirituality and culture.

Enthralled by the Tibetan concept of tulpa, an entity you could manifest into physical existence by mentally conceiving it, David-Neel decided to explore the discipline of creating one herself. In her mind she conceived a round, pleasant little monk, kind of a Friar Tuck clone, as harmless and friendly as he could be. She then began practicing a routine of intense visualization and concentration, and over time she was able to see the small monk as not just a mental image but as a living, tangible being, separate from herself, as real as the rest of the world it began to inhabit. The more she continued to visualize him, the more solid and visible he became and, she was increasingly upset to discover, the less she was able to control him. He started making appearances at his own convenience, whether she willed him to or not, and within a few weeks, other people who knew nothing about her tulpa experiment began asking her about the diminutive stranger who seemed to be coming and going out of nowhere.

Most alarming to David-Neel, though, was that the longer her creation existed, the more he began developing his own persona that had nothing to do with the one she'd originally visualized. The pleasant, cherubic little monk began to evolve into a stronger, more slender version of himself, and as he did he slowly became sullen, dark and menacing. Finally David-Neel knew she had to destroy this potentially dangerous being she'd created but could no longer control, and she also knew she could destroy him only by absorbing him back into her mind, where he came from. The monk tulpa put up a fierce fight, so self-sufficient by then that he felt completely entitled to exist, and it took over a month of the same intense concentration that created him for her to eliminate him. The process was so debilitating that David-Neel's health was almost destroyed right along with the sinister little creature she'd brought into this world.

Tulpa, then, are powerful projected thoughts and emotions that become telescoped into physical forms. The more thoughts, emotions and credibility that are invested in the tulpa, the more real and alive they become. It's important to remember that once they've begun to exist on their own, without those who created them controlling when they appear and disappear, they're no longer imaginary, and no longer all that easy to control or get rid of.

The yeti, or Abominable Snowman, of the Himalayas is a brilliant example of a tulpa, created by rumor and legend and then given life by increasingly widespread fear of it and belief in its existence. Its huge footprints have been photographed in the deep mountain snow, but even though it has reportedly been seen, fleetingly, from a distance of 300 yards, its full form has never been captured on film. The native Sherpas of the high Himalayas firmly believe that the yeti lives among them and that it can make itself appear and disappear whenever it chooses, exactly like Alexandra David-Neel's monk, who began to decide for himself when and if he wanted to be seen.

I believe the Loch Ness Monster is a tulpa. I also strongly believe that anyone who claims to have seen the devil in physical form has simply allowed fear, negativity and evil to become such powerful forces in her life that she's created a tulpa that's guaranteed to terrorize her, with no one but herself to thank.

Which is why I believe that a tulpa, created out of greed and a misguided interest in fame, was the only thing that ever haunted the infamous house in Amityville, New York, where the supposed "Amityville Horror" took place.

In case you're not familiar with the story of the Amityville Horror, its real horror took place on November 13, 1974, when a deeply troubled young man named Ronald DeFeo murdered six members of his family in their three-story house. He was convicted of all six murders.

In the summer of 1975, the DeFeo house was bought by George and Kathy Lutz. The young couple and Kathy's three children moved into the house in December of 1975. Within either ten days or twenty-eight days, depending which account you read, they were allegedly driven from the house by ghosts, flying pigs and other terrifying embodiments of evil. Their accounts of exactly what those ghosts, flying pigs, etc. looked like and did to them continued to change even after their best-selling book and the hit movie *The Amityville Horror* based on that book leapt onto movie screens, claiming to be a true story. To this day the Lutzes can't seem to land on a story they're comfortable with. In one interview, for example, George Lutz said that on their last night in the house, before they ran for their lives, abandoning everything they owned, he was in bed, helpless, unable to move or even cry out, for reasons he couldn't quite articulate, while his wife levitated above the bed and he could hear his children's beds upstairs slamming against the floor as if they were being lifted in the air and then suddenly dropped. In another interview George Lutz said that what happened in that house on their last night there—which he clearly described in the above-mentioned interview—was simply too horrible to describe. Beats me.

I've never been to the Amityville house. Warner Brothers Studios offered me a very generous amount of money to go there for a filmed paranormal investigation, but I declined. I believed then and I believe now that George and Kathy Lutz thought that moving into the Amityville house might be their ticket to fame and fortune. I doubt that they meant any harm. Opportunism often starts with innocent intentions. I'm sure what started out as a potentially profitable publicity stunt kept snowballing until it was out of control and far too late for the Lutzes to back out of their story gracefully, especially with a movie studio determined to include the words "a true story" in their ads for *The Amityville Horror.* But there's no way around the fact that anyone who tries to cash in on someone else's tragedy will always pay too high a price in the long run to make it worth the effort. If the Lutzes are now stuck with a tulpa or two from their time in the Amityville house, that increases the price to astronomical, and I truly wish them well.

And if you still find it hard to imagine that an actual tangible living being can be created through something as simple as the power of the mind, please take a moment to realize that there's nothing human-made that exists on this earth that didn't originate with a single thought.

The Tunnel

Yes, *that* tunnel. The tunnel you've heard about all your life, the one with the bright white light at the end, the one you're a little uncomfortable thinking about but hope to God isn't just another feel-good fairy tale.

I can personally assure you that the legendary tunnel is very real. You can assure yourself, for that matter, if you can access your past lives through meditation, regressive hypnosis or exercises I've included in other books—you've been through the tunnel yourself, probably dozens of times but definitely at least once for every lifetime you've lived on earth. But I know firsthand how easy it is for your conscious mind to forget what you had for dinner last night, let alone how you got Home after your last incarnation. So I have the benefit of my own experience with the tunnel in this life to draw on, and I'm happy to tell you everything I know about it.

I was forty-two years old. I was on the operating table, going through what was supposed to be postoperative "routine" surgery. I'll spare you the physiological details and skip to the important part: With no warning, I flatlined.

I can't tell you a thing about the drama my body and the surgical team went through. All I can tell you is what happened to *me* from that moment on:

* The tunnel appeared, right on cue. Like many people, you may have always pictured it suddenly dropping down from some invisible trapdoor in the sky. As it turns out, it doesn't drop down and lead up at all. It rises from us, from our own etheric substance, and leads across our bodies, at about a twenty- or thirty-degree angle. It makes complete sense when you know that our destination on the Other Side isn't far, far away past the clouds, moon and stars. It's right here, a whole other dimension and frequency level, just three feet above our ground level.

* I don't remember entering the tunnel, but I remember everything about moving through it. I was alive. Completely, thrillingly, vibrantly alive. I felt free and weightless, relieved to be rid of my body and rid of the pull of gravity. And without effort, I was infused with peace, bliss and total recall of the truth of eternity. With it came a release of all worry about the loved ones I'd left behind. I knew they'd be fine. They would see to that, and so

would God. And in what would seem like no time at all to me, we'd be together again on the Other Side, so there was no sad sense of loss, or missing them.

* The sacred brilliance of the white light appeared ahead of me. Everything I'd heard and read about it was true—for reasons that defy description, it did seem that all God's love and infinite knowledge were pulsing through it, and it was as familiar to me as my own soul.

* The figure of a loved one appeared in the large opening at the end of the tunnel. In my case it was my cherished Grandma Ada, whom I'd yearned to see again since I was eighteen. Beyond her I could see hints of a grassy, flower-filled meadow, in magnified jewel tones that have no comparison on earth.

Now, in my case, this was obviously a *near*-death experience. The rest of that story is simply that I heard the distant voice of a friend by my hospital bed crying, "Sylvia, don't go, you're so needed." I was just reaching for my Grandma Ada's outstretched hand when that voice intruded, upon which she calmly turned her hand so that her palm was toward me, a firm, silent, adoring order for me to stop. There was no discussion, no conscious decision on my part, only the friend's plea, my hand inches from my grandmother's, and then I was slammed back into my body, waking up on a hospital bed, as if a giant rubber band around my waist had been stretched to its limit and yanked me back.

What I know from my Spirit Guide Francine, though, and from more regressive hypnosis sessions than I can count over the last four decades, is that when we do take our loved one's hand and step into that light beyond the tunnel, we experience the most joyful reunions with loved ones from Home and past lives, with our Spirit Guide and with all the animals we've ever adored. (No disrespect to the people I love, but I can't wait to see my animals again.) And from that breathtaking meadow where those reunions take place we proceed to the familiar vast marble steps of the Hall of Wisdom where our transition to the Other Side officially begins.

To clear up a couple of issues I'm asked about by clients several times a week:

No matter where on this planet we are when our bodies die, no matter what our official religion or if we have one at all, no matter if we were formally baptized, or if we had a proper burial, or if our bodies have even been found—*the tunnel doesn't have to find us; it comes from us, wherever we are and whatever the circumstances of our death. And all tunnels, from everywhere on earth, lead through God's infinite white light to the same familiar steps of the Hall of Wisdom on the Other Side.* I know the agony some of you are in, unable for countless tragic reasons to hold a deceased loved one just one more time to say goodbye. But whatever part of your pain has to do with the peace of your loved one's spirit, I swear, and you know I won't lie to you, even when you wish I would—your loved one is Home, safe, sound, and healthier than ever, in the joyful peace of God's arms.

U

Ultraterrestrials

We all know that extraterrestrials are visiting life-forms from other planets. And then there is the great debate about ultraterrestrials. There must be hundreds of theories about ultraterrestrials, starting with such basics as whether or not there are such things, who they are if they do exist, where they come from and whether their intentions toward us are good or evil.

I have my own theory about ultraterrestrials, based on an experience in which I came in actual physical contact with one.

Several years ago I managed to start a grease fire in my kitchen. Like an idiot, I was so busy trying to put out the fire that I did not notice how much oily black smoke I was inhaling, until the realization hit me that I was about to suffocate. Panicked and gasping for air, I started running toward the balcony about twenty feet from the kitchen, but about halfway there I knew I wasn't going to make it, and I started to pass out.

Suddenly some superhuman force tackled me from behind and hurled me out onto the balcony. As I lay on my stomach, gratefully breathing fresh air again, a shock of golden blond hair fell into view over my shoulder for just a split second before I felt the weight of the force who'd saved me dissipate.

When I sat up again, only moments later, I was alone on the balcony, staring in at the lingering tendrils of smoke from the fire that had burned itself out by now.

Since Francine's hair is jet-black, I knew I couldn't give her credit for rescuing me, so I assumed it was one of my Angels. I was shocked when Francine told me that no, my heroine had actually been my beloved grandmother Ada Coil, who'd died three decades earlier. In fact, to be honest, "shocked" isn't exactly the right word. I didn't believe her.

"It couldn't have been Grandma Ada, Francine. Grandma Ada's hair was white, remember?" I said, frankly a little pleased that finally, for once, I was going to prove Francine wrong. Being smug lasted for two or three seconds at most. Then it hit me that Grandma Ada's hair had turned white in her seventies and eighties, from the golden blond it had been throughout her life, including when she was thirty years old—the age we all are on the Other Side, from where my grandmother rushed to save my life. Rescuing me was such an urgent, loving impulse that instead of transforming into a persona I'd recognize, she came as she was, thirty years old, blond and younger than I was at that time.

And that is what I believe ultraterrestrials are. I believe that they are visitors from the Other Side—the Angels, the Spirit Guides, the departed loved ones—who, in our moments of great need and crisis, find such strength from the sacred love within themselves for us and our safety that they manage to manifest from their spirit form on their dimension to a physical form on this dimension, just long enough to accomplish some heroic act on our behalf. I don't believe ultraterrestrials can or will intercept our charts; nor do I believe that's their intention. In fact, I believe they come to help ensure that we complete them. I know that's what my Grandma Ada did for me that day, and that I wouldn't be here if it weren't for her. So yes, I believe in ultra-terrestrials, I believe they are our heroes from Home, manifested briefly on earth when we desperately need them, and I believe that more often than we probably know, we owe them our deepest, most heartfelt gratitude.

The Underworld

Let's start with what the Underworld is *not*. It is *not* hell. It is not a distant cousin of hell, it is not where Satan lives, it is not a place where some eternal fire of damnation burns. There is no Satan. There is no hell. There is no eternal damnation. No perfect, loving God would be capable of creating such a place, let alone banishing one of His children there.

What the Underworld *is* is a creation of God that is essentially a mirror image of the Other Side. Each of them is comprised of seven levels. On the Other Side the levels ascend to the highest possible advancement, which is the seventh. In the Underworld, also called the Seven Lower Levels of Creation, the most highly advanced beings are found on the First Level, and the advancement descends from there.

The First Level of the Underworld is populated with what we on earth call "the little people." Yes, *those* little people—the fairies, the gnomes, the elves, the sprites, the leprechauns, all the beings some swear to have seen and others swear exist only in myths and, pardon the expression, fairy tales. And it's on this First Level of the Underworld that unicorns live, in case you've ever had a sneaking suspicion that they're not as fictional as skeptics like to claim they are.

Presiding over this very beautiful and appropriately diminutive First Level is the Queen of the Fairies, Lilith, who's been given her own section in this book. The First Level entities are their own phylum, with life spans lasting hundreds of years. They procreate, but they never reincarnate, for the same reason, in a way, that animals never reincarnate—their spirits are complete and fully evolved at the moment they're created, so they have no journey to accomplish, no learning left to do.

The First Level exists on the same frequency as earth, and it's not just a lot of overactive imaginations who are responsible for the rumors that "the little people" make appearances on earth. They do, and because their dimension and ours are vibrationally identical, we're able to see them more easily than we can see the spirit world from the Other Side, who have a lot of frequency adjusting to do to become visible. They are not evil, either in their own world or in ours. They mean no harm and they cause no harm, while being accused of the lowest, nastiest crimes against nature imaginable. (I admit, it makes me chuckle when I hear someone scoff at how ridiculous it is for anyone to believe in such a thing as gnomes, and then a sentence or two later adds that "everyone knows" gnomes steal and eat people's babies. I wonder why it is that when we don't know much about a subject, we almost always fill in the blanks with something negative.)

The Second Level of the Seven Levels is a nebulous and frankly unpleasant place to visit, not because it's evil but because it's noisy, it's loud and it sounds like a thousand radios at full volume playing different stations at the same time. The best way I know to describe its purpose is to call it the Underworld's audible version of the Akashic Records. Start with the recognition that as soon as any thought is complete, it becomes a thing, with an energy of its own. Then look back at all the thoughts you've had within the last two hours, let's say. Would you consider each and every one of them worthy of going on record on the Other Side? (I would have to answer "no" to that myself, by the way.) But energy can't be destroyed, so it has to go somewhere, and where the energy of those particular thoughts goes is to the Second Level of the Underworld. It's a pulsating, nerve-shattering mass of weeping, hysterical laughter, words, phrases, moans, screaming, threats, wailing and expletives in every language that ever existed, and I'm convinced that Dante was primarily referring to the Second Level when he wrote his *Inferno*.

The Third Level to the Seventh are a bit hard to delineate, at least for me, and in all my research I have yet to read a description I would completely endorse. In general, though, the denizens of the five lowest levels are those creatures, monsters and the projected ugliness humankind has energized into being. It's a vast, animated mental garbage dump, where demons really do exist, but only because humans keep creating them like otherworldly tulpas. (And tulpas are discussed at length in their own section too, by the way.)

The most important fact to understand about the hideous demons of those lowest levels is that *they are incapable of visitations to earth*. You will never actually see one on this planet, and you'll certainly never be harmed by one. Where they will appear from time to time, unfortunately, is in nightmares—the perfect, most descriptive place for them. But even their presence in nightmares is not because they come to us; it's because we get too curious for our own good sometimes and astrally go to them, with the result that we scare ourselves silly. Even on their own turf, the lowest-level entities can't and won't do us any physical harm. They're just a shocking jolt of manifested negativity, not something we could ever be prepared for or something we can easily shake off after we've been exposed to it.

If you find yourself having recurring nightmares that sound like the astral trips to the lowest levels I've just described, the second place to turn for help is Lilith. (The first place is always God. *Always*. And Lilith, for all her beauty and power, is worthy of admiration but not of worship—she is not a god.) As guardian of the First Level, she is able to seal off the levels below hers from our access, and all we have to do is ask. Just petition Lilith to cement the door closed that leads beyond the beautiful fairyland of the First Level and she'll be happy to oblige. She knows what's down there, and she knows it's not really evil, satanic or dangerous. She's just eager to spare you the needless psychic trauma, and so am I.

Urantia

Whether you consider it a possibility or hold your sides laughing about the inception of *The Urantia Book*, you'll have to admit it's interesting and worth acknowledging in a collection of paranormal terms.

As the story goes, there was a man named Dr. William Sadler who was a professor at Chicago University and a lecturer in counseling at a nearby theological seminary. In the late 1920s, Dr. Sadler was visited by a new counseling client who'd begun talking in his sleep—not random, idle words and phrases, but long dissertations from a group of supermortal beings who called themselves "revelators." These revelators seemed to have chosen this man as their channel for communicating with humans on earth, but only while he slept. When the client was awake, he not only lost his channeling ability; he was completely disinterested in his channeling ability, the revelators and what the revelators had to say.

Dr. Sadler, on the other hand, was fascinated, and began transcribing sessions with his client while the client slept. The result of those transcriptions evolved into *The Urantia Book*, a massive 2,000-page tome, comprised of four separate sections, all of them directly or indirectly relating to Urantia, which according to the revelators was the name by which Earth was known in ancient times.

Part I of *The Urantia Book* discusses God, the existence of paradise and the order of the many universes. Part II introduces Michael, the Son of God and Son of Man (Jesus) as the ruler of Urantia's/Earth's universe, called the Local Universe. There's also a central universe where God himself is manifest. Part III is the history of Urantia/Earth, from its creation to its many geological transformations through the evolutions of humankind, civilizations, cultures and religions. And Part IV is devoted to the life of Jesus.

When I first heard of *The Urantia Book* and how it was conceived, and then heard that it had been translated into about fifteen languages and sold more than a quarter of a million copies, my curiosity got the better of me, and I settled in to read it. I made it about a third of the way through before I started screaming, "What's your point?!"

I promise you, I'm no lightweight when it comes to reading. I've labored my way through volumes so thick and densely written they make *The Urantia Book* look like a pamphlet. I'm not about to claim there's no worthwhile information to be found in all those pages. There probably is. And I give *The Urantia Book* credit for not presenting itself as a new religion, or even as a religion at all. It seems to be nondenominational, embracing of a variety of faiths and, like the philosophy of my church Novus Spiritus, it doesn't appear to be campaigning for recruits.

It's entirely possible that I'm too pedantic, or logic-driven, to have an endless amount of patience with hypotheticals. And I guess revelators transmitting information through a sleeping man to a pastoral counselor aren't likely to waste their time dictating light reading. But I love exploring new angles on my own beliefs, and on new beliefs entirely. It widens my view, opens my mind and deepens my spirit's appreciation for God and the countless ways His children find to adore Him. I guess that was my biggest disappointment with *The Urantia Book*. I was expecting it to be spiritually thought-provoking. Instead, it felt so intentionally complex that I just found it provoking.

By all means, if you love to read, you're up for a challenge and you're even remotely curious about *The Urantia Book*, don't hesitate. I'm sure you can find it online, in more than a dozen languages. And if there's some brilliant God-centered wisdom in it that I either didn't get to or didn't understand, you have my word, I'll stand up in a heartbeat and say I was wrong.

Vampires

In December of 1431, in a Romanian fortress, a child was born whose name was Vlad Tepes. His father, military governor of Transylvania, was named Vlad Dracul. As Vlad Tepes grew up, he adopted the nickname by which he was often called: "Dracula," which was simply a diminutive that meant "son of Dracul."

In 1442, the young Vlad Dracula was kidnapped by political enemies of his father's and held for six years in Turkey. On his release he learned that both his father and his older brother had been tortured and assassinated. With that news, the now seventeen-year-old Dracula vowed revenge, and he finally achieved it in 1456, killing the assassins and taking over the Wallachian throne of Romania in the process.

During his six-year reign, he was a cruel, merciless, often sadistic ruler, with a preference for impaling, decapitating, blinding, boiling, burning or skinning those who opposed or annoyed him. He also forced an assembly of his enemies to build a fortress for him in the town of Poenari, ruins of which exist today as "Castle Dracula." Dracula once invited the local vagrants and homeless, without mentioning that he considered them all to be lowlifes and thieves, to a great feast in one of the halls of his court. As the meal ended, Dracula ordered the hall sealed and torched. All the guests burned to death. Another story goes that, in order to intimidate a sultan who was trying to capture the throne, Dracula poisoned enough wells and rivers and set fire to enough villages that when the sultan and his forces finally reached the outskirts of the city in what would have undoubtedly been a successful siege, they were confronted by the impaled bodies of tens of thousands of Turks. The site of this horror came to be called the "Forest of the Impaled," and the sultan, by the way, retreated.

Dracula was eventually assassinated in 1476.

And if you're wondering where in that story Vlad Dracula's thirst for drinking blood is mentioned, triggering his status as the world's most famous and historic vampire, don't bother browsing back through it. It's not there. There's no reference in the life of Dracula, unspeakable human being that he was, to his having the slightest interest in drinking blood. Novelist Bram Stoker, who created that particular fictional vampire, simply chose Dracula as the model for his books, and thus was born one of the great franchises in literary and film history.

Of course, the vampire myth dates back thousands upon thousands of years, in virtually every culture on earth—some variation on the dead rising from their graves during the night, sometimes in formal wear and capes, moving through villages and countrysides sucking the blood of humans and animals and, at will, turning their prey into vampires as well and ushering them into the land of the undead.

Opinions varied on how they could be stopped. Piercing their hearts, particularly with a cross, was rumored to be effective. Or you could decapitate them and place their heads between their feet. Pouring holy water on their graves and/or burning them often worked, according to legend. And then there's my particular favorite: Vampires theoretically loved to count things. So if you simply spread poppy seeds around the graves of vampires, they would be so enthralled with counting the seeds, they would simply forget to go on hunting and blood-drinking sprees.

What keeps all this fascinating, colorful mythology and fiction from being enjoyable is that there have been believers, and believers have led to too many tragedies to imagine. People throughout the centuries were accused of being vampires if they were simply born with some oddity like a caul or pointed teeth, or born out of wedlock, or if they died before they were baptized, or if they died in some unexplainable way. Exhumations were common as believers checked corpses for signs of vampirism. There was even a French theologian named Dom Augustine Calmet who, in 1746, composed a long, logical treatise on the validity of the existence of vampires. What prompted him is anyone's guess (although I'm suspicious that a hallucinogen called laudanum, which was common at the time, might have been involved), but he lent still more credibility to a myth that had no business becoming anything beyond that.

Applause goes to a member of the Austrian royal family, Empress Marie Theresa, who finally sent her own physician throughout the land to do a thorough investigation. He did. And he returned to her with a report stating in no uncertain terms that no such thing as vampires existed, nor had they ever. With which Empress Marie Theresa enacted a series of laws making it a punishable crime to tamper with graves and desecrate corpses.

That there are still those today who take vampirism beyond its rightful place as a myth is an unfortunate fact, but for the record, I promise you, there are no true vampires, only pretenders who've adopted a violent legacy of fiction as an excuse for their own violence and disturbed behavior.

Visage

I used to take casual polls during readings, lectures and salons, so I'm aware of the myth that when we leave our bodies and become part of the spirit world again, we either look like wispy vapor blobs or we look like nothing at all.

It pleases me to assure you that we each have very distinctive physical personas on the Other Side, and those personas are called our visages. We have bodies, we have eyes that blink and we have hearts that pump blood through our veins. I find it fascinating that we also have organs that are a mirror image of our human bodies on earth, the identical placement but reversed from left to right. Why we have organs when we no longer have to bother with such bodily inconveniences as digestion and waste elimination, I have no idea. I asked my Spirit Guide Francine, whose answer was, "Because that's the way God made us." She's a hard woman to argue with.

Similarly, I asked her why it is that no matter what age we are when we die, we're all thirty years old on the Other Side. Why thirty? "Because we are." See what I mean? Just like on earth, visages at Home come in all heights, weights, nationalities, hair colors, eye colors and skin colors. At Home, though, we can change our visage styles whenever we choose without ever losing our identities, and without spending a moment in a salon, at a makeup table, or under a plastic surgeon's scalpel, through simple thought projection, which is as natural to us on the Other Side as breathing.

For example, Francine tells me I occasionally adopt the appearance of an Asian woman on the Other Side, for no other reason than that I find it attractive. It doesn't throw everyone into hopeless confusion about who I am, and I don't have to run around reintroducing myself to my friends. The other spirits think nothing more about it than, "She's wearing her Asian look today." That might explain why I spent hours in front of a mirror when I was a small child, pulling on my face, trying to adjust my eyes, nose and mouth so that I'd look familiar to myself. I'm sure I kept sitting down at my vanity expecting to see the reflection of a thirty-year-old Asian woman staring back and didn't appreciate finding a strange little red-haired Caucasian girl instead.

Our ability to easily change our visage on the Other Side is especially apparent when we decide to pay a visit to a loved one on earth. We all recognize each other through any number of looks at Home, but human beings need all the visual aids they can get when it comes to figuring out an unexpected appearance from the spirit world. If we died at the age of five, or ninety-five, but appeared to a loved one as the happy, healthy thirty-year-old we are on the Other Side, their chances of recognizing us would range from slim to none. We eliminate the problem by simply thought-projecting ourselves back to the physical appearance they remember us by.

On the other hand, I can't tell you how many clients have astrally traveled to the Other Side to spend time with a deceased loved one and found themselves talking to a thirty-year-old stranger who somehow seemed familiar. If and when it happens to you, pay attention to those strangers. Chances are they're exactly who you were longing to see; they just weren't expecting you and didn't know to adjust their visage to match your memory of them.

While there's a lot of freedom in our ability to choose our visages on the Other Side, a few mandates apply too:

* No visible scars, injuries, marks of illness, or disabilities from our most recent lifetime—life on the Other Side means total and complete healing.
* If we repeatedly abuse our bodies during an incarnation, though, our bodies on the Other Side will reflect that abuse as a reminder that we have more to learn about overcoming self-destruction.
* The more spiritually advanced we become, the more physical beauty we're given, as a badge of our progress.
* No matter how physically beautiful our visage becomes, we always retain a tiny physical flaw of some kind, a blemish we accept gladly, to remind us that the only true perfection is God's and God's alone.

Voodoo

This may come as a surprise to a lot of people, but at the heart of voodoo lies a belief in one God, supreme and omnipotent.

Voodooists further believe in a legion of spirits, called the Loa, who reside in all nature and all natural phenomena, giving all living things sanctity, and a connection to all other living things throughout the universe. We are all parts of the same One, in other words, so any action we take toward anyone or anything around us—kind or cruel— is an action we've taken toward ourselves. Practitioners of voodoo revere their ancestors, whose spirits they believe are alive and present among them, and pay frequent ceremonial homage, through music and dance, to their connection to the spirit world and to the Divine.

Now, I ask you, is that even close to a description of what you think when you hear the word "voodoo"? I'm not trying to solicit converts; I'm just pointing out yet another religion that's tragically been misunderstood and condemned for the acts of a few extreme splinter groups who have nothing to do with the origins, the core beliefs and the intentions of the voodoo faith itself.

It has its roots in ancient Africa and is one of the world's oldest religions. It traveled from there to the Caribbean through the European colonization of the island of Hispaniola, which Haiti and the Dominican Republic now share. The Europeans brought African slaves with them and, in order to keep them under constant control, made sure they were impoverished. But the anguish of slavery and poverty created a great, lasting unity among the Africans on Hispaniola, built around the common faith they brought with them from across the ocean.

It's our nature, I guess, to mistrust what goes on in secrecy and assume it must be evil or it wouldn't be hidden. And I don't pretend to have a vast area of expertise on voodoo rites and rituals. What I do know, though, is that there have been more than enough times and places throughout the history of voodoo since it arrived in the Caribbean in which its practice was punishable by imprisonment, torture and death. That voodoo has been strong enough not just to survive so much cruel injustice but to thrive, to the point where Haiti officially sanctioned it as a religion in 2003, is a testament to the depth of its courageous commitment to its faith in the sanctity of nature and of one almighty God.

Vortex

Several definitions in this book—especially "chakras," "imprints," "psychometry" and "tulpa"—make reference to the word "vortex." Just to clarify and give you an image in case you're not familiar with vortices, they're most commonly seen in nature in the form of tornadoes and water spouts—masses of air or water spinning with such speed and force that they're able to pull any objects in their path into the void or "eye" at their center.

These spiraling masses of energy also exist in swirling vortices of the earth's power, usually unseen but dramatically perceived—there will be sudden gravitational anomalies, seemingly impossible light and sound distortions, inexplicably contorted plant life, and human effects ranging from dizziness to sudden deep introspection to euphoria.

According to some studies, there are up-flow vortices, in which the energy flows out of the earth toward space, and in-flow vortices, where the energy flows from space toward the earth. And it's the in-flow vortexes that have been known for millions of years by other worlds throughout the universe as convenient gateways into our atmosphere—the Great Pyramids, Stonehenge, Roswell and the Bermuda Triangle, to name a tiny handful.

Certain areas of the Grand Canyon, Superstition Mountain and the Mount Shasta vortex in the United States and Mt. Bego in France are wonderful vortex exploration sites for a unique vacation theme you won't forget.

Walk-Ins

In 1984, Ruth Montgomery released a book called *Strangers Among Us*, in which she introduced a concept of soul/spirit switching called "walk-ins." It was a New Age blockbuster, with walk-ins from around the world stepping up to be identified, forming support groups and subgroups and offshoots called "starseeds," I believe, for the late teens/early twenties set. My office phones started ringing off the hook the day that book hit the stands, as they always do when a new theory comes along, and twenty-plus years later I still have clients who are worried they might be a walk-in, or be vulnerable to a walk-in, or their child might be a walk-in . . .

Let's get a few things straight:

I've been a huge fan of many of Ruth Montgomery's books, and I always will be.

The fact that I don't happen to believe one word of the idea of walk-ins doesn't detract from my overall respect for her and her amazing body of work.

I don't doubt for a moment the sincerity of her belief in the walk-in theory, or the sincerity of those who read it or heard it and suddenly were afraid it might apply to them or a loved one. They wrote to Ruth

Montgomery literally by the tens of thousands, begging her, as the acknowledged expert on the subject, to tell them whether or not their suspicions were true. Before long she was so overwhelmed with mail that she responded with nothing but preprinted cards saying, essentially, "Wish I had time to answer every letter, but I don't. Good luck with it." Now, believe me, I know better than anyone what it's like not to be able to respond personally to every letter that comes in. But you can't yell "Fire!" in a crowded theater and then complain about the crowd you get stuck in trying to get out of there.

And so, since there does seem to be some lingering fear about it, when we all have more than enough other things on our minds these days, this seems like as good an opportunity as any to explain why walk-ins make no spiritual sense to me at all.

Before I do, here's Ruth Montgomery's premise:

Two souls make a deal. Soul #1, which is always an adult, is no longer interested in being around for one reason or another—it's developed as much as it feels it can in this life, the body it's in has been badly injured or disfigured, it's despondent and considering suicide, it's simply become overwhelmed and stagnant with unhappiness and is in need of new challenges, whatever. Soul #2 says it would love to take over this body and get some earthly work done if Soul #1 is finished with it, thank you. So Soul #1 moves on to "continue its journey" in "another place," and Soul #2 steps into the vacant adult body. This, of course, creates a lot of confusion for Soul #2, who's suddenly in completely alien surroundings in the midst of total strangers who already have established relationships with the occupant of that body and have no way of knowing that there's now a "stranger among them." Soul #2 struggles to establish its own identity, an advantage most newly arrived souls are allowed by entering the body of an infant and getting to start with the even playing field of being as strange to everyone around it as everyone around it is to it. Entering an adult body in the middle of a life means that, by definition, there are expectations and predispositions that Soul #2 may have no interest in at all. The changes feel so jarring and sudden that the walk-in can find itself very disoriented for a while until it gets accustomed to its new surroundings.

Okay. So. First of all, if you've read the section on the Chart, you know how strongly I believe that we write a detailed blueprint for our lives, usually filled with a lot of challenges so that our spirits can progress while we're here. Among other things, our chart is tantamount to a contract we make with God. I can't imagine either God or us being so cavalier about the journey of our souls that we'd add a walk-in clause that says, "And then, if we get bored or fed up, we can just move out and let someone else deal with it." What possible learning or growth would there be in that, and why would God, whose love for us is immeasurable, expect so little of us and wish so little for us?

There's also the fact that the whole idea of walk-ins comes way too close for comfort for me to the idea of possession, which, if I haven't made it clear elsewhere, I believe is physically, physiologically and spiritually impossible. I believe that the whole myth of being possessed by the devil, or anyone else, good or bad, has been used as a scare tactic/threat from various churches who've found that fear can be very effective in keeping a congregation in line, as a very cheesy publicity stunt, as a tragic misinterpretation of mental illness or even something as ordinary and benign as kinetic energy or some combination of the above. And yes, I'm familiar with *The Exorcist*. Loved the book and the movie. Really wonderful pieces of fiction.

Again, if the walk-in issue makes sense to you, and it's something you believe in, I'll never agree with you, but I'll defend your right to your beliefs as if they were my own.

If it's still on your mind as a kind of looming question mark that makes you uneasy or frightens you, though, please just ask yourself what the logic of walk-ins would be from the perspective of our souls' best interest? And if it's not in our souls' best interest, it's a safe bet that God didn't create such a thing to begin with.

Werewolves

According to Greek mythology, the great god Zeus once paid a visit to an earthly king named Lycaon, who was rumored to be a thoroughly despicable human being. In the course of the visit, Lycaon served a feast, which Zeus recognized to be human flesh. Enraged, Zeus exacted punishment on Lycaon by turning him into a wolf.

Brilliantly colorful and dramatic myth, and in fact, the word "lycanthropy" bears an uncanny, not coincidental resemblance to "Lycaon." Lycanthropy is the mental affliction that makes its sufferers believe they've turned into wolves. It's actually from the Greek *lycos*, which means "wolf," and *anthropos*, meaning "man."

Wolves have been revered and feared for their cold, cunning stealth and hunting prowess by countless cultures for countless thousands of years. Tribal dances in which wolf skins were worn to ask the gods for a successful hunt have been common since ancient times throughout the world.

Put the mental affliction together with humankind's endless fascination with wolves; then add the powers of rumors, legends and crowd hysteria and it's not a huge stretch to figure out how the myth of werewolves was born and continued to spread. Tragically, especially during the Middle Ages, literally thousands of people were tortured and executed for being accused of being werewolves, sometimes for no other reason than the fact that they had too much body hair and were thought to be either odd or suspicious, whether they actually had the disorder of lycanthropy or not.

Compounding the hysteria was the increasing popularity of an unfortunate drug called laudanum. It was first experimented with by a sixteenth-century Swiss physician named Paracelsus and included in a wide variety of medicines throughout Europe in the nineteenth century. It was a very effective pain reliever, cure for insomnia and general mood elevator. Hopefully unbeknownst to its creator and subsequent developers, it was also fatally addictive, being nothing more than dressed-up and cleverly nicknamed opium.

It's impossible to know how many laudanum addicts there were on the European continent and its surroundings from the sixteenth to the early twentieth centuries, until someone finally caught on that it was opium, and horribly dangerous. We do know that Samuel Coleridge, Charles Dickens, Lewis Carroll, Edgar Allan Poe, Lord Byron and other brilliant literary figures battled laudanum addictions throughout their adult lives, and most suffered from one of laudanum's most dramatic side effects: raging, uncontrollable hallucinations.

According to my Spirit Guide Francine, who's my most reliable source on subjects like this, lycanthropy, fear/fascination with wolves, humankind's vulnerability to rumors and crowd hysteria and, sadly, our tendency toward initial mistrust of those who look and behave in ways we consider odd all made major contributions to the widespread belief in werewolves. But an equally widespread and insidious use of and addiction to laudanum and its inevitable hallucinations were what fixed it as "fact" based on "eyewitness accounts" in many cultures.

The bottom line: Nowhere in God's logical, orderly creation do any of us ever change species—not during one lifetime on earth, not from one lifetime on earth to the next. Watch all the movies and read all the books you like in which werewolves are on a rampage, but don't ever forget, *they're pure fiction*.

White Light

The White Light, put most simply, is God's aura. It's infinite love, infinite wisdom, infinite compassion and infinite power, contained in a brilliant, fathomless glow. It's the Light that waits for us at the end of the tunnel that leads us Home. It's the Light we can mentally surround ourselves with every minute of every day on earth to protect ourselves and tell the darkness it has no future where we are. It's the Light in the core of our being that is a genetic legacy from our Father, our Creator, that unites us all to each other and to Him, as children of the Divine. It's the White Light of the Holy Spirit, into which all our grief, pain, burdens and missteps can be eternally resolved, simply by our asking.

The White Light is God's sacred aura, at our disposal whenever we need it, whether we believe or not, because whether we believe or not, He never stops believing in us.

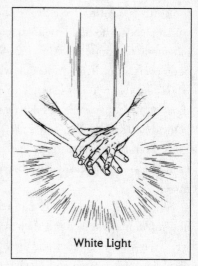

White Light

Wicca

Wicca is simply a frequently used synonym for "witchcraft," which you'll find under its own listing.

Witchcraft, Witches and Warlocks

Did you know that at the heart of true witchcraft in its original form is a worship of nature and the search for an ecologically balanced Mother Earth? And that it is no more common for witches to practice Satanism than it is for us Christians to frequent prostitutes, as we can't deny some avowed Christians have confessed to? And that they keep their rituals to themselves not because they involve unspeakable evil but because we "civilians" have been historically intolerant of suspected witches to the point of executing them?

It shouldn't surprise you that I'm ready and willing to defend witchcraft, or Wicca, as it's also called, if you stand back and look at what witches and I have in common. True witches and I share a deep love of the earth, its animals and this planet, and a belief that abusing the earth is a form of sacrilege. They and I are pacifists. They and I worship gods who build, nourish, create and embrace without malice, judgment or prejudice. Most of all, they and I have most certainly been accused of being in league with the devil, but never by anyone who spent two minutes learning the slightest bit about us. In fact, I've thought more than once, if I'd lived in Salem, Massachusetts, in 1692, being exactly who I am, with exactly the same gifts, doing exactly what I do—even being exactly as active and passionate a believer in God as I am now—I could easily have been executed during the Witch Trials myself.

Witchcraft is thought to date back to the Stone Age, and for several millennia witches and their male counterparts, called warlocks, were the village doctors and herbalists, while in private practicing their rites of honoring and praying to the nature goddess. Then along came the Church. And God bless them, while I cling to the belief that they meant well and continue to mean well, the Church doesn't always take kindly to those who seem to prefer their privacy. And for an institution whose Bible clearly reads, "Judge not, lest ye be judged," it's not always adept at a live-and-let-live attitude toward those whose way of living seems odd, untraditional or, worst of all, heathen, meaning any other belief system than that ordained by the Church. So it's fair to say that the Church viewed witches and warlocks with open contempt. This, of course, drove the witches and warlocks even farther behind closed doors, which, of course, made them look even more suspicious, bizarre, potentially evil and guilty of acts more heinous and amoral than decent minds could even foul themselves to imagine.

Out of which ultimately evolved the tragic injustice of the Salem Witch Trials. What began as two young girls pretending to have fits, which were diagnosed as bewitchment, took form in the Puritan belief that witches' powers were bestowed by the devil; progressed with the insistence that the girls identify the witches responsible for their fits so the witches could be hunted down and killed; and went horribly out of control as the girls fell in love with their newfound attention and power, as they began naming any old "witch" that sprang to mind, including a four-year-old child. Witch hysteria swept through Salem, husbands turned in their wives as witches just to punish them for some minor marital infraction, "positive identifications" were made up out of thin air, the mentally ill were brought in and easily coerced into confessions without having the slightest idea what they were being accused of, and with the momentum of fear on their side and no one to oppose them, the Puritan magistrates were in judgment heaven.

It's hard to say how long this might have gone on if the two young girls who started it all hadn't finally pushed their luck too far. Having exhausted all their accusation fun in Salem, they were sent on a literal witch hunt to the surrounding areas, where eventually, in some sort of insane attempt at a grand finale, they claimed that the governor's wife was a witch. And that, at long last, was the beginning of the end of the Salem Witch Trials.

But by the time it was over—and remember, this all started from an imaginary incident in which not one single crime was ever committed—141 people were arrested, one elderly man was crushed under a pile of rocks in an effort to torture him into a confession he refused to give, and nineteen other innocent people were hanged.

And we wonder why witches are reluctant to this day to "come out of the closet."

One of the kindest, gentlest people I've ever had the pleasure of meeting was a full-blown, unapologetic warlock. Goodness just radiated out of him, and I could tell as I shook his hand that there wasn't a dark, mean or hurtful bone in his body. Whatever rituals his coven practiced (covens are groups of never more than thirteen witches and/or warlocks), they definitely didn't involve anything dark.

And who am I, by the way, who grew up in Catholic school, to pass judgment on a group for loving their rituals?

As for those anomalies of witchcraft who branch off and stick pins in dolls and cast evil spells and whatever other destructive ugliness they indulge in, I wish them the same karma I wish the Puritan magistrates of the Witch Trials, the Christian Crusaders and everyone else who inflicts cruelty of any kind in the name of a god or goddess they claim to love.

There's a quote I've heard all my life that makes me deeply appreciative of true witches, and true practitioners of voodoo, and the Aborigines, and Native Americans, and countless other cultures whose faith may look foreign to us and who may call God by other names than we do, but whose kind, tender love for our Mother Earth should be an example for all of us who live here.

May it do the same for you, because it's just the truth:

> *"Treat the earth well:*
> *It was not given to you by your parents,*
> *It was loaned to you by your children.*
> *We do not inherit the Earth from our Ancestors,*
> *We borrow it from our Children."*
>
> —Ancient Indian Proverb

X

Xenoglossy

It was decades ago. I was newly certified as a master hypnotist in California. In addition to the psychic readings I'd been doing for years, I was testing the waters of a hypnosis practice, knowing how effective hypnosis could be in solving a vast range of common problems, from smoking and fear of flying to sleeping disorders.

One afternoon Mr. A arrived in my office, wanting help with a chronic weight problem. We were about ten minutes into a completely routine hypnosis session when suddenly, with no warning, Mr. A appeared to lose his mind before my eyes. He never moved from the couch he was sitting on, and his relaxed posture and calm tone of voice never changed. He simply went from telling me about his eating habits to describing his life in Egypt and his work on the pyramids as if they were all part of the same story. He then launched into a dissertation on a subject he seemed to be very passionate about. The problem was, he was delivering it in some kind of unintelligible nonsense language, and I couldn't understand a single word he said. My training had taught me never to interrupt or stop a patient who might be experiencing a psychotic episode. So I let him carry on, nodding politely to reassure him that I didn't find this odd, while keeping my hand near the alarm button under my desk that would cue my staff that I needed help.

And then, after about half an hour of incomprehensible blather, he was suddenly back, finishing the details of his eating habits, in English, as pleasant and normal as when he'd arrived, seemingly oblivious to what had happened.

Fortunately, I've always taped every reading and hypnosis session of my career, giving the tape to the client when we're through. In this case, with Mr. A's permission, I sent a tape of this session to a psychology professor friend at Stanford. I didn't say a word about what was on the tape; I simply asked him to listen to it and tell me what he thought, fully expecting a diagnosis that whoever this Mr. A was, he needed professional help.

The professor called me back three days later. He was so excited he was a little short of breath. "Where did you get this tape?!" he almost yelled into the phone.

"Why do you ask?" I said.

It turned out he and some Stanford colleagues had spent those three days listening to and researching what they heard on that tape, and they'd reached a conclusion with one hundred percent certainty: My client's "unintelligible nonsense language" was actually an ancient (seventh century B.C.), obscure Assyrian dialect consisting of word pictures, almost like spoken cuneiform.

I went through the motions of calling the client and asking him, without explanation, if by any chance he happened to be fluent in any ancient Assyrian dialects. I'm sure he hung up convinced that *I* needed professional help.

That session was a turning point for me: It was my cue that hypnosis could be a bridge for my clients to the lives they've lived before. And if I did some intensive, focused study on how to help, instead of sitting there gaping at them with one hand on the alarm button, whole new worlds could open up, literally, for my clients, and for my ongoing research into past lives.

It wasn't until years and years later that I came across the word "xenoglossy" and discovered there's an actual term for what had happened and many other people it's happened to.

Xenoglossy, it turns out, is the ability to speak or write in a language never learned by the person exhibiting skills in it. Unlike glossolalia (which is described in its own section), or speaking in tongues, xenoglossy is a spontaneous, inexplicable fluency in a traceable, if sometimes obscure, language or dialect.

To no one's surprise, there are legions of skeptics who insist that any and all demonstrations of xenoglossy are either faked or coached, and that there's really no such thing as xenoglossy.

Yes, there is.

Yin and Yang

The concept of yin and yang, which is at the core of many Eastern theories about the metaphysical laws of the universe, originated with philosophers in the Chinese Han dynasty that ruled from 207 B.C. until A.D. 9. As exotic as that might make yin and yang sound, it's not unlike basic universal principles accepted by cultures and religions around the world in the twenty-first century.

Western religion in general believes that God created a universe of dualities—male and female, good and evil, light and dark, land and sea, etc.—and those dualities are interdependent on each other for their existence. God's universe is also cyclical—physically, as with the seasons, the movements of the stars and planets, the day following the night which follows the day, etc.; and metaphysically, as with the absolute karmic law that can also be stated, at its most basic, "what goes around comes around."

Han philosophers asserted that the universe is ruled by one principle, which they called the Great Ultimate, or the Tao. That principle is divided into two equal and opposite principles called yin and yang, and all the equal opposites in the universe belong to one of those two principles. Yin encompasses such elements as femaleness, darkness, the moon, submission, the earth, cold, etc. Yang encompasses maleness, light, the sun, dominance, heaven, heat, etc. And no element of one could exist without its counterpart or opposite in the other. We couldn't know darkness, for example, if it weren't for light, or light if it weren't for darkness. Harmony would be unrecognizable without the existence of discord, and vice versa.

Yin and Yang, the Chinese symbol of opposite yet balanced energy forces

One of the most fascinating aspects of the yin/yang concept is known as "presence in absence." Basically (and I do mean *basically*), it goes like this:

* All the elements of yin and yang cyclically change into their opposites.
* Since each element inevitably evolves into its opposite, then each element must contain some hint of its opposite—good health, for example, must contain some hint of illness, and illness must contain some hint of good health.
* So even though an element's opposite may not be conspicuous as one of its components, no element can exist without that hint of its opposite. In other words, there's no such thing as perfect health, let's say, since health has to contain a hint of illness according to the principles of yin and yang.

Using the health/illness example, then, "presence in absence" means that even in its seeming absence during good health, illness is present in that absence—an element's opposite is always present whether or not its absence looks completely conspicuous.

The symbol of yin and yang is a circle in which two fish—one black, one white—are encircling each other. Their eyes are made prominent by the fact that the black fish has a white eye and the white fish has a black eye. The two fish, yin and yang, represent the

opposite, equal and complementary nature of the male/female principle of yin/yang, wrapped around each other and interdependent as
they are, neither of them more dominant than the other. Both fish's
eyes being open and visible represents the yin/yang belief that both
the feminine and masculine points of view are essential in the fullest
possible understanding of life and its mysteries.

Yoga

I love yoga, and no matter how overloaded my schedule is or how non-
stop my travel, I practice it two or three times a week.

I'm not opening with that statement to say, "I practice yoga, so you
should too." Instead I'm saying, "If I can do yoga, you can do yoga,"
and/or, "If I have time, you have time."

Yoga is a system of exercise designed to bring the body and mind
together as one united entity in complete harmony with itself. It dates
back a minimum of 5,000 years and has developed into more than a
hundred different disciplines or schools. All of them, though, work
from a base of the same three primary elements of exercise, breathing
and meditation. It's not a religion, nor are there any required behaviors
or beliefs, except for one: According to the yoga philosophy, we already
have within us everything we need for our greatest fulfillment.

The most commonly practiced schools of contemporary yoga are
variations on Classical Yoga, a system compiled by a scholar named
Patanjali at around the time of Christ. Classical Yoga at its purest addressed itself to eight different facets or "limbs."

* *yama,* or "restraint"—abstinence from violence, crime, dishon-
  esty and uncommitted sex
* *niyama,* or "observance"—aspiring toward purity, peace, study
  and understanding
* *asana*—the physical exercises

* *pranayama*—the breathing techniques
* *pratyahara*—"withdrawing the mind from the senses," which means preparing to meditate
* *dharana*—concentration
* *dhyana*—devotion, meditation
* *samadhi*—experiencing one's essential nature

Sometime in the second half of the 1800s yoga made its way to the United States, where its popularity began to grow very slowly but even more surely. It's probably no surprise that as it evolved and took its own forms in the Western world, the eight limbs of Classical Yoga for the most part narrowed themselves down to the three that involved the least self-deprivation: physical exercises, breathing techniques and meditation.

Even the most traditional members of the western medical community are finally endorsing yoga as being legitimately beneficial to physical health and well-being. The exercises and breathing postures definitely stimulate specific parts of the body corresponding to the endocrine glands, which affect everything from our metabolism to our immune system to our abilities to process blood sugar, effectively deal with stress and develop constructive sleep patterns.

The news that there are more than a hundred forms of yoga, with volumes of information available on each of them, can be enough to make a mildly curious beginner throw up his hands and head back to his couch and TV before he's even started. The good news is, there are a few basic, popular "schools" that are easily accessible, not mystifying and honestly enjoyable, even for someone like me, who—yes, I'll say it—loathes traditional exercise. (It's a running joke between me and Lindsay, inspired by a party that's too long a story, to call each other and announce we've just signed the two of us up for kickboxing classes. We'll be doing that right after we build a log cabin from scratch.)

You should have no trouble finding basic, comprehensible reading material and classes on the following types of yoga:

* HATHA, the one we most often picture when we think of yoga, a blend of physical postures, movements and breathing exercises.
* RAJA, a blend of exercise, breathing and meditation, with some teachers offering a series of studies as well.
* KUNDALINI, which incorporates some of the postures of Hatha yoga but in continuous movement rather than held positions; also known for a cleansing breathing exercise called "Breath of Fire" and use of the chant "sat nam," which translates to "truth is my identity."
* TANTRA (my personal preference), with an emphasis on the disciplines of meditation and visualization toward a blending of the physical and spiritual bodies into one.

The late, magnificent teacher/mythologist Joseph Campbell wrote a beautiful description of the idea of yoga in his essay on Hinduism (and interestingly, yoga preceded Hinduism, by the way) that I'm going to beg my editor to let me include.

"Yoga is the intentional stopping of the spontaneous activity of the mind stuff. . . . We are all, as we sit here and stand here, the broken images, the broken reflections, of a single divine perfection; but all that we ever see when we look around with our mind stuff in its usual state of spontaneous activity, is the broken rainbow-reflection of this perfect image of divine light. Let us now open our eyes, let the waters stir again, let the waves come into action—and we shall know that all these flashing sights before us are reflections, broken images, of that one divine radiance, which we have experienced."

Zarathushtra

It seems unfair that, considering his contribution to world religion, Zarathushtra is not exactly a household name. He should be, and I'm here to help.

Zarathushtra was born in what is now Iran, around 8000 B.C., and he was the first prophet to embrace and spread the word of monotheism, or the concept that there is one and only one God. He called this Supreme Being "Ahura Mazda," which is a combination of words meaning "Lord Creator" and "Supremely Wise." He believed that Ahura Mazda/God created humankind with the freedom to choose between good and evil, and the responsibility to face the consequences of the choices we make. That means that we, not Ahura Mazda/God, are the cause of the good and the evil in this world we've been given—not an actual evil being. Zarathushtra didn't believe in the devil.

He believed in the coming of a messiah who would be born to a virgin. He believed in an eventual apocalyptic battle that would purge the world of evil and result in a resurrection of Ahura Mazda/God's kingdom on earth. He believed that each of us possesses the divine within ourselves and that it is our obligation to honor and act on our own divinity by respecting the natural and moral laws of the universe.

He believed that when we leave life on earth, our essence leaves our body. If we've made good choices throughout our lives, treating ourselves and others with love and faith, our essence goes to the House of Songs, also called the Realm of Light. If we've lived in opposition to the natural and moral laws of the universe, our essence goes to the Realm of Darkness and Separation. Those realms weren't actual physical places, according to Zarathushtra. They were eternal states of either oneness with or separation from Ahura Mazda/God.

He believed that our purpose in life is to be among those who renew the world as it progresses toward perfection. He believed that, just as the way to fight darkness is by spreading light, the way to fight evil is by spreading goodness, and the way to fight hatred is by spreading love.

Isn't that beautiful? And awfully familiar, even though it originated from a prophet in 8000 B.C.? Zarathushtra's followers are called the Zoroastrians, and many scholars consider Zoroastrianism to be the mother of all the contemporary world's religions. All things considered, it might be a richly deserved title.

Zombies

Zombies are mythical—*mythical*—undead beings whose bodies walk around robotically among the living as if they're still one of them, no one realizing until it's too late that their souls and minds and consciences no longer exist.

In truth, there have been many drugs through many centuries whose effects simulated blank, catatonic states and slowed the body's natural functions so dramatically that they sometimes appeared to have stopped breathing. As with such other myths as werewolves and vampires, there have been too many disease- and drug-induced tragedies associated with the zombie legend to consider it harmless—people buried alive, severe brain damage, the autistic misinterpreted and either shunned or stoned, etc.

Enjoy the fiction of zombies if it appeals to you. But leave it at that and, for God's sake, literally, don't let it enter your mind that it might be real, worth simulating or worth perpetuating.

ACKNOWLEDGMENTS

Special thanks to:

Mr. Willy Dufresne, for his reliably cheerful help and advice;

Kirk Simonds, for the honor of allowing us to showcase his artwork in another of our books;

Brian Tart, for a seemingly impossible eight books in six short years;

and Bonnie Solow, for gracefully keeping her door open.

With our gratitude,
Sylvia and Lindsay

Please read on for an excerpt from

Sylvia Browne's new hardcover

INSIGHT

Available now from Dutton

This book is my Golden Anniversary celebration. As most of you know by now, I've been psychic since the day I was born, a family legacy that can be traced back at least three hundred years. But not until I was almost twenty, half a century ago (you do the math), did I allow myself to ease, informally at first, into a life of private readings: one-on-one sessions, in person or on the phone, with those who have an infinite variety of questions and are willing to hear the answers that come not *from* me, but *through* me, from the Source of all answers, wisdom and life itself.

Fifty years of readings. In a threadbare storefront office in San Jose, California, so tiny that I actually hung drapes on a blank wall to create the illusion of a window. In an equally tiny space in my cramped house, with my sons' diapers drying on a clothesline just outside the door. In countless hospital rooms and nursing homes and pediatric care facilities. In five-star hotel suites, mansions, mud huts and deerskin tents. On riverbanks, desert sand dunes, glistening beaches and freezing cold mountaintops. At the foot of the Sphinx, the Great Pyramids, the Eiffel Tower and a grove of baobab trees. On six of seven continents (Antarctica and I seem to be maintaining a mutually respectful distance), I've done thousands upon thousands of readings in this past half century, for clients of every age, race, creed and circumstance. And at this fifty-year road mark, I'm looking back with profound gratitude and coming to some indisputable conclusions about that part of my life that continues to be devoted to my clients: I've received far more than I could ever give, and learned far more than I could ever teach.

When we cut through the superficial differences between us, the meaningless variations in geography, skin color, cultural traditions, and the specific words by which we worship God, we citizens of this earth who haven't turned away from Him, we're all the same at our core. We yearn to love and be loved. We yearn to hear that we're on the right path, or how to find our way back to it if we feel we've wandered off. We yearn to be stronger, wiser, healthier, more courageous and less afraid. We yearn to understand what confuses and debilitates us. We yearn to experience our connection to our Creator, and our own eternal spirits, rather than just hope against hope that they exist. We yearn to know beyond all doubt that there's more than this, that *we're* more than this, and that, for ourselves and for everyone we've ever loved, there really is no end. We yearn for peace of mind, and access to the ultimate peace our spirits possess through our divine birthright.

In varying forms, those are the issues with which my clients have entrusted me through all these years. And again, the answers I offer have nothing to do with me, other than my willingness to stay out of the way, accurately repeat the information I'm given (whether it makes the slightest bit of sense to me or not) and rest assured that I'm only given whatever information my clients are meant to know, which is not my call to make.

As essential to my readings as God Himself are the affadavits I ask for from every client I "read." I don't just want validation. I *need* validation. I need to know if what I've passed along is accurate and helpful. If it's not both of those things, it's time for me to close my doors. I'm not talking about 100 percent accuracy. God is the sole possessor of that phenomenon. My accuracy level has been clinically tested, and frequently, at somewhere between 85 percent to 90 percent. That's my yardstick, and the standard to which I expect my clients to hold me each and every day.

Contained in this book is just a fraction of those affadavits, from clients who've come to me for help with everything from health and relationship problems to missing and murdered loved ones to grief issues to spiritual confusion to the perpetual and ever-popular "When will I meet Mr./Ms. Right?" These written validations and thousands more are on file in my office, thanks to my tireless, meticulous staff, and the comparative handful I've included in these pages are limited to those who specifically indicated their permission for me to quote them. Still, because I consider my clients' privacy to be sacrosanct, I won't use their real names as I tell their stories. If they care to "go public" about it, that's their call to make, not mine.

Just to clarify, by the way: Some of the validations you'll read are addressed to me directly. Others are accounts of readings that were sent to my staff, and they refer to me in the third person. It might have been less confusing for me to transform them all into "Dear Sylvia" letter form, but I had my heart set on re-creating these validations in the form in which they arrived in my office.

In case you're wondering what accounts of other people's readings could possibly have to do with you, there are a couple very simple answers to that question. For one thing, some of the greatest insights we can achieve in this life come from the best and the worst of shared experiences. For another, far more important thing, these stories offer a steady stream of reassurance that whatever you've been through, or are going through, or are bracing yourself to go through, someone else has been there too, and you're not alone.

To every client over this past half century, with or without an affadavit, whether you're contained in this book or not, I thank you from the bottom of my heart for all you've taught and given me, and for the courage it took to ask me the questions that mattered most to you, knowing I would never lie to you or give you false hope even when that's what you might have thought you wanted.

God bless you and love you. I do.

*   *   *

As long as humankind has occupied this planet, we've felt a little vulnerable, a little afraid and more than a little homesick for the Other
Side, where we're accustomed to living in God's perfection. We've
looked, listened and prayed for something or someone to tell us with
some authority that life on earth isn't as random and illogical and
pointless as it often seems.

Prehistoric man hoped to increase his odds of success at hunting
food for his family.

Kings, pharaohs and warriors sought divine guidance on upcoming
battles.

Presidents and prime ministers throughout history, eager to maximize their power; doctors, scientists, psychiatrists, and law enforcement officers in search of solutions to mysteries that have eluded
them; loved ones of the missing, the murdered with no suspect, the
critically ill with no diagnosis; the singles in search of Mr. or Ms.
Right; children with night terrors, or genius far beyond their years;
adults with debilitating fears, or simply the quiet, urgent need to know
that they matter, if only to God . . .

In doubt, in desperation, in grief and in spiritual hunger, humankind of every circumstance, in every culture, religion and civilization since time began has turned to those who seem to have some sort
of special insight, an "inside track" from some Greater Power, to answer their most practical and most intangible questions.

By whatever name they've called them, they've turned to psychics.

It's not easy to narrow down exactly what a "psychic" is. In general,
a psychic is anyone who's able to receive and accurately interpret messages that originate from sources that are normally imperceptible to
the five senses of sight, hearing, touch, taste and smell—in other
words, sources that are "extrasensory." That would correctly mean that
every person on earth is psychic, since every one of us has "gut feelings," "impulses," "instincts," "intuitions" and other signals we act on
that have nothing to do with the five senses. I like to use the analogy

that the difference between "being psychic" and "being *a* psychic" is like the difference between "playing the piano," which anyone can do, even if they use their foot or elbow, and having the gifts that elevate some to becoming concert pianists.

Compared to the earth's psychic history, which has existed "since humankind first set foot on this planet," my family's three-hundred-year psychic lineage makes us seem like a bunch of newcomers. Be that as it may, as many of you know, I was born in Kansas City, Missouri, on October 19, 1936, and I've been genetically psychic since that day.

I'm asked all the time what it's like to be psychic, and the best I can do to describe it is to answer the question with a question: "What's it like to be *you*?" I've never experienced not being psychic, so I have nothing to compare it to, just as you've never experienced being anyone but you. I did learn very early in my childhood that I was seeing and hearing things that those around me weren't. If my wise and brilliantly psychic grandma Ada hadn't been there to explain what I was experiencing, and to help me think of it as a gift rather than a burden, I'm sure I would have grown up frightened, self-conscious and desperate to hide my apparent insanity from the rest of the world.

Instead, with Grandma Ada's comforting guidance, I learned to pay attention to the sights, sounds and silent knowledge that seemed to be seeking out me of all people, this child who yearned to be "normal." I learned to pray that I not be given information I could neither handle nor do anything about: no visions of melting faces on those who were about to die, please; no random violent "movies" of plane crashes with no telltale flight numbers or twisted mangled cars full of bleeding accident victims without enough details to warn someone ahead of time; no involuntary collage of crime scenes unless they were accompanied by the names or faces of the criminals involved. I learned to accept, and ultimately embrace, my Spirit Guide, who burst into my life from the Other Side one night when I was eight years old and, once I recovered from my initial terror of her, even accepted my insistence on changing her name from Iena to Francine. I learned that the nuns at the Catholic school I attended were insistent on the reality of spirits who survive death, and of Angels, but had no patience whatsoever with my announcement that I routinely saw and communicated with those same spirits and Angels. (I thought the nuns would be delighted that I was able to confirm the existence of this spirit world they kept carrying on about. Instead, it inspired them to consider me a discipline problem who needed to keep her fairy tales to herself.)

Nuns and confusion aside, I decided that if I had to be stuck with "knowing things," as the euphemism went, I might as well stop keeping those things to myself, whether anyone wanted to hear them or not.

Sometimes it caused problems: like when I informed my mother that my father had a girlfriend, and what she looked like and how long he'd been seeing her, even though there had never been the slightest hint that a girlfriend existed.

Sometimes it was literally a godsend: like the day my father and I were sitting in a movie theater, and in the middle of the movie, I felt a sudden, ice-cold panic and screamed at him that we had to go home *right that second*. My baby sister, Sharon, couldn't breathe, I told him. She was turning blue, and she would die if we didn't get there to help her. We were met in the driveway by the mother, who managed to tell us through her frantic sobs that something was desperately wrong with Sharon. She was burning up with fever, and gasping for air. Mother had tried to call an ambulance, but the phone was inexplicably dead. Daddy sped Sharon to the hospital with only minutes to spare, the doctors told him later, but she did successfully recover from what turned out to be double pneumonia.

Dispensing both important and trivial unsolicited information to everyone around me became second nature to me throughout my childhood. But to this day, I remember the first time someone actually sought me out for an answer to something that had been troubling her. Technically speaking, it was my first official "psychic reading."

I was eight years old. My Spirit Guide, Francine, and I were beginning to communicate with some regularity, still a bit hesitantly and skeptically on my part, but there was no denying the fact that she was interesting and seemed to know what she was talking about.

One day a classmate named Mary Marguerite approached me after school, pulling me aside so that we'd be out of earshot of the other children. Mary Marguerite and I had been friends since we were five years old. She'd become completely accustomed to my psychic gifts, which translated through the lovely, simple acceptance of a child's eyes as my just knowing things that other people didn't. Looking back, I don't think she or any of my other childhood friends thought any more of my "knowing things" than we thought of the fact that our friend Louise could touch the tip of her nose with her tongue and our friend Cindy could voluntarily burp.

"Sylvia," Mary Marguerite whispered, "I'm really worried about my mom. She doesn't seem very happy, and I don't know why. Is there something wrong with her?"

I had no conscious awareness of asking Francine, or Anyone Else, for that matter. And in retrospect, I wish I'd had a more insightful answer to give her. But an answer did come to me instantly, and I shared it with her. "I don't know, but she needs to be careful, because she's going to fall down and break her arm." I admit I was amazed at how clearly I saw and knew that, on command, in response to a question, rather than simply at random as usual. And it turned out I wasn't finished. "Your father's going to lose his job, too."

Within two months, Mary Marguerite's mother had broken her arm and her father had lost his job. My first official "reading," and even though I was eight years old, it didn't count as far as I was concerned until and unless I turned out to be right.

*   *   *

I "read" my way through high school, for girlfriends anxious to hear if their boyfriends were faithful and/or would marry them someday, for a few sheepish members of the faculty who couldn't resist privately checking out their supposedly psychic student, for virtually everyone but myself—and if my teenage years proved nothing else, they proved that I don't have a psychic bone in my body when it comes to my own life. As high school ended and college began, I was mourning the loss of my cherished grandma Ada and the end of a relationship with a man I was sure would be the greatest and the last love of my life. (Not even close, needless to say.) And as much as I appreciated the challenging stimulation of my college courses at St. Theresa's College, tackling double majors in education and literature, with a minor in theology, I felt lost, empty, afraid and alone.

I can't trace exactly when depression compelled me to start actively "tuning out" my psychic gifts in general and Francine in particular. But I do know that denying the essence of who I was made me physically ill, persistently flat on my back with everything from the flu to bronchitis to full-blown pneumonia. I also know that the self-doubt I was struggling with took root and flourished as I began adding abnormal psychology courses to my already overloaded curriculum and discovered that at least four of the seven primary levels of mental illness seemed to describe me perfectly.

Believe me, I'm well aware that most of you who've taken psychology courses were as unnerved as I was by the creepy suspicion that those infernal lists of psychotic symptoms hit a little too close to home. I had some added bonuses, though, that many of you had the luxury of ignoring. All my life I'd seen visions no one else saw. All my life I'd heard voices no one else heard. The conclusion seemed unavoidable and paralyzing: I was obviously schizophrenic.

That realization would have been devastating enough all by itself, but as far as I was concerned, it also meant the end of my dream of becoming a teacher. It was the only career I'd ever imagined for myself, and I truly believed I'd be good at it. There wasn't a chance, though, that I was going to jeopardize innocent children by exposing them every day to a teacher who also happened to be a raving lunatic. I'm sure Grandma Ada would have "grounded" me and pulled me back on track, but she was gone, and I plugged my ears to Francine by re-defining her as the ultimate proof of my terrible mental illness. I finally confided in my doctor and in a priest I'd known for many years, both of whom were compassionate, understanding and insistent on sending me to a psychiatrist. I went, convinced that he would confirm my self-diagnosis. My doctor and my priest admitted later that they fully expected what actually happened: after an endless barrage of interviews and tests, the psychiatrist sat me down, pulled his chair close to mine and calmly concluded, "You're perfectly normal, but something paranormal is going on as well."

It was better than "In my professional opinion, you're nuts." But I still wasn't completely persuaded that I could safely unleash myself on hapless classrooms full of children. After all, I had proof of my dementia: that constant, chirping presence named Francine who'd been part of my life, part of *me*, since I was eight years old; that haunting voice that no one else could hear. The more I read, the more I studied, the more I agonized over her, the clearer it became that not only was Francine not a being from the spirit world, not only was she not my Guide, but she wasn't even real. That's why I was the only person who'd experienced her. She was imaginary, just some alternate personality my own pathetic mind had created as an escape, a diversion from my abusive mother, a textbook coping mechanism I'd been foolish enough to indulge. If I could get rid of her once and for all, it would mean I'd managed to integrate myself into one cohesive being again, and I could maybe even look forward to being sane someday.

It sounded so logical to me, and I was so convinced that saying good-bye to the imaginary Francine was a giant leap toward mental health, that I actually gave her a ceremonial farewell speech. I explained everything I'd been going through and everything I'd been thinking, building to the grand finale of unmasking her Spirit Guide facade and telling her that finally, thank God, I knew my imagination had conjured her up, which meant that it could just as easily eliminate her.

She listened with her characteristic patience, neither defending herself nor resenting me. She didn't say a word until I was finished. Then she made a suggestion, which I was free to accept or reject, completely my choice: if the issue was that no one had ever experienced her but me, and she was unable to make that happen, then I could go right ahead and dismiss her as imaginary and she'd never bother me again. But if she really was my Spirit Guide, an actual living entity from the Other Side as she claimed to be, and others besides me could experience her as a being completely separate from me, it should prove once and for all that my sanity was perfectly intact.

"What are you suggesting?" I asked her, almost afraid to hear the answer.

"Gather your family," she said. "I will show myself to you, and to them. Then you will know."

In all these years, I'd never seen Francine. She'd described herself to me: five feet nine inches tall, slender, with olive skin, very large dark eyes, and black hair that she wore in a thick braid that fell to her waist. Oddly, the subject of her manifesting herself had never even come up. Now she was offering to do so, as the ultimate proof of my own mental health or lack of it, which made it an offer I couldn't refuse.

"When?" I asked.

"Tonight," she replied. My hands were shaking as I dialed my parents' number.

It was raining. Of course. Daddy, Mother and my sister Sharon were with me in the darkened room full of candles Francine had asked for. (Spirits can see candlelight more clearly than electric lights, by the way, in case you've ever wondered.) They were almost giddy with the anticipation of meeting and actually seeing this woman I'd been carrying on about for all these years. In sharp contrast, I was anxious, almost terrified, torn between an odd fear of Francine materializing and a dread of her not materializing, of the four of us sitting there hour after hour, waiting and watching for nothing at all, which would prove beyond all doubt how nuts I really was.

There was an empty rocking chair beside me. Daddy, Mother and Sharon were sitting across from me. We were all silent. The only sound was the heavy rain outside my small apartment windows. It was Daddy's eyes I noticed first, as they moved to the rocking chair and began widening in amazement. Within moments, Mother's and Sharon's eyes were fixed there too, mirroring Daddy's look of something approaching awe.

I couldn't bring myself to look directly at the rocking chair, where their stares were held. Instead I just watched peripherally as, very slowly and gracefully, without a sound, a pale blue dress began to take shape, its soft opaque folds draping from the seat of the chair to the dark wood floor.

Then the long, slender fingers of a hand with impossibly smooth burnished gold-olive skin appeared against the pastel blue, resting in the lap of the dress. An arm, thin and muscular, revealed itself gradually above the hand, as if a transparent veil was being lifted.

At that point my father suddenly blurted out, "Don't anyone speak until she's gone so we won't take a chance on influencing each other about what we saw." No one answered him. He seemed to be the only one of us in the room who was able to find his voice.

As I continued to watch out of the corner of my eye, a long, thick braid of black hair fell without warning from the front of the shoulder to lay against the arm.

And that was all I could take. While my enthralled family continued to gape, I turned away and never glanced back. That's all I saw of Francine, all I wanted to see and I've never seen her again in the half century since.